BANKING AND FINANCE IN THE ARAB MIDDLE EAST

Commercial banking is expanding more rapidly in the Middle East than in any other area of the world, but the increasing complexity of regional finance perplexes many, not least bankers themselves. This book explains how Arab banking has evolved since the mid-nineteenth century and traces the development of many key institutions such as Bank Misr and the Arab Bank. The historical dimension helps put later changes in perspective, such as the nationalization measures of the Nasser era in Egypt and elsewhere, as well as the efforts to establish effective central banks. Recent developments discussed include the rise of Islamic banking, and the significance of Koranic teaching on usury for banking practice. The role of regional financial centers is assessed, including the rise and demise of Beirut, the current importance of Bahrain as an offshore money market center, and Kuwait as an investment center. Not only is the penetration of the Western banks in the Middle East examined, but also the increasing impact of Arab banks in international financial markets, including London. This is the first published book to consider the role of the Euro-Arab joint venture banks in recycling petro-currency. The comparative material on the increasingly important Middle Eastern aid agencies can also not be found elsewhere in published form.

Rodney Wilson has been a Lecturer in the Economics of the Middle East at the University of Durham since 1973. He has travelled extensively in the region in the course of his research, and has lectured at universities in Cairo, Kuwait, Riyadh and Jeddah. He has written numerous articles on Middle Eastern economic topics for *The Times,* and is author of *Trade and Investment in the Middle East* (1977) and *The Economies of the Middle East* (1979).

Also by Rodney Wilson

TRADE AND INVESTMENT IN THE MIDDLE EAST
THE ECONOMIES OF THE MIDDLE EAST

BANKING AND FINANCE IN THE ARAB MIDDLE EAST

Rodney Wilson

St. Martin's Press   New York

© Rodney Wilson 1983

All rights reserved. For information, write:
St. Martin's Press, Inc., 175 Fifth Avenue, New York, NY 10010
Printed in Hong Kong
First published in the United States of America in 1983

ISBN 0-312-06630-9

Library of Congress Cataloging in Publication Data

Wilson, Rodney.
  Banking and Finance in the Arab Middle East.

  Includes bibliographical references and index.
  1. Banks and banking – Arab countries.
2. Finance – Arab countries.   I. Title.
HG3366.A6W53 1982   332.1'0917'5927   81-21432
ISBN 0-312-06630-9   AACR2

Contents

List of Tables

Preface

During the last two decades commercial banking has been expanding more rapidly in the Arab Middle East than in any other area of the world. As recently as the early 1960s much of the region remained unmonetised and the existing financial institutions were small in size, catering primarily for the requirements of the limited domestic markets. The region's only financial links with the outside world were through foreign-owned banks, and no indigenous commercial bank had internationalised its operations to any significant extent. Apart from Beirut there was no centre which served wider regional needs, and even the Lebanese capital was of only limited importance internationally. Yet today the whole Arab Middle Eastern financial scene has been transformed, with a tremendous proliferation of local banks, a rapid expansion of branch networks, and an enormous widening in the range of financial services provided by indigenous institutions. The region's banks are now strongly represented in major international financial centres, and there are already twenty Arab Middle Eastern banks included in the world's top five hundred banks. At the same time, although expatriates still occupy many key positions in commercial banking, a new generation of bankers native to the region is playing a growing role in Arab finance. Overall a solid foundation for financial activity has been laid, and there is little doubt that, barring political catastrophes, the remainder of the present decade and the 1990s should witness further sustained progress.

An historical approach has been taken in this study in order to portray the development of Arab banking in the context of an unfolding story. It is the author's belief that there are many lessons to be learnt from each of the episodes, and that present conditions can only be understood with reference to past experience. For example, in so far as Arab banks have a distinctive character, this can best be understood by an examination of traditional banking practice, and in particular by looking at the pattern of moneylending and moneychanging activity. The dominance of nationalised financial institutions in some states, and privately owned banks in others, is also best viewed in the historical context, as are the varying attitudes on permissible activity for foreign banks. Involvement of foreign banks in the region's financial affairs dates back to the middle of the last century, and it is interesting to study this early penetration, not least because there are many parallels between the role of European capital then and that of today. The experience of Egypt in particular is instructive, and its financial history in the nineteenth century still has relevance in the modern Arab world.

Although it is perhaps ambitious to treat the development of banking over as wide an area as the Arab Middle East, a multi-country approach has certain advantages. The countries of the region have much in common, most particularly their Islamic inheritance which has important implications for banking practice. Given the common language of the region, the movement of banking personnel from one country to another has been considerable, and financial integration is generally much more advanced than political co-operation. The degree of capital mobility intra-regionally in recent years has been remarkable, and in this sphere of activity co-ordination between the various states has been much more effective than in other potential areas of mutual assistance. Some banks and financial institutions regard themselves as regional entities rather than belonging to any single country, and many others have a strong presence throughout the Arab world. Even the foreign banks tend to treat the region as a distinct unit, some being specifically created to serve trade links with the region as a whole, while many multinational banks have a separate Middle Eastern division within their organisations, and staff are frequently transferred around the area.

Inevitably in a study of this kind, some selectivity has been necessary in the coverage. Geographically the area has been restricted to the Arab Middle East, which excludes Israel, Iran and Turkey. Although some of the foreign banks include the latter two countries within their Middle East divisions, for linguistic and cultural reasons they tend to be cut off from the emerging Arab financial community. In many respects the Magreb countries are more integrated with the Arab Middle East than these non-Arab countries, but they are also excluded, as it was feared depth of coverage would be sacrificed if there was too wide a geographical spread. Historically the approach has been to concentrate on those areas which have excited most interest at a particular time, and to examine developments which have subsequently proved significant in determining future banking patterns. Hence more details are given of the nationalisation experience in Egypt and Syria than of their current banking operations, which have evolved relatively slowly since the state takeovers. Attention is focused on institutions which have been especially influential in the Arab Middle East, such as Bank Misr of Egypt and the Arab Bank. A whole chapter is devoted to recent financial trends in the Gulf in view of that area's importance for both the regional and the world economy. The impact of Islamic ideas on banking is also discussed in detail, as it seems probable that they will become increasingly significant in the future. Much illustrative material is drawn from Saudi Arabia as the centre of Islam, but new Islamic banks are being opened throughout the region as the chapter on Islamic banking shows.

Although this study is primarily academic, it is anticipated that many of the readers will be practising bankers, concerned with everyday financial affairs rather than monetary theory. The book has been written with a minimum of economic jargon, and it should be readily comprehensible for those with only an elementary knowledge of economics and finance. It is designed not only to be of interest to those currently involved in Middle Eastern banking, but also to provide a useful introduction to the region for those whose career leads them there. In the last few years there have been numerous articles written about Middle Eastern banking in the financial press, but this is the first book devoted exclusively to the subject. Surprisingly, there is even a conspicuous absence of country studies on banking, except for some dealing with Lebanon which are rather dated now. As the evolution of financial institutions is a critical aspect of development, it is also hoped that this work will be of interest to all those concerned with the Middle Eastern economies generally, whether in universities, government departments, or state planning agencies.

In preparing this book I owe a considerable debt of gratitude to all those bankers and financial experts who gave so generously of their time in those Arab countries where I conducted extensive interviews. I should like to mention in particular the assistance I received in Saudi Arabia, Bahrain and the United Arab Emirates from both the central banking authorities and the commercial banks. On my numerous visits to the city of London the representatives of the Arab banks and financial institutions whom I saw were extremely helpful and gave me much encouragement with my work. In Durham I should like to thank the staff of the Middle Eastern Documentation Unit and its director Dr Dick Lawless, for the assistance they provided in locating material, and I should also like to acknowledge the financial support I received from the Middle East Travel Fund for my visits to the region. Once again I must thank Mrs Lovaine Ord for her tireless efforts in typing the manuscript, and Mr John Tavlin for his assistance in proof-reading. Last, but certainly not least, I must express the debt I owe to my wife Barbara for her invaluable help.

September 1981   R.W.

1 Traditional Banking Practice

The financial system of the Middle East dates back long before the advent of modern banking, which has only had a presence in the region for just over a century. As soon as a barter economy gives way to a monetary system, in which some type of specie is used for transactions purposes, a need for financial institutions inevitably arises. Several reasons can be advanced for this need. Firstly, unless all payments and receipts take place instantaneously, some individuals and businesses will end up with holdings of cash, precious metals, or whatever other monetary instruments are used for transactions purposes. These holdings can of course be hoarded, but this involves a security risk, and a cost if protective measures are taken to minimise the risk. However, if centralised deposit facilities are provided, the need for hoarding is reduced, as well as the costs involved. Most societies find it is more convenient, and cheaper, to have such facilities, and the individuals who historically specialised in this task were the moneylenders or the moneychangers.[1]

A second reason for financial institutions is that where there is a delay involved between payments and receipts the resultant deficit has to be financed in some way. The credit to bridge this gap has traditionally been provided by moneylenders. Of course even in an unmonetised barter economy some credit needs will exist, as although a cultivator for example may be prepared to barter his crops for seeds and other productive inputs, his family's subsistence between planting and harvesting has to be covered. These needs can be met out of the hoarded surpluses from previous harvests, but in the Middle East historically, as in other agrarian based societies, it was the landlords who acted as hoarders, and provided their tenants with credit in terms of commodities. The cost of such credit was naturally high, given the opportunity cost which the landlords had to bear as a result of their assets being tied up in hoarded commodities. With monetarisation, credit costs are reduced, as the moneylenders, unlike the landlords, do

1

not keep large amounts of unutilised assets, but lend out as much as possible, subject only to a small reserve for contingencies. With the change from a barter economy, some landlords of course become moneylenders, but the aptitudes and specialisations needed to deploy funds effectively as a moneylender are rather different from those of the landlord, and many were unwilling, or unable, to enter the new profession. The moneychanger needs some skill as a portfolio manager to succeed, and has to judge the character and ability of his borrowers, as well as assess the worth of any security they may offer. A landlord is more concerned with cultivation techniques and water resource management, especially the latter in the Middle East.

A third rationale for financial intermediaries was because not all transactions were carried out using the same monetary instruments. Different types of precious metals were used, gold and silver being the most important, but even these were in various forms, ranging from metal minted in the form of coins, to that manufactured as jewellery. Hence the need for brokers, to arrange the exchange of one financial instrument for another. Some knowledge of the metals themselves and their different qualities was obviously required for such a task. At the same time the moneychangers would have to make sure they obtained sufficient quantities of the assets which were widely used to meet all likely demands. Hence some forecasting ability was needed, or an aptitude for anticipating the market's requirements. Clearly, although the demand for exchange facilities was to meet transactions needs, it would be as unprofitable for the moneychangers as it was for the landlords to merely hoard their assets, unless of course the assets were appreciating rapidly in value. If the latter was not the case, the financial instruments were frequently lent out or invested for some kind of return, either in terms of an interest payment or a profit share. Given this obvious way in which moneychanging and moneylending activities complement each other, it was scarcely surprising that the two activities tended to be performed by the same people. Some of the tasks were identical, and similar financial skills and aptitudes were required for both occupations.

A widening of trading opportunities will of course increase the demand for moneychanging facilities. This may result from greater specialisation in different types of economic activity within a country, or internationally as trade routes are extended with improved methods of transport. In the case of the latter there is likely to be a heightened derived demand for various exchange mediums which the countries involved use, and which the moneychangers will aim to provide in sufficient quantities. Even as early as the lifetime of Mohammed fourteen hundred years ago, the cities of the Hijaz obtained supplies from a wide variety of geographically dispersed sources, and the moneychangers of Mecca, Medina[2] and Taif were able to provide appropriate mediums of exchange which could be used to meet import payments. Gold and silver coins were used to purchase grain supplies from the highlands of Yemen, fruit and vegetables from the Nile Valley, and cloves and spices from as far away as the East African coast.[3]Coins minted from such metals were durable, compact and easy to carry, while in addition they had a certain value because they could be melted down by local silversmiths and goldsmiths and made into decorative jewellery. Like all mediums of exchange, however, at least part of their value came from their acceptability for transactions purposes. To a considerable degree silver and gold were regarded as desirable because of their dual function, and at least part of their preciousness as jewellery was because they were also regarded as the best instruments for exchange.

RANGE OF MONEYCHANGING ACTIVITY

Historically the moneychangers have played a much more significant role in Middle Eastern finance than conventional commercial banks and, even today, they continue to serve a wider section of society than the banks, which tend to cater for the middle and upper classes only. With the spread of the monetary economy their activities have steadily increased, and their business has reached record proportions in absolute terms, even if in relative terms the conventional banks are gaining ground. So long as the majority of transactions in the economies of the Middle East continue to be carried out on a cash basis there is little doubt traditional moneychangers will continue to thrive, and while resistance to the spread of chequing facilities and other modern methods of payment remains, the scope for ordinary banking activity will be restricted. The banks cater for the more westernised citizens, and large modern sector businesses, including state-owned companies, but most private individuals, the numerous small trading and manufacturing establishments of the souk economy, and virtually the entire agrarian sector, deal almost exclusively through moneychangers. The banks certainly have started to dominate in terms of the total value of financial business in recent years, but in terms of the absolute numbers of clients and customer contacts, moneychangers still conduct more business than the banks in the majority of Middle Eastern states.

Most employees in the Middle East are paid by cash rather than cheque or direct transfers, even in relatively sophisticated economies such as those of Egypt and Turkey. For the majority of people these cash payments are themselves an innovation, as the major progress they have experienced is monetarisation, not the advent of cash substitutes as in the West. For many employment in a non-family enterprise marks a considerable change, as hitherto most of those even in urban areas were either self-employed or worked in enterprises for their fathers, grandfathers, or other relatives. Payments were often irregular, family members being paid according to their needs rather than in relation to effort, and frequently payments were made in goods, including food. Some were provided with housing and furniture when they married by senior family members, and household goods were often obtained from craftsmen and workmen in the souk or bazaar in exchange for services rendered by the family business on a barter basis. Gifts between family members were a substitute for regular wages or salaries. In this type of economy there is little need for financial intermediaries even of the traditional moneychanging kind.

Yet moneychanging and moneylending activities are widely carried out in many centres in the Middle East, and some of the traditional moneychanging businesses have been run by the same families for hundreds of years, often on the same sites where the establishments are found today. Major centres included the bazaars and souks[4] of Constantinople, capital of the Ottoman Empire, Beirut, an important trading centre since Phoenician times, Cairo at the hub of the Nile Valley, Isfahan and Shiraz the major merchant cities of Persia, and the sheikhdoms and emirates across the Gulf, as well as in the cities of the Hijaz as already mentioned. All of these cities were important transit centres, as there has always been considerable movement of people in the Middle East.[5] The deserts of the region rather than being barriers to movement instead served as links, with camel caravans regularly plying long distance trade routes. The routes to Mecca were particularly important, with pilgrims being attracted from the entire Muslim world, even beyond the Middle East, and in these circumstances it is not surprising that moneychanging activities were particularly well developed in the cities of the Hijaz. A wide range of coins and precious metals were exchanged by the pilgrims, partly to cover their subsistence needs when in the holy cities, but also to purchase presents and souvenirs for relatives at home. Some of these goods were supplied by other pilgrims, who would of course wish to obtain payment in a medium of exchange which they could use in their country of residence.

There is little doubt the traditional moneychangers became extremely skilled in organising the exchange of coins and precious metals, and there was even some degree of specialisation in the mediums of exchange handled, with particular moneychangers concentrating on coins from one region and a specific type of precious metal. Hence there were moneychangers in the Khan Al-Khalili souk in Cairo that specialised in coins and jewellery from the highlands of Ethiopia far up the Nile Valley, while others accepted mediums of exchange which were used in kingdoms such as Buganda, two thousand miles away in central Africa in what has become Uganda. Some of this activity dates back to the fourteenth century. Those in Beirut accepted coins and precious metals from throughout the Mediterranean area, and even from West Africa, where some Lebanese traders had settled in an attempt to expand their businesses. In Constantinople particular moneychangers handled different European currencies, while a similar pattern prevailed in Dubai where some moneychangers dealt mainly in Indian silver rupees, while others accepted currency from even further east, as well as mediums of exchange from the Indian Ocean periphery of East Africa.

Not only did moneychangers serve as retailers, having direct contact with their customers, but because of the degree of specialisation in the system some acted as wholesalers, catering for the demands of other moneychangers. Long before any inter-bank markets had developed, in many major moneychanging centres there was a considerable amount of business conducted between those involved in coin and precious metal dealings. Thus those who specialised in a particular type of coin or precious metal would be approached by other moneychangers who had been asked for supplies of these by one of their clients. These might be arranged on a swap basis within a particular souk or bazaar, but often deals involved moneychangers from other souks. The major centres of moneychanging activity were in fact linked, and some moneychangers employed regular couriers who could travel hundreds, or even thousands of miles in the course of their business. For example the Maria Teresa silver thalers or dollars[6] were commonly used in the Arabian Peninsula for transactions purposes during the nineteenth century and in the first half of the twentieth century, in the absence of local coins or currency which were widely accepted for international, or even inter-regional payments. Yet these silver coins had been the currency of the Austro-Hungarian Empire, and they were supplied to the moneychangers of the Hijaz and the Gulf by moneychangers in Constantinople who acted in a similar capacity to that of correspondent banks. Interestingly, until the foundation of the Yemen Arab Republic in the 1960s, the Maria Teresa silver thaler actually served as the official currency of royalist Yemen, even though these coins bore the bust of a long deceased Austrian Empress, and the Empire itself had collapsed with the First World War.

In the sheikhdoms and emirates of the Gulf the Indian silver rupee circulated widely, and currencies from the Indian sub-continent were generally used as the major mediums of exchange until separate Gulf currencies were established. Again it was the moneychangers who obtained supplies of these currencies from affiliates in India and what has now become Pakistan, and many of the dhows crossing the Indian Ocean carried couriers amongst their passengers, representing the moneychangers of the Gulf souks. Within the Gulf region there was a degree of specialisation in the coins and precious metals traded by the various moneychangers. The souk in Dubai for example, the most important moneychanging centre in the Gulf, specialised in the exchange of Maria Teresa thalers for Indian rupees, but coinage from the cities of Persia was relatively less important. Fine filigree silver from the Omani metalsmiths of Zanzibar and from Lamu[7] was also freely traded in the Dubai souk, and was provided to some extent as a money substitute, although probably more for precautionary than for transactions purposes. Further north in Bahrain the Shia moneychangers[8] provided Persian coins which they obtained from affiliates in the bazaars of Shiraz and Isfahan, but Bahrain's direct contacts with the Indian subcontinent were less, and most of the rupees which circulated came through the moneychangers of Dubai.

Many moneychanging businesses are not solely concerned with currency exchange, but are also involved in other fields of economic activity outside the sphere of monetary matters altogether. Historically this was also the case, as many of the moneychanging establishments evolved from souk retailers selling precious metals for jewellery, or even small manufacturing workshops where silversmiths and goldsmiths practised their trade. The conversion of gold coins and bullion into jewellery and vice versa was an important activity for such establishments, and it was only a natural progression for some of the goldsmiths and silversmiths to start dealing in the coins themselves. In the souks and bazaars of the Middle East today, the moneychanging establishments are found in close proximity to the gold and silver merchants, and many of the latter continue to undertake some moneychanging business as an adjunct to their main business as jewellers. There are still frequent dealings between the moneychangers and jewellers, with the latter bringing foreign currency and travellers' cheques to the former for conversion into local currency, and in addition some personal cheques for acceptance, which the moneychangers will pass on to the relevant conventional banks. The moneychangers for their part will hand over gold and silver bullion they receive, and even some coins and jewellery to the silver- and goldsmiths, either for reselling or for melting down for conversion into other forms of jewellery.

THE PLACE OF MONEYCHANGERS IN THE SOUK ECONOMY

In the majority of cities and towns in the Middle East with major souks or bazaars, the moneychanging establishments are usually found in the centre of the souk, or at least in as close proximity as possible to the other souk traders. The spatial distribution of moneychanging establishments corresponds to that of other types of souk activities, with a number of moneychangers doing business in one particular area of the souk, so that customers know exactly where to go if they have financial dealings to arrange. This clustering of establishments carrying out similar activities is an important characteristic of souk organisation, and also applies to establishments selling cloths and clothing items, fresh meat, fish, fruit and vegetables, carpets and other household goods. One reason for the clustering is to ensure a rapid flow of information about potential supplies reaching the market, and the dissemination of views about price trends as well as other factors likely to affect business. Clustering has its disadvantages of course, as local customers may find a greater dispersion of moneychangers saves them time because there is a greater likelihood of an establishment being nearby. For travellers, or occasional visitors this is seldom the case however, and they are more likely to remember the location of zoned establishments. The latter may be of more consequence in nomadic societies where people are constantly on the move, and have only a slight acquaintance with many towns and cities.

In some respects the clustering of moneychanging establishments in the souks of the Middle East is analogous to that which occurs in major western financial centres, and there is little doubt that the traditional spatial concentration of economic activity is particularly well suited to any financial community. In so far as there is a degree of specialisation amongst the moneychangers on the lines already indicated, and some development of a wholesale market in financial services, then clustering is certainly beneficial. The moneychangers of the Middle East collaborate with each other in the souks and, although there is inevitably some rivalry, the degree of competition can easily be exaggerated. Hard bargaining may take place between individual moneychangers and customers over charges for particular financial services, but there is little variation in charges amongst different moneychangers in the same souk.[9] Identical exchange rates are usually quoted by all the moneychangers, and the cost of borrowing may vary according to the customer, but there is no significant differentiation between moneychangers themselves. Western concepts such as price wars and special discount offers are unheard of in the traditional souk economy, and moneychangers are not aggressively trying to take over the whole business and drive their rivals into liquidation.

Traditional moneychangers do not actively attempt to entice away each others' customers, and the emphasis is on maintaining customer loyalty. The close proximity of establishments within the souk promotes price conformity, with information on exchange rates freely swapped. Customers frequently go to a moneychanger who is a member of the same family, tribe, or religious sect, as is the case with other souk business. In Bahrain, for example, Shia Muslims always dealt with Shia moneychangers, and Sunni with their co-religionists, and the same religious loyalty was found amongst the Coptic Christians and Muslims of Cairo, and the Marionite Christians and Muslims of Beirut. Customers from other towns and cities often knew by the names of the establishments who belonged to what religion, and their sect or tribal grouping. Only the Jewish moneychangers appear to have a diverse clientele and there are few of these left in the Arab world or Iran. There is little sign that such affiliations are breaking down, indeed in many parts of the Middle East they seem to be growing stronger.

Not only do the traditional moneychangers favour customer loyalty, but staff allegiance is also viewed as important, and there are few instances of any staff leaving one moneychanging establishment to take up work in another. Most staff of course in the past were family members, usually sons and grandsons, and sometimes nephews, cousins, or other more distant relatives. Few women relatives were engaged however, as most male customers in the Middle East would not like to conduct their financial affairs with a member of the opposite sex. [10] It was rare that people were recruited from outside the family, and where they were it was mainly members of the tribe and co-religionists. At the same time at least one family member from each generation was encouraged to enter the business, so that there would be a constant line of succession. Those who wanted to broaden their horizons through travel were given jobs as couriers, but sons who wanted to go into other fields of business activity within the souk, or in neighbouring souks, were often given finance through the firm to get them started in their own businesses. The latter would of course remain clients of the moneychanging firm even after they had repaid any money advanced, and in this way the moneychangers would extend their fields of contacts into new areas. It was not unusual for a high proportion of the clients of the particular moneychanging business to be related to the founder of the establishment.

To a large extent the distribution of moneychanging establishments in Jeddah's main souk is representative of the type of clustering which occurred historically, hence it may be instructive to examine its pattern of activity as a case study. [11] As the detailed souk plan in Figure 1.1 shows, there are thirteen moneychanging establishments in a fairly restricted area of the central souk only 40 metres long, and two adjacent side alleys. The clustering of moneychangers is so close that other types of business activity cannot be carried out to any great extent within the area, the only exceptions being the fruit and vegetable stall on the north side of the souk between the moneychanging establishments of Ahmed Abdul Qani Bamaodah and Mohammad and Abdul Al-Subeaei, and Mukairin the jewellers. The latter is on the other side of Al-Subeaei, between his establishment and the Saleh Seirafi Corporation for Commerce and Construction, yet another moneychanger. The main concentration of jewellers is round the corner from the main pedestrian thoroughfare of the souk, but still well within the confines of the pedestrianised souk, and less than 30 metres from most of the moneychanging establishments. Precious metal objects and gold and silver bullion are to be seen within some of the moneychanging establishments themselves, but if advice is needed about the value of a particular article brought in for exchange, then advice can normally be quickly obtained from a

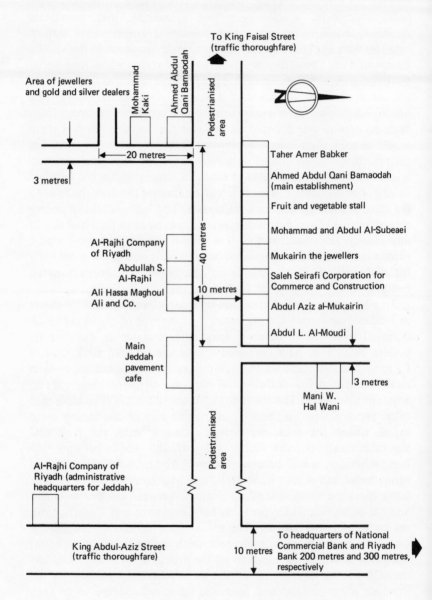

Figure 1.1   Moneychangers of Jeddah souk

neighbouring jeweller. Moneychangers seldom keep scales to weigh precious metals and bullion, given the proximity of the jewellers who always have carefully checked and accurate scales. No payment is made by the moneychangers to the jewellers for services rendered, but exchange facilities will be offered at favourable rates to the particular jeweller with whom a moneychanger customarily deals. Such a discount is especially useful for jewellers in Jeddah, as customers will pay in a variety of currencies and travellers' cheques or other medium, of exchange.

Not all the moneychangers in the Jeddah souk confine their activities solely to exchange of currency and precious metals or even to banking matters such as the provision of credit. Some take part in trading activities to varying degrees, which gives them another line of business to fall back on when exchange activity is slack. In Jeddah of course, as the main port (or airport in recent years) of arrival for pilgrims visiting Mecca, exchange activity is highly seasonal. An establishment such as that of Taher Amer Babker sells mainly cigarettes in the quieter season, while during the pilgrimage season the concentration is on finance. Some of the large cartons of cigarettes are still sold during the pilgrimage season, however, as the pilgrims themselves may find the Taher's prices compare favourably with those at the airport. Other moneychangers sell rare coins, which have a value in excess of their metal content and are collectors' items for many visitors to Jeddah, both from within Saudi Arabia and internationally.

Many customers, including pilgrims visiting Jeddah, head for the Al-Rajhi moneychanging establishments, two of which are found in Jeddah's central souk area as the plan shows, while another is located nearby. The Al-Rajhis have a reputation for offering more favourable exchange rates than the commercial banks in Saudi Arabia, which draws most visitors and residents to their establishments. Often casual customers go to the Al-Rajhi establishments in preference to the other moneychangers because of their reputation, even though as already indicated the other moneychangers normally offer identical rates. However, at peak times the Al-Rajhi establishments often become so busy that rather than queue, potential customers will try the other moneychangers. Given this crowding-out effect, the clustering of moneychangers which occurs in the souk brings business to all. Hence to some extent the reputation of the Al-Rajhis is a favourable externality as far as the other moneychangers are concerned. In fact the Al-Rajhis often have access to exchange rate information through their international contacts which the other moneychangers lack, but which they can soon discover by seeing what the Al-Rajhis are doing with their rates. In so far as it is possible to apply terms such as price leadership to the context of a souk economy, then the Al-Rajhis are the family who perform that function.

The Al-Rajhi Company of Riyadh has become the largest moneychanger in the world, and their Jeddah branch represents only one of 120 offices found throughout Saudi Arabia.[12] This is a more extensive network than even the kingdom's leading conventional financial institution, the National Commercial Bank, can boast. As the plan shows there are two Al-Rajhi establishments in the central souk area of Jeddah, both trading next to each other under different names. The Abdullah S. Al-Rajhi Establishment for Exchange, Commerce and Commission was founded by a nephew of the owners of the Al-Rajhi Empire, who decided to go his own way in 1975 at the age of twenty-seven, and founded his own independent moneychanging business. Like his uncle Suleiman Al-Rajhi, one of the brothers who founded the original firm, young Abdullah soon prospered, and by 1980 had twenty-three branches of his own moneychanging firm.[13] His business is the greatest rival to the Al-Rajhis of Riyadh, although of course there is no price competition, but there is considerable rivalry over the range of services provided.

The rise of the Al-Rajhis to their present dominant position amongst Saudi Arabian moneychangers is itself a fascinating story, as in the 1960s Suleiman Al-Rajhi used to walk round the Jeddah souk with an old suitcase full of banknotes which he supplied to the other moneychangers.[14] Yet only a decade later the family had become one of the richest in Saudi Arabia, as the fully paid-up capital of their main business alone is almost $200 million.[15] The family has long since diversified from the original wholesaling business of supplying foreign banknotes to the other moneychangers, and their establishments perform most normal banking functions. As deposit takers they rank third in the kingdom after the National Commercial and Riyadh banks, their deposits being worth almost $1500 million by 1979. In addition the Al-Rajhis have their own construction and contracting business, and act as timber merchants and builders' suppliers. Saudi Arabia's oil boom has undoubtedly been a major boost for the business, which has also helped the other local moneychangers expand, if on a more modest scale. Of those represented in the plan, Al-Subeaei had fifteen branches by 1980, Abdul Aziz Al-Mukairin three branches, Ahmed Abdul Qani Bamaodah three, and Mohamed Kaki ten. The latter is also related to the owners of the National Commercial Bank. Another family represented in central Jeddah, but outside the plan area, the Bagalafs, own eight moneychanging establishments.

The Al-Rajhis not only made fortunes in moneychanging, but have also made considerable amounts out of property as a result of land grants made by King Abdul-Aziz Ibn Saud in the vicinity of Riyadh. Once Riyadh became the kingdom's capital and started to expand, land values soared, and as a result so did the wealth of the Al-Rajhis. As a devout Muslim, King Saud had always mistrusted banks, and he left many of his financial affairs to the Al-Rajhis. They had the advantage of coming from the desert of the interior, and had a similar background to the King himself. The traditional moneychangers of the Hijaz were always viewed with some distaste by the King, given the money they had made from the pilgrimage traffic over the years, but the Al-Rajhis of Riyadh were untarnished in the King's view. The Al-Rajhis did not use their privileged position and growing wealth however to take over the other moneychanging establishments or drive them out of business. Such cut-throat methods would be out of keeping with the teaching of the Koran, and hence any trend towards monopolisation was avoided. Instead of expansion being through acquisition and merger, it was through opening further branches in new commercial areas as the economy of the kingdom grew.

BANKERS VERSUS MONEYLENDERS

The relationship between traditional financial institutions and modern commercial banks has never been cordial, or even relaxed, and nowhere is this more evident than in Saudi Arabia where moneychangers and moneylenders still play a very significant role in financial activity. Those employed in the commercial banks seem to treat the moneylenders as if they were rather primitive institutions, and are at best patronising. At the same time the more conservative moneylenders assert that their neighbourly operations are more in accordance with the spirit of an Islamic society, and that the bankers are impersonal and remote from the customers they serve.[16] In addition it is alleged that because the conventional banks are essentially westernised institutions, they are therefore inappropriate in an oriental society.[17] In contrast the moneychangers and moneylenders adopt the business methods of the souk economy, and their financial relationships with at least some of their clients are also seen as part of a wider personal friendship. Family relationships have been built up over generations with other merchants in the souk whom they serve, and they are often related by marriage to these customers. Hence they have not only a knowledge of the business history of their customers but also detailed information on their family backgrounds.

The moneychangers of the Jeddah souk, like those in other parts of the Middle East, do not merely exchange currency, but also continue in their traditional role as moneylenders. Conventional bankers often assert that customers are ill-advised to seek credit from such sources, as the charges for borrowing are higher than those levied by the banks. There is little doubt that there is some truth in this assertion, yet many customers, even those with modern businesses outside the traditional souk economy, often prefer to deal with the moneylenders rather than conventional banks. Several reasons can be advanced for this preference, one being the flexibility of the loan terms offered by the moneylenders. Whereas the banks offer fixed terms on business and personal loans, the duration of which is normally agreed in advance, the moneylenders are prepared to allow more flexible arrangements, with the customer making repayments when it suits him, rather than the cash flow position of the lender. Conventional banks of course have overdraft facilities, but these are only made available to their more affluent customers in the Middle East, while most bank customers are encouraged to keep their accounts in credit. These less affluent customers often find the moneychangers more helpful than their own banks.

A further attraction of the moneylenders is the informality with which credit can be arranged. When a potential borrower approaches a bank, there will often be a considerable amount of paperwork involved, and the loan will take time to arrange, perhaps involving two or more appointments with the bank even for minor requests. Admittedly most Middle Eastern banks do not probe too far into the purposes for which loans are utilised, at least as far as valued customers are concerned, given the emphasis on personal and even business privacy in the region. However, the banks have to satisfy themselves about the financial status of their client and the value of any security being offered, all of which can prove a lengthy process. In contrast the moneylenders, because of their close acquaintance with many potential borrowers and their families, are able to respond instantly to requests for credit. There is a minimum of paperwork, and clients do not usually need to make appointments in advance.

Even those clients whom the moneylenders do not know can obtain credit immediately provided they offer security; and unlike the banks, the moneylenders will act as pawnshops, directly accepting jewellery or precious metals themselves, and advancing cash or other forms of credit required. The security offered in this way can be immediately valued by a neighbouring jeweller, goldsmith or silversmith in the souk, if the moneylender has any doubt about its worth.

The premium for the service provided by the moneylender compared with a conventional bank is often modest, since, because the moneylender's costs are lower, he can afford to give more favourable credit terms than might otherwise be the case. The premises which a moneychanger operates from are usually far from plush, unlike those of many Middle Eastern banks, and they are usually of a similar basic standard to the other establishments in the souks. Property taxes where these are applied are minimal, and as many moneychangers own their premises, or hold them on permanent leases, rental payments are either nil, or negligible. Staff costs are also low, as employees in moneylending and moneychanging establishments are not on bank pay scales.[18] Disputes over pay or conditions are unheard of within such family businesses, but arguably there is some intra-family exploitation, although in the long run, as the younger generation will inherit the business, there is little cause for dissatisfaction. In any case the emphasis is on the fortunes of the family, and of the parents in particular, not on the personal wealth of individuals from its younger generation.

The moneylenders have distinct advantages over conventional banks in being unregulated, which reduces their administrative work, and in having no official reserve requirements. Conventional banks have to keep a portion of their reserves, usually from seven to fifteen per cent, deposited with the central bank or monetary agency of the country in which they operate. These deposits earn no interest, or other return, and are therefore completely unprofitable from the bank's point of view. Them moneylenders do not have to bear this opportunity cost and can deploy all their funds profitably, which gives them a competitive edge over the conventional banks. This naturally arouses resentment in the banking community and in Saudi Arabia since 1980 there have been some rumours of regulations being imposed on moneylending activity.[19] Although these would enable the authorities to have greater control over the money supply, and indeed a better knowledge of the actual magnitude of the money supply, there is little need for such regulation in the interests of sound lending activity or financial institutional stability. No moneylenders have gone out of business in recent years in Saudi Arabia due to imprudent lending practice, whereas one of the kingdom's banks nearly went into liquidation in the mid-1960s. Nor is there much evidence that credit from the moneylenders is used for less economically desirable purposes than that advanced by the conventional banks. In these circumstances regulation would appear unnecessary, and if it reduces flexibility or raises the moneylenders' costs, then this burden will only be passed on to the whole community.

It is worth noting that much of the credit advanced by the traditional moneylenders is tied to the purchase of particular goods or services, unlike that granted by conventional banks which is usually untied. Those obtaining credit from the Al-Rajhis, for example to finance construction ventures, will be expected to purchase materials and equipment from Al-Rajhi companies which act as builder's suppliers.[20] Credit may even be given in kind rather than cash, and no money may change hands in the course of the transaction, but rather a note may be provided authorising the supply of particular items which the affiliated company may then present to the moneylender. Even when the moneylender himself has no outside trading interests, he may encourage, or even require, borrowers to use suppliers who are his relations, or who are at least his clients even if unrelated. It is argued that by tying credit in this way, which helps the moneylender's associates, it will ultimately benefit the moneylenders themselves. They have long realised that prosperity is indivisible, at least as far as their clients and themselves are concerned.

Moneylenders like conventional banks obtain most of their funds for lending from deposits, but many augment their deposits with capital injections from other businesses with which they or their relatives are involved. As much as a third of all resources are obtained in this way in some cases such as the Al-Rajhis, but such internal financing is never practised by conventional banks. There is in fact no rigid distinction between ordinary deposit accounts and paid-up share accounts, except that the moneychangers and their relatives may in effect hold the latter, and take a share in the profits of the business. Ordinary depositors do not get a dividend return, nor do they earn interest. They know however that their funds are secure, and can be withdrawn on demand, while in addition depositors receive first preference in obtaining loans, on which they have to pay only modest amounts of fees. For those without deposits or with minimal deposits, charges are much higher for borrowing.

Most of the moneylenders maintain considerable liquid resources, but in the event of a sudden spate of withdrawals, they can request funds from neighbouring moneylenders in the souk in much the same way as bankers help each other out on a day-to-day basis over liquidity. Their close proximity to each other in the souk facilitates such operations, and it means that each can see how neighbouring businesses are faring. Given the importance of a degree of mutual confidence, this is an additional reason why moneylenders do not strive to drive each other out of business, and the emphasis is on collaboration rather than competition as already indicated.

From the customers' point of view one advantage of the moneychanging and moneylending establishments compared with conventional banks is their extended hours of opening. In Saudi Arabia, for example, the banks are generally open from only 8.30 a.m. until noon, and from 5 p.m. till 7 p.m., and close on Thursday afternoon and all day Friday. Most moneychangers, however, open from 8 a.m. till 8 p.m., with a two-hour lunch break, and they remain open all day on Thursdays. [21] The moneychangers also have longer hours of opening during Ramadan and the pilgrimage season, and as Ramadan and its aftermath can extend to six weeks, this can be a significant convenience. There are no cash dispensers outside banks in the Middle East despite the growing sophistication of banking methods; but even if these are eventually installed, there will still be a demand for the other financial services which only the moneylenders and moneychangers can provide when the banks are closed.

Although the moneylenders and moneychangers were the earliest type of financial business in the Middle East, they are far from being old-fashioned. Today they still maintain some of their traditional methods, and most have little desire to be transformed into conventional banks. Yet at the same time the leading establishments are modernising their businesses, and innovating to take advantage of new opportunities. None may yet have computerised accounting systems, but even the humblest establishment uses calculating machines, and the Al-Rajhis and some of the larger exchange dealers have telex equipment. Exchange operations are conducted extremely efficiently, and the moneychangers usually offer more favourable rates than the banks, as already indicated. They are able to do this partly because of their excellent communications with the world's major financial centres, indeed often it is asserted that the moneychangers of Jeddah's souk know more about movements of the riyal than the Saudi Arabian Monetary Agency, the kingdom's central banking authority.

Unlike the banks in Saudi Arabia which obtain much of their foreign exchange from the Saudi Arabian Monetary Agency or else from Bahrain, the Al-Rajhis deal directly with centres in Europe, especially Zurich. Special couriers are sent to Switzerland on a regular basis to obtain foreign banknotes and gold to augment the supplies which the moneychangers obtain from the currency changed by foreigners within the kingdom, and that from Saudi citizens returning from abroad. These jet-hopping couriers are in many ways performing a similar function to those who traditionally travelled with the camel trains. The method, however, enables the Al-Rajhis to obtain their currency and gold at more favourable rates than the conventional banks, and as they also act as suppliers to the other moneychangers, they can obtain the standard discounts for bulk purchase. In fact the Al-Rajhis find it worthwhile to maintain a permanent link with Zurich through an associated company headed by an Iraqi, Mahmoud Kasim Shakarchi, who conducts exchanges when conditions are optimal. Before the Lebanese civil war much of this business was conducted through Beirut, but since the moneychangers have discovered just how efficient Swiss markets can be, it is unlikely they will revert to using that troubled city again. [22]

In terms of exchange dealings the Al-Rajhis are more important than any of the Saudi banks, as they not only handle moneychanging within the kingdom, but also many of the remittances repatriated by the foreign workers. Although most of the European and American workers deal with the Saudi-ised institutions that represent national banks from their countries of origin, such as the Saudi British Bank [23] or the Saudi American Bank, [24] most of the Arab workers, and those from the Indian sub-continent and the Far East prefer the moneychangers, who now have an extensive network of correspondent institutions abroad. The moneychangers have clearly developed considerably and, although their role in Saudi Arabia, as already indicated, is more significant than in other Middle Eastern states, they are still a force to be reckoned with throughout the region. Of course the entry of European banks into the Middle East has transformed the financial system since the last century, as the next chapter will show, but traditional institutions remain and even flourish. It would certainly be premature to write their epitaph, and their continued presence certainly adds colour to the Middle Eastern financial scene.

2   Emergence of Modern Banking

As Egypt had the earliest modern banks in the Arab Middle East, it seems appropriate to examine its financial institutions in detail, even though initially they were foreign rather than locally owned. It was in any case the rapid penetration of foreign banks which eventually resulted in moves to found indigenous institutions, whose business practices correspond to those found in the West. That Egypt should be the instigator of modern banking in the Arab Middle East is not altogether surprising, as the country boasted the largest number of educated people, had considerable commercial dealings both internally and externally, and possessed an economic and financial sophistication not found elsewhere. Despite the fact that nationalism in Egypt was strong even in the early nineteenth century, foreigners took most of the initiative in financial dealings, and there was a marked absence of local competition.[1] It was only in the 1920s that a belated attempt was made to emulate European banking practices and establish a wholly indigenous institution.

Although Egypt was nominally part of the Ottoman Empire in the nineteenth century, it enjoyed considerable political autonomy under its vigorous ruler Mohammed Ali, which was reflected in the independence it exercised in the financial sphere. The Ottoman Bank of course operated within the country, its Alexandria branch being opened as early as 1867; but its activities were confined to the finance of trade, and it did not have the privileged position *vis-à-vis* the local Egyptian authorities which it had in Constantinople. Other foreign-owned banks carried out similar trading business, including the Egyptian Bank, the first modern financial institution established in Cairo, which started operating in 1856.[2] Overall this British-owned institution probably received greater patronage from the Cairo authorities than even the Ottoman Bank, as they engaged its services to arrange several major loans, though it did not have any exclusive rights to government business.

19

The main instigator of the Bank of Egypt was a Greek merchant from Izmir (Smyrna) named Pasquali. Thanks to his convincing and persuasive personality, he was able to get financial support for his new venture from prestigious and influential backers, including the London-based East India Company, the Westminster Bank, the Oriental Banking Corporation, and even the British Treasury,[3] which encouraged English investors to provide the rest of the capital. Conflict soon developed however between the bank's conservative-minded English backers, and the rasher Pasquali, who had initially convinced the directors to appoint him as resident manager. The directors were unhappy about loans made to the Egyptian royal household, and their fears proved well-founded when repayments were not forthcoming, and the bank found most of its assets tied up. Owing to the efforts of the arduous Pasquali the bank nevertheless managed to survive; but he received little thanks and was soon dismissed by the board. Out of spite Pasquali decided to set up another venture with himself as manager, this time with French support; but the institution established in 1881, the Société Financière, never became active.

As the Société Financière was stillborn, real competition for the Bank of Egypt only came in 1864 when the Anglo-Egyptian Bank was founded, which was later to become part of the Barclay group. Its original sponsors were the Agra and Mastermans Bank, an important Anglo-Indian concern, and a French finance company belonging to Samuel Laing which was heavily involved in railway development.[4] The Anglo-Egyptian Bank started with LE500,000 (Livres Egyptienne – Egyptian pounds, originally on a parity with sterling). This was more than twice the capital of the Bank of Egypt, consequently the Anglo-Egyptian bank succeeded in attracting commercial business on a modest scale, mainly from the French community in Egypt, despite the institution's name. Its main business, however, was with the Egyptian government, in discounting Egyptian treasury bills, and in syndicate participation in long-term loans for the government, which meant its profitability tended to fluctuate with the standing of the government, although in no sense could it be regarded as a central bank. Nor was the bank really competitive ultimately, as by the 1870s it acted in association with the Bank of Eygpt in handling government business and, as with the Imperial Ottoman Bank and the Deutsche Bank in Constantinople, there was no question of the authorities playing off one institution against the other.

Several additional major foreign banks established offices in Egypt from 1870 onwards, as cotton exports expanded rapidly, resulting in a growing demand for trade finance. A prime cause of this was the ending of slavery after the American Civil War which enabled Egypt, with its low-cost labour, to compete more easily in world cotton markets against the former Confederate States whose production was disrupted by the war. In addition, the opening of the Suez Canal was also a major boost to the Egyptian economy, both through its effect on trade, and by generating revenue for the new canal towns, as well as the Cairo authorities. Amongst the earliest banks established was the Yokohama Specie Bank which started business in Port Said in 1870.⁵ This Tokyo-based bank was the first of the Japanese financial institutions to establish overseas branches, and the Port Said branch was one of its earliest ventures abroad. The Suez Canal was of considerable significance for Japanese trade, making Port Said an obvious location for any institution involved in export credit or import finance. Port Said's position as a banking centre was further enhanced in 1872 when the Ottoman Bank opened its second Egyptian branch there. Three years later the Paris-based Crédit Lyonnais also opened an office in the port, an event which had long been expected in European banking circles in view of France's shareholding in the Suez Canal and its growing commercial links with Egypt.

A further five years was to elapse, however, before another largely French-inspired institution started business in Cairo, Crédit Foncier Egyptien, but this new locally incorporated institution functioned as a mortgage or land bank, rather than specialising in ordinary commercial banking transactions and the finance of trade. Hitherto in Egypt most of the moneylending to landlords had been in the hands of the traditional moneylenders who were frequently Greek rather than local Muslims, even at village level. As these traditional moneylenders often charged usurious interest, the creation of Crédit Foncier was a welcome development for the landowners, as it meant that they could obtain credit on reasonable terms. Only the larger landlords benefited, however, as it would have been administratively expensive for the bank to deal with numerous smallholders, who frequently did not have their lands registered in any case. Thus the creation of the new bank probably reinforced the inequalities which existed in Egypt's rural community, strengthening the financial position of the large landowners *vis-à-vis* those with smaller acreages who continued to rely on expensive moneylenders.

By the 1880s merchants and traders in Egypt were expanding their businesses, which created a demand for further larger-scale modern banking facilities. In response to this demand the Cassa di Sconto e di Risparmio was started in Cairo in 1887, while the Banque d'Athenes opened an Egyptian branch in 1895 to serve the Italian and Greek communities respectively.[6] This type of ethnic loyalty in financial dealings in Egypt was to persist until the Revolution under Nasser, and it certainly inhibited the development of indigenous banks, given the financial power of the foreign communities. There is little doubt that, if financially sound local institutions had been developed in Cairo at an earlier stage, the phenomenon of ethnic banking would not have arisen to the same extent. Even during the first decade of the twentieth century new banking business went to the foreign banks rather than local institutions, with Le Comptoir National d'Escompte de Paris, the Ionian Bank, the Deutsche Orientbank and La Banque d'Orient opening offices in Egypt.[7] These latecomers had little difficulty in entering the financial market, as there was no real competition from the established banks who were content to serve their own communities and did not actively seek other business.

It is worth emphasising how much of the early banking activity in Egypt was located in Alexandria and Port Said rather than Cairo, which only later developed as a financial centre. To a large extent this reflected the ethnic nature of the banking system as Alexandria was a cosmopolitan city, whose inhabitants regarded themselves as belonging to the Mediterranean rather than the Arab world, and where there were large numbers of Greeks and Italians settled. Much of the population of the city was Christian rather than Muslim, and even many of the Arabs were either Christian immigrants from the Levant, or members of the Egyptian Coptic Church. Similarly Port Said was an international town, and most of its wealthy residents likely to use modern banking services were foreigners, normally involved with the Canal either directly or indirectly. Cairo in contrast was essentially Arab and Muslim, although the foreign community grew substantially in number in the 1890s when attempts were made to establish a local textile industry, which soon failed owing to European competition and an absence of tariffs. It was to serve this community that the Ottoman Bank established its Cairo office in 1887, over twenty years after its first branch in Alexandria had been opened, and fifteen years after the founding of its Port Said branch.[8]

A NATIONAL BANK OF EGYPT?

After 1856, as already mentioned, much of Egyptian government finance was raised through the main Cairo-based, but British-owned financial institution, the Egyptian Bank, rather than through the Alexandria office of the Ottoman Bank. The Egyptian Bank was less soundly based than the Ottoman Bank, however, as its eventual failure in 1911 showed; and even as early as 1876 there had been some discussions between the British, French, Italian and Egyptian authorities concerning the establishment of a national institution to act as central banker for the Cairo government. Each of the three European powers was to select a commissioner to control the bank, but there was no provision for Egyptian representation on the control body. Such interference in the affairs of another country allegedly worried Lord Derby, the British Foreign Secretary, yet Britain was to occupy Egypt only six years later. It seems more likely that his main fear was that French influence would soon dominate in the new institution, as had proved to be the case with the Ottoman Bank. Whatever the reason for Derby's opposition, however, the idea of a new institution was dropped, as Britain refused to nominate a commissioner.[9]

Only in 1898 therefore was a National Bank established in Egypt, this time as a result of a wholly British initiative by Lord Cromer, who had originally been involved in discussions twenty-two years earlier.[10] By this time Britain had established itself as the dominant foreign power in Egypt, so there was little to fear from the French, but the foreign banks continued to function as a power unto themselves. Under the Capitulations originally granted by the Ottoman Government when they exercised overall legal authority over Egypt, foreigners were not subject to Islamic legal codes, and this was extended to include banking. The enactment of the mixed court legislation in Egypt in 1876 confirmed this position, as the new courts, rather than the local courts, adjudicated on legal matters affecting non-citizens and even the judges in them were foreign. In practice the banks were given a free hand in the absence of legislation on financial affairs, but it was to regulate this position, and establish virtual British management of the banking system, that Cromer had proposed a National Bank. Its foundation consequently was a result of British rather than Egyptian national interests, although Cromer would have argued that the local financial climate could be substantially improved under British direction, with mutual benefits.

The National Bank never succeeded in its objective of becoming a banker's bank, however, as legally it did not have the power of a central bank, and in the complete absence of any banking legislation, it had little control over the other foreign financial institutions. Indeed its privileged position and pretensions to power aroused the resentment of the other banks, and they successfully thwarted any attempts it made to control their activities. Nor was the bank popular with local Egyptians as its entire senior staff were foreign nationals, and although by the 1920s one or two Arab professional politicians were asked to serve on its board of directors, this was seen by many as merely a gesture to win favour with the Egyptian authorities.

From the start however the National Bank had close relations with the Egyptian authorities in any case, as its first Governor was Sir Elwin Palmer, who was formerly Financial Adviser to the Cairo government.[11] Although power was in theory exercised from the bank's Cairo head office, a committee of directors was set up in London, which had to approve all loans of LE100,000 or over, any augmentation of capital, changes to the bank's statutes, and the annual dividend. The most powerful director was Sir Ernest Cassel, whose shareholding amounted to LE50,000, representing half of the bank's initial capital. For one individual to own such a share in what was supposed to be another country's central bank was certainly incongruous, and in the circumstances it was scarcely surprising that the Egyptian authorities felt increasing unease about their National Bank's position and loyalties, despite the initial close relationship. The only locally-owned shareholdings in the bank were those of two cotton exporting firms, C. M. Salvago and Co. and Suares Frères and Co., but neither of these was run by Egyptian citizens. Although the bank was granted a monopoly right of note issue on its foundation,[12] it never assumed the dominant role in other government business which the Imperial Ottoman Bank or the Imperial Bank of Persia enjoyed. The National Bank made advances to the Egyptian and Sudanese governments at national and local level, and discounted Egyptian government bills with one year or less to run, but it had no exclusive rights to this business which all the banks operating in Cairo, Alexandria and Port Said shared to a greater or lesser degree.

Despite the National Bank's abortive effort to become a banker's bank, and its failure to become a fully fledged central bank, in its commercial dealings the institution was nevertheless a success. By 1907, nine years after its establishment, the number of depositors had risen to 5901, while by 1911 it had over 10,147 clients, and it had opened a network of sixteen branches in Egypt and the Sudan. Advances to the Cairo and Khartoum Governments accounted for less than 11 per cent of assets, but private loans in the two countries accounted for almost 58 per cent of assets, the remainder consisting of cash and bank notes (14 per cent) and foreign bills and securities.

Almost half of all deposits were accounted for by the Egyptian Ministry of Finance and the mixed courts, the remainder representing the current account holdings of foreign residents, and those of a small minority of wealthy local traders, large landowners, and high-ranking public servants. Given the high ratio of government deposits to total deposits, but the low ratio of government borrowing in relation to private loans, to a large extent the bank served as a mechanism for channelling funds from the public to the private sector.

Not only did the National Bank aid inter-sectoral transfers, particularly, its supporters asserted, the more directly productive activities within the private sector, but it also went to considerable lengths to lend money in the rural areas. An experimental agricultural credit scheme was launched in the Belbeis district of lower Egypt only one year after the bank's foundation, with 1580 advances made to tenants with smallholdings and owners of small plots.[13] Repayments of these limited advances, which averaged a mere LE3 each, was made the concern of the government tax collectors as part of their normal professional duties. This minimised the administrative overheads for the bank, and made the scheme more viable from its point of view, as in effect the government was subsidising the whole operation by covering much of the wage expenses. The venture proved a success as virtually all of the loans that had been made at sowing time in the spring of 1899 were repaid the same year after the autumn harvest. Therefore Sir Elwin Palmer, the scheme's instigator, decided to extend lending operation throughout the delta region of Egypt, and by 1901 over 34,000 loans had been made.[14] Of the 15,269 loans outstanding in September 1901, 3326 were repayable within a year, and 11,943 within five years. The new five-year loans were of course for greater amounts than the annual loans, but the average amount of credit granted still only worked out at under LE30, well within most peasants' capacity to pay over the longer period.

There is little doubt that Palmer's venture was of considerable benefit to many in the rural areas, and encouraged the spread of cotton cultivation by smallholders which added to Egypt's export earnings. Not all of the money may have been of course used for productive purposes or even for farming, but those who used their credits as they were supposed to found their cash incomes augmented. Apart from those who gained directly, there were also indirect benefits as moneylenders were forced to lower their interest charges, although others stopped lending altogether rather than reduce their rates. The Crédit Foncier Egyptien was forced to lower its minimum advance to

LE100, but this was still more than most of those in the rural areas could afford to repay.[15]

As the National Bank's agricultural lending scheme grew in both scope and scale, it was forced to go to the government for more funds, and as a temporary measure LE250,000 was advanced early in 1902 to help finance more loans, as those already outstanding amounted to over LE400,000. Later the same year however the decision was taken to establish a separate agricultural bank with its own funds, to be wholly owned by the National Bank, which would also exercise ultimate control. In June 1902 this new institution, with its capital fixed at LE2.5 million, took over the National Bank's agricultural business. Part of this capital was subscribed by the government, and the rest issued in bonds, which freed the National Bank's own capital for more directly commercial purposes. This was no doubt a major reason why Sir Elwin Palmer of the National Bank had argued the case for the new institution extremely vigorously.

Under article four of the Agricultural Bank's statutes it was empowered to make advances of up to LE300 for a maximum of five and a half years, to be secured by first mortgage on lands worth at least twice that amount, or alternatively it could grant unsecured loans of up to LE20 for a period not exceeding fifteen months.[16] The new institution was however less well run than the parent bank, and some of its advances were used for land purchase. This only added to the speculation already building up in Egypt's rural areas due to the large inflow of foreign capital attracted by opportunities for the profitable development of cotton. When the land boom collapsed in 1907, the debt burden on landowners both large and small became onerous, and many were threatened with dispossession. In order to prevent widespread rural unrest, the government finally passed the five feddan law in 1912, which prevented foreclosure on land below that amount. This effectively halted the granting of secured loans to small farmers, and after that the bank stopped providing new credit and concentrated on collection of debts, many of which were still outstanding twenty years later.

The difficulties facing the Agricultural Bank from 1912 onwards did not seriously undermine its parent company however, as its activities continued to expand rapidly in the commercial banking field, especially with respect to trade finance. As Table 2.1 shows even the First World War did not seem to affect the bank's activity, despite a crisis in the Egyptian financial community immediately prior to the outbreak of hostilities when many worried about the possible effect of the war on Egypt's trade. During the war in fact many European financiers exported funds to the comparative safety of Egypt as the deposit figures for the National Bank show, but this caused an accompanying increase in advances, as the bank wanted to profitably deploy its funds. This in turn accentuated Egypt's inflationary problems on the demand side, which were aggravated already on the supply side due to wartime shortages. The National Bank felt impelled to lend nevertheless, despite these inflationary implications, otherwise it might lose its share of Egypt's financial business to its rivals. Thus the conflict between the role the bank should have been playing as a central bank controlling the economy, and its commercial ambitions and worries was becoming more obvious.

The figures cited in Table 2.1 refer to the turnover of advances and deposits in each calendar year rather than the amounts outstanding at any given time, as it was the size of its business which the National Bank sought to emphasise. In practice assets barely covered advances, and the National Bank, in line with other Egyptian banks, allowed its

TABLE 2.1 *The National Bank of Egypt: turnover of advances and deposits (LE million)*

	Advances	Deposits
1914	39.1	123.2
1915	52.4	155.5
1916	50.5	234.9
1917	63.4	290.6
1918	112.0	410.0
1919	136.9	553.3
1920	158.3	611.4
1921	69.6	454.7
1922	69.8	385.1
1923	87.3	404.5
1924	96.1	417.5
1925	94.1	449.7
1926	85.1	443.4
1927	148.9	557.0
1928	144.1	578.2
1929	126.1	847.2

SOURCE Mohammed Ali Rifaat, *The Monetary System of Egypt* (London: Allen and Unwin, 1935) Table XXIII, p. 123, and Table XXXI, 127.

cash ratio to fall dangerously low, as there was no legislation governing such matters or the activities of the foreign banks in general. The banks did not appear to have learnt any lessons from an earlier crisis in 1907 when the Cassa di Sconto suspended payments, and there was a run on all Egyptian bank deposits, which the National Bank could do little to stem because of its own precarious position. Only when a belated syndicate was formed between the banks was disaster avoided, yet the same mistakes were being repeated again during the 1912–20 period.

After the good fortunes of the war years for the Egyptian banks, 1920 saw a sudden change, partly due to a repatriation of deposits back to Europe, but mainly because of a dramatic fall in cotton prices which severely cut Egypt's export earnings, and caused a sharp decline in economic activity in general. This is reflected in the fall for advances and deposits cited in Table 2.1, with advances declining by 57 per cent between 1920 and 1921, and not regaining their 1920 peak for over a decade. With business in a state of depression, customers no longer wanted credit, especially for the finance of the cotton trade, the mainstay of Egypt's economy. The decline in deposits was more gradual and less severe in magnitude, but nevertheless serious, with their value declining by a quarter between 1920 and 1921 alone, and with a further 14 per cent fall the following year. The National Bank fared less badly during the crisis than most of its competitors, but as the supposed central bank in Egypt, it was blamed by many for the financial crisis, and out of expediency soon fell out of political favour. By the 1920s the heyday of the National Bank had already passed, and despite it being only partly to blame for events, it had little hope of even retaining its privileged position *vis-à-vis* the government and the other banks.

THE START OF INDIGENOUS BANKING

Since the 1907 Cassa di Sconto crisis there had been increasing dissatisfaction amongst the local Muslim bourgeoisie with Egypt's banking system, as the growing educated class felt the need for modern banking facilities rather than traditional moneylenders, but they were unhappy that all the main financial institutions established in their cities and towns were foreign-owned. Following a debate on banking in the Egyptian congress when the Cassa di Sconto affair was discussed, in 1911 Mohammed Talat Harb, an influential Cairo financier, wrote a book arguing the case for an Egyptian bank, which would be owned by the local citizens whom it would serve.[17] He was unable to get sufficient financial support at that time however to put his ideas for a new institution into action, but the experiences of the First World War years persuaded many that a locally owned and controlled bank was needed. Although there was a substantial inflow of funds during the war years as already indicated, the banks were reluctant to commit these funds on a long-term basis to Egyptian borrowers in case, once peace was restored, the money was repatriated.

After the end of hostilities in 1919 Talat Harb, feeling the time was right to get his proposed banking venture finally started, sent a circular to prospective shareholders urging their support for a new financial institution to be known as Bank Misr (Bank of Egypt). As this was at the height of the immediate post-war boom there were Egyptians around with money to invest, especially the large landowners and rich merchants who dealt in cotton, as it was not until a year later that cotton prices dramatically fell. These people had previously merely hoarded surplus funds, or deposited them in foreign banks, or invested in land, but in the new mood of confidence following the war, there was a desire to be more venturous, and when offered the prospect of taking part in a new national scheme which could also bring personal reward, investment funds were soon forthcoming. Altogether 128 rich Egyptians bought shares in the bank, raising LE80,000 between them, a considerable sum for the time for such an untried and largely uncertain undertaking.[18]

The dominance of landowners and merchants was reflected in the Board of Directors of the Bank, as of the ten initial members, four were large landowners, two were rich merchants and a further two were high-ranking government officials. The remaining two directors were already involved with finance, including Talat Harb himself, as both were also directors of Crédit Foncier Egyptien, the institution founded in 1880 which granted loans to those who mortgaged their land. As the share capital of Bank Misr was increased, three additional directors were appointed from the same type of social background, as one was a merchant and owner of an important silk factory, the second was a high-ranking government official, and the third was a large landowner.[19] Therefore in no sense, despite the bank's name, could it be looked upon as a bank representing the ordinary Egyptian people, but instead it was essentially an institution owned by, and under the direction of, the local bourgeoisie.

The bank was nevertheless an immediate success with its capital more than doubling in its second year of operations, and expansion throughout the 1920s as Table 2.2 shows. By the beginning of 1928 the bank's capital amounted to one million Eygptian pounds, representing 250,000 shares worth LE4 each. As shares were restricted to Egyptian citizens and were not quoted on overseas markets, there

TABLE 2.2   *Augmentation of Bank Misr's capital*

	Number of shares	Value of shares (LE)	Reserves (LE)	Profits
1920	20,000	80,000	—	3,249
1921	43,777	175,108	1,622	16,981
1922	50,132	200,528	4,660	38,323
1923	67,296	269,184	10,912	68,521
1924	78,307	313,228	19,541	92,298
1925	118,731	474,924	112,879	116,375
1926	180,000	720,000	124,634	125,592
1927	180,000	720,000	278,201	153,499
1928	250,000	1,000,000	293,101	163,866

SOURCES   Share figures from Mohammed Ali Rafaat, *The Monetary System of Egypt* (London: Allen and Unwin, 1935) Table XXXII, p. 133; reserve and profit figures from M. Kamel A. Malache, *Etude Economique et Critique des Instruments de Circulation et des Institutions de Credit en Egypte* (Paris: Presses Universitaires de France, 1930) pp. 314–15. Reserve figures refer to statutory amounts, which were augmented by extraordinary reserves amounting to LE10,000 in 1922 and LE90,000 by 1929.

was little trading in the shares in the absence of a stock market in Cairo. There was much buying as new issues were offered, but little selling, and the price of shares remained fixed at LE4 throughout the 1920s. Regular dividends were of course paid but monetary considerations may not have been paramount for all subscribers, as many would have been prepared to wait for rewards, and were pleased to have the opportunity to back a wholly Egyptian enterprise for the first time.

Although Bank Misr was largely owned by Egypt's richer classes, its depositors represented a much wider section of the local community, many of whom viewed the institution as a kind of savings bank. People who hitherto had little use for banks were encouraged to open deposit accounts rather than hoard their cash balances, and there is little doubt that whereas accounts with the other banks were primarily kept for transactions purposes, the precautionary motive was significant in explaining the growth of Bank Misr deposits. Ordinary Egyptians, especially the Muslim majority, had been wary of dealing with foreign-owned and essentially Christian-run financial institutions, but once there was a national institution controlled by local Muslims, their apprehension about modern banking practice disappeared. As Table 2.3 shows the number of customers increased rapidly, from under five hundred when the bank first started, to almost forty thousand by 1929.

The average size of deposit with Bank Misr was much smaller than with the other banks, indicating the type of customer the bank was attracting, frequently of only very limited financial means. There was actually a decrease recorded in the average deposit size over the 1920–29 period as Table 2.3 illustrates, from over LE400 to under LE200, although most of the decrease was in the first two years of the

TABLE 2.3   *Accounts with Bank Misr*

	Number of accounts	*Average holding (LE)*
1920	492	409
1921	1,717	236
1922	5,114	192
1923	8,705	203
1924	12,795	205
1925	17,710	180
1926	23,680	187
1927	29,335	188
1928	34,218	197
1929	39,694	183

SOURCES   Mohammed Ali Rifaat, *The Monetary System of Egypt* (London: Allen and Unwin, 1935) Table XXXIII, p.136; M. Kamel A. Malache, *Etude Economique et Critique des Instruments de Circulation et des Institutions de Credit en Egypte* (Paris: Presses Universitaires de France, 1930) p. 319.

bank's operation. Owing to this small size of average deposits, the total value of deposits at Bank Misr was considerably less than those of the National Bank, even as late as the early 1930s as Table 2.4 indicates. Bank Misr had more customers than any other bank in Egypt, but it still ranked a poor second in terms of its deposits. Nevertheless the rapid rise in the value of deposits was remarkable, from a mere LE200,960 in its first year of operation to almost LE9 million twelve years later.

It is interesting to note that whereas deposits at Bank Misr doubled in 1921 and again in 1922, those with the National Bank fell with the exodus of foreign capital, as shown in Table 2.4 and already discussed with reference to the turnover figures cited in Table 2.1. As the

TABLE 2.4   *Bank Misr and the National Bank of Egypt compared*

	Volume of deposits (LE)	
	Bank Misr	*National Bank*
1920	200,960	17,272,377
1921	405,405	11,183,212
1922	981,217	11,121,433
1923	1,769,355	12,792,402
1924	2,623,953	14,611,469
1925	3,189,919	12,611,609
1926	4,424,707	15,921,358
1927	5,517,815	16,490,017
1928	6,732,558	15,616,286
1929	7,259,867	14,769,798
1930	7,202,393	15,874,726
1931	8,033,073	16,722,885
1932	8,898,966	19,289,426

SOURCES   Mohammed Ali Rifaat, *The Monetary System of Egypt* (London: Allen and Unwin, 1935) Table XXXIV, p. 138; cross check and more detailed comparative accounts for 1923 and 1924 in E. Papasian, *L'Egypte Economique et Financière* (Cairo: Imprimerie Misr, 1926) p. 146 and pp. 358–60.

Slightly different figures for Bank Misr are recorded by Albert N. Forte, *Les Banques en Egypt* (Paris: Librairie Technique et Economique, 1938) p. 149.

turnover figures deal with flows over time rather than stocks at a particular point of time, this explains the differences between the sets of National Bank deposit data. Whatever data is used however, the advantage Bank Misr derived from having Egyptian citizens as depositors was evident, as it was unaffected by international capital flows. Bank Misr's deposits were also more stable because although two-thirds were classified as demand rather than savings deposits, much of the former in fact represented savings which were seldom withdrawn.[20] The Bank therefore found it less risky to advance funds for longer periods, or even invest directly in equity, than most of its commercial rivals.

BANK MISR AS A
DEVELOPMENT INSTITUTION

Initially Bank Misr concentrated on lending for agricultural projects, reflecting the interests of its landowning shareholders, and its first few annual reports emphasised the importance of lending for farm improvement. Unlike Crédit Foncier, however, few funds were advanced for land purchase, and it did not encourage mortgage business, but instead preferred to help as much as possible cultivators who were already established in developing their own land. It was keen to promote agricultural co-operatives for marketing produce, both by providing them with direct financial assistance and through giving advice, as it believed such institutions would benefit cultivators at the expense of the middlemen. Notwithstanding this support for co-operatives, the bank was far from being socialist in outlook, and it was essentially the large and medium-sized farmers who received credit rather than the smallholders whom the National Bank and its agricultural subsidiary had supported at the turn of the century. The bank's goal was the modernisation of Egyptian agriculture through technical and institutional innovation, but not socialisation.

By the 1920s Egypt's large landowners were not only interested in the cultivation of cotton and other cash crops, but were also becoming increasingly involved in activities outside farming. At first their concern was in fields related to agriculture, especially vertical or downstream activities involving the processing of agricultural produce. Cotton spinning and weaving was an obvious field to enter given the local availability of raw materials, the plentiful supply of low-cost labour, and the potential market outlets for the products both at home and abroad. It was not surprising therefore that Bank Misr, and the landlords who backed it, soon became involved in the local textile industry. The bank's first venture in cotton had been in 1924, only two years after its foundation, when it helped establish Société Misr pour le Commerce et l'Egrenage du Coton by investing LE30,000 of its resources.[21] This company, as its name implied, was mainly concerned with the collection and marketing of raw cotton, but three years later in 1927, the bank helped launch another company, Société Misr pour la Filature et le Tissage du Coton.[22] The bank subscribed most of the LE300,000 initial capital of this spinning and weaving company, which alone accounted for almost one third of the bank's total finance for commercial enterprises.

By taking a direct equity stake in new industrial ventures Bank Misr was following French and German financial practice rather than that of the United Kingdom, whose banks refused to tie up their funds in such a way. Even the essentially British National Bank of Egypt preferred to advance credit on a short-term basis rather than undertake longer-term financing. From a development point of view, however, short-term credits were inappropriate to the needs of a country such as Egypt, as it took infant industries time to establish themselves, and achieve consistent production of acceptable quality. There was therefore a conflict between the British banker's desire to keep his institution's asset holdings fairly liquid, and the requirements of a country in its initial stages of industrial development where the profitability of investment is inevitably long-term. Given the stability of Bank Misr deposits, however, long-term lending presented less of a risk for them than would have been the case for the National Bank or the other foreign-owned financial institutions whose funds were highly volatile.

Although Bank Misr was innovative in its early years of operation, and was willing to back untried undertakings, it was nevertheless conscious of its responsibilities towards its depositors, and tried to minimise risks as far as possible. This was done partly by taking an active role in the ventures it was supporting, as bank employees sat on the boards of directors of the Misr companies, which enabled them to monitor all progress and give advice, especially on financial questions, when it was thought necessary. British banks traditionally did not participate in this way in the internal affairs of other enterprises, and if the National Bank had attempted to do likewise in Egypt, its activities would have been resented as foreign interference in national affairs. In contrast the presence of Bank Misr representatives on the boards of companies was welcomed, not only as local businessmen respected its advice, but also because its involvement increased public confidence in particular ventures, and made financing from other sources easier to arrange.

Indeed Bank Misr tended to view itself as a catalyst, which would come in at the start of a new venture, but then gradually withdraw once the enterprise became established and was able to find alternative funding. The bank hoped that its presence would encourage other investors to become involved, which would not only reduce its own risk, but also eventually free its commitment, so that finance could be redeployed for other purposes. Thus, although the bank's initial commitment to the Société Misr pour le Commerce et l'Egrenage du Coton amounted to only LE30,000, by 1934 the total paid-up capital of the company stood at LE250,000. Similarly by the same year the paid-up capital of the Société Misr pour la Filature et le Tissage du Coton amounted to LE450,000, yet Bank Misr's initial subscription was under LE300,000 as already pointed out. [23]

The first company supported by Bank Misr was a printing works, established in 1922, with only LE5,000 paid-up capital initially, which increased by over tenfold within a decade. A related paper industry company, founded in 1924 with a capital of LE30.000 was unfortunately less successful. Apart from the cotton collection and marketing company, and the spinning and weaving company, other companies involved in the cotton trade and supported by the bank included the Société Misr pour le Transport et la Navigation, founded in 1925 with a capital of LE40,000 and the Société Misr pour l'Exportation du Coton, established in 1928 with its capital worth LE160,000. Those landlord interests involved in the cultivation of cotton and connected with the bank hoped that by founding these two companies, middlemen could be avoided, or at least there would be competition which would reduce their margins and help those more directly involved in production. The performance of the cotton export company was however disappointing compared to that of the collection and internal marketing company, largely because exporting required considerable experience and knowledge of the working of overseas markets.

As well as cotton-related projects Bank Misr also financed other processing ventures which made use of local raw materials, including a small silk weaving factory in 1927 by advancing LE10,000, and a linen mill the same year with the same amount of investment. The linen mill was the larger of the two projects, as its total paid-up capital amounted to LE45,000 compared to LE30,000 for the silk factory. As local fisheries was another obvious venture for Bank Misr to back, LE20,000 was invested in a new company in 1927, which had a total capital of LE75,000. Other diverse new ventures which illustrate the range of Bank Misr interests included a cinema company in 1925 with an investment of LE15,000 and in 1934 two projects: an insurance company (LE200,000 invested) and a shipping company (LE100,000 invested). [24]

Overall there was general agreement that Bank Misr had proved extremely successful as an institution in providing new venture finance, and in harnessing local funds for national development which would otherwise have been hoarded or used for basically unproductive purposes. At the time of Egypt's nationalist revolution in 1919 there were no purely locally-owned companies, whereas by 1934 the total assets of Bank Misr and its related companies amounted to almost three million Egyptian pounds,[25] and the group had become the dominant force in manufacturing activity, as well as playing a significant role in the country's trade, with Société Misr pour l'Exportation du Coton the largest single exporting concern, despite its initial difficulties. The group's assets of course represented not only the bank's investments, but also those of local citizens who were prompted to invest because of the bank's initiative and example. By 1932 in fact, when the bank had already sold off some of its equity investments to the general public, its direct industrial investments only amounted to LE200,000 whereas its loans to industry and agricultural corporations amounted to almost LE800,000.[26] As the 1930s progressed its asset structure in terms of the shares of investments *vis-à-vis* loans displayed increasing similarity to that of other banks operating in the Middle East.

Despite its undoubted success, Bank Misr had its critics, especially amongst the foreign community, although this may have been because its activities and those of Egypt's new business and professional class threatened their own interests. It was frequently alleged that the Egyptian authorities showed favouritism towards Bank Misr, allowing it to handle government financing in preference to the National Bank for essentially political reasons in the aftermath of the 1919 nationalist revolution. Certainly the accounts of the municipalities and the native courts were transferred from the National Bank to Bank Misr in 1925, and although the National Bank regained them with the suspension of parliament later that year, they were kept permanently with Bank Misr after the restoration of parliamentary government in 1927. Central government accounts continued to be held with the National Bank, however, which retained the right of note issue. Admittedly the authorities viewed Bank Misr as their main industrial development institution, but that merely reflected the failure of the other banks to perform that role, and in no sense was Bank Misr a mere arm of the government. The government is also alleged to have favoured the Misr companies in the award of contracts and in other business, but as the companies essentially served the private sector, and as the functions of Egypt's government were fairly restricted in any case, the significance of state business was probably limited.

The hostility displayed by the foreign community in general towards Bank Misr in its early years is perhaps surprising, especially in retrospect, as, although the rise of the new bank affected the fortunes of the National Bank, it was not really competing with the other banks. These, as already mentioned, primarily served their own ethnic communities. Gradually, however, Bank Misr became an accepted part of Egypt's financial scene, even for those who opposed its development at the outset, and many saw the advantage of a local institution which had done much to spread the banking habit. For its part the attitude of Bank Misr towards foreign interests grew more tolerant once it became firmly established and self-confident, and its original strident nationalistic character gradually mellowed. In addition the Bank saw the need to bring in foreign expertise if it was to expand the range of activities of the Misr group, as in many fields there was a lack of suitably qualified Egyptians. Therefore foreign partners were sought from 1932 onwards, although Egyptian control was maintained in all ventures, with just one exception. The Misr Air Works, formed in 1932, was the first joint venture between Bank Misr and foreign partners, with the bank holding 60 per cent of the initial capital of LE20,000, while British shareholders bought the remaining shares.[27] The Misr General Assurance Company, formed in 1934, involved a similar ownership arrangement, with the 40 per cent foreign holding owned by the British Bowring Company and the Assicurazioni Generale di Trieste. Other joint ventures started in 1934 included the Misr Navigation Company in partnership with Cox and Kings of Britain, and the Misr Tourism Company with a capital of LE7,000 comprising 1400 shares, of which 830 were held by foreigners. The most ambitious joint venture however was established in 1938 involving the development of two factories, one for the spinning and dyeing of fine cotton and the other for dyeing alone. The capital required, LE500,000, was provided in equal shares by the Misr Group and the Bradford Dyers Association.[28]

Although Bank Misr had made an exception for the spinning and dyeing project in allowing joint control in order to gain British expertise which would otherwise have not been forthcoming, the policy of establishing purely Egyptian ventures whenever possible was never abandoned. Wholly Egyptian-owned ventures established in the 1930s included the Société des Tabacs et Cigarettes (Capital LE40,000), founded in 1937, Société Misr pour l'Industrie et le Commerce des Huiles (capital LE30,000) and Société des Mines et

Carritères (capital LE40,000) formed in 1939.[29] All these ventures were relatively small in size however in comparison to some of the deals involving foreign participation, especially the spinning and dyeing company. Notwithstanding this one fifty-fifty venture, there is little doubt that Bank Misr played a leading role not only in promoting Egypt's industrial expansion during the 1920s and 1930s, but also in ensuring that local people became involved in these new developments. Egypt was the first Arab country to succeed in establishing an industrial base, and subsequent development of manufacturing from the 1950s onwards owes much to the experience gained in those early years for which Bank Misr must take the credit.

THE SPREAD OF INDIGENOUS BANKING

The early success of Bank Misr in the 1920s attracted attention in other Arab countries, particularly in Syria and Lebanon, whose banking structure was broadly similar to that of Egypt prior to the foundation of Bank Misr, but where local citizens wanted indigenous institutions. Foreign banks, especially French institutions, undertook most banking business, as at that time both Syria and Lebanon were under French mandate and administered jointly. The dominant institution was the Banque de Syrie et du Grand Liban, which was mainly owned by private French interests who had bought the eight branches of the Ottoman Bank in Syria and Lebanon in 1919 on the dissolution of the Ottoman Empire, although the Ottoman Bank still retained a residual holding of 11,000 shares out of a total of 51,000.[30] The Banque de Syrie et du Grand Liban inherited the Ottoman Bank's right of note issue, and it acted as central bank for the French administration, as well as being involved in commercial lending, mainly trade finance, the expansion of which enabled it to open seven further branches during the 1920s.

Unlike the National Bank of Egypt, which at least had its head office in Cairo, the Banque de Syrie et du Grand Liban had its headquarters in Paris and an office in Marseilles, and its operations were governed by French law. The bank was therefore even less of a national institution than its Egyptian counterpart, and its sixteen directors together with its senior staff were all French citizens. Despite the privileged position the Banque de Syrie et du Grand Liban occupied, like the National Bank of Egypt it exercised little control over the other banks operating locally, who viewed it as a commercial competitor rather than as an agent of government. These other banks included the Banque Française de Syrie, which was a subsidiary founded by the Société Générale of Paris in 1919 to profit from business in the new French dependencies.[31] Although this subsidiary company only had four branches in Lebanon and Syria, and a head office in Paris, the assets of its parent company greatly exceeded those of the Banque de Syrie et du Grand Liban, and it exercised considerable influence in French banking circles, including those in the Orient.

The French also used their North African banks as instruments for financial penetration into Syria and the Lebanon, as Crédit Foncier d'Algérie et de Tunisie established an office in Beirut in 1921, and three others in Syria in the early 1930s, when Compagnie Algérienne, its main commercial rival, also opened two offices.[32] Both these banks of course operated primarily in Arab and Muslim environments, but neither served the indigenous inhabitants in Algeria or Tunisia, instead dealing mainly with the French settler communities, a pattern which was to be repeated in Syria and the Lebanon, although there was some limited lending to large local landowners. Other ethnic banks operating locally included the Banco di Roma with branches in Beirut, Aleppo and Damascus from 1919 onward, which served the Italian community, while the Anglo-Palestine Bank, which had operated in Beirut since the beginning of the century, primarily catered for the Jewish community. The main interest of the latter, which was the official banker for the Zionist movement, was in financing Jewish settlements in Palestine, and it worked in association with the Palestine Jewish Colonization Association.[33] Its interest in Syria and the Lebanon was therefore at best peripheral.

Although foreign-owned and -controlled institutions played the major role in Syrian and Lebanese banking in the 1920s, there were a number of locally owned institutions which had existed since Ottoman times, including in Beirut George Trad and Co., Banque Alexandre P. Haddad, Faroun and Shiha, and Robert Sabbagh and Co., and in Damascus Banque Asfar, Sara and Co., Banque Ernest Asfar, and Siouffi and Sabbagh, while in Aleppo the main names were Albert Homsi, Nasri Gazali, and Nihmad Brothers and Baida.[34] The resources of these local family banks were small, however, and, like the moneylenders described in Chapter 1, many were the financial offshoots of trading businesses who would lend solely to their established customers. Only the firm of Alexandre P. Haddad published annual accounts, and none of the institutions energetically sought new depositors, yet it was only by attracting additional funds that they would have been able to lend the substantial amounts required for industrial projects and other modern economic ventures.

It was the obvious deficiencies in the services provided by both the foreign banks and the small local establishments that prompted a group of Lebanese and Syrian financiers to draw up a plan for a new indigenous banking institution. [35] Local citizens concerned with their country's development could not fail to notice the lack of industrial progress in contrast to Egypt, yet Lebanon in particular had traditions of craftsmanship and entrepreneurship which were much stronger than those found in Cairo or Alexandria. A few local Muslim financiers decided therefore to approach Bank Misr, to enlist its help to set up a venture in Syria which could perform a similar function to that undertaken in Egypt. A delegation was dispatched accordingly in 1929 from Beirut to Cairo to study Bank Misr's structure and working arrangements, which it was believed could be the model for the Syrian institution. Naturally Bank Misr welcomed this approach from fellow Muslim Arabs, and promised to help the Beirut delegation in any way it could, pointing out that it had been looking to widen its field of activities in any case.

Banque Misr Syrie Liban was subsequently established in 1930 as the first modern pan-Arab financial venture, with half of its share capital owned by Bank Misr and a small group of wealthy Egyptians, and the other half subscribed by the group of Syrian financiers. [36] No group had overall control, and as Bank Misr had only a minority share of the paid-up capital, in no sense was the bank to be a mere subsidiary of the Egyptian parent, as the French and other foreign banks were in relation to their overseas owners. Instead the bank was essentially local in character, an institution for the promotion of national development, and the role of Bank Misr of Egypt was mainly confined to the provision of technical assistance. Consequently, although many of the administrative staff were Egyptians seconded from Bank Misr, they did not see it as their job to further the Cairo bank's interests, but to repeat in Syria what had been achieved in Egypt. Article two of the bank's statutes for instance emphasised the importance of financing new industrial ventures, which had been the Egyptian policy.

Unfortunately the achievements of Banque Misr Syrie Liban were much less impressive than those of its Egyptian counterpart, although in its first year of operation it not only developed its Beirut headquarters, but also opened other branches in Damascus and

Tripoli (of Lebanon, not Libya).[37] After the initial enthusiasm for the new institutions however, its backers became less active, and by the mid-1930s only half of its limited initial capital of one million Syrian pounds had still been subscribed. As the Egyptian pound was worth five Syrian pounds by the 1930s, owing to the depreciation of the French franc to which Syria's currency was tied, the subscribed capital of Banque Misr Syrie Liban was only worth LE100,000, a mere tenth of the capital value of Bank Misr of Egypt. The low rate of capitalisation reflected the slow growth in the bank's commercial activity, as to a considerable degree local trade finance was already handled by the small family banks, which were more developed than those in Egypt. In addition in Egypt the cotton industry generated a considerable amount of trade both directly and indirectly involving people not previously needing the facilities of a financial institution, whereas in Syria and Lebanon business remained in the hands of well-established families who had longstanding connections with local financiers.

To some extent the bank's lack of success was also due to its Eygptian staff finding it difficult to work in a foreign environment, even though it was still Arab, and subsequently a high staff turnover. A more crucial factor however was the lack of opportunities for industrial development which the bank could support in Syria and Lebanon compared with Egypt. There were no obvious resource-related activities on which to concentrate apart from cotton textiles, and building up these industries would have meant direct competition for the Egyptian ventures which Bank Misr supported. Although Banque Misr Syrie Liban was supposed to be a nationalistic institution whose prime loyalty was to its own country rather than Egypt, it still felt constrained in backing any project which might interfere with the other interests of its shareholders. Yet as the local market for industrial products in Syria and Lebanon was much more restricted than in Egypt, and with the European powers restricting imports even from their own dependencies in the 1930s, the only hope for industrialisation in Beirut and Demascus lay in the context of an integrated Arab market. Such ideas would have been too far ahead of their time however even for the Misr group to accept, despite it being and important instigator of inter-Arab financial co-operation.

3 Growth of Arab Financial Expertise

With the spread of education in the Arab world, especially in the first three decades of this century, many young Arabs started to enter the modern sectors of their own economies. They began to take over some of the jobs which had formerly been carried out by foreigners, either expatriates from Europe serving in the area for short stays, or more permanently resident foreign nationals, such as those living in large numbers in Beirut, Alexandria and Cairo. In the field of banking and finance many young Arabs already worked for the foreign banks represented in the Middle East even in the closing decades of the nineteenth century, but most did not rise above the lowest clerical positions, and many were employed as messengers and in other similar menial tasks. By the 1920s however this situation was changing and, although few Arabs had reached the position of branch managers in the commercial banking system, many of the jobs up to cashier level were filled by local citizens. These moves went furthest in Egypt and the Levant, as school-leavers from the foreign colleges, where many wealthy local merchants sent their families, were in heavy demand by the banks. Teaching in schools such as the American College in Cairo was entirely conducted in English, and the basic numerate and literary skills imparted were the same as those taught in western schools.[1]

In general developments within banks tend to reflect those in the societies in which they are located, and the Arab world is no exception. As more local nationals started to play a prominent role in modern economic activity, the clientele of even the foreign banks tended to change, and there was a greater need for bilingual staff. The work of the banks was gradually Arabised, with an increasing number of records and accounts kept in Arabic rather than in English or French. Given the extremely restricted numbers of graduates in oriental languages from European universities, and the aversion of many of these graduates to careers such as banking in any case, the banks were virtually forced to recruit local nationals and promote them into higher positions than hitherto. Essentially it was supply and demand forces in the labour market that put the banks into this position, although there is little doubt they were also conscious of their image in the societies in which they operated, and the banks wanted to be seen as agents for imparting skills to local nationals.[2]

The pressure to employ local nationals in increasingly senior positions intensified with the rise of popular indigenous banking, especially in Egypt with the growth of Bank Misr in the 1920s. However, even in Syria and the Lebanon similar pressures were felt, and Bank Misr soon spread its activity to the Levant as Chapter 2 describes. Bank Misr remained essentially an Egyptian institution, however, but as modern banking started to have a greater impact on domestic economic activity, there was a desire that locally-owned rather than foreign-owned banks should at least get a share of the new business. At the same time some of the local nationals employed by the foreign banks felt their promotion would be faster, and prospects better generally, if they worked for Arab-owned banks. However, they had little desire to work for the traditional moneychangers or moneylenders, who usually paid wages below bank rates, and ran their businesses on family lines, with preference given to close relatives for employment and promotion. The more educated Arabs tended to view the moneychangers and moneylenders as rather primitive financial institutions, whom nobody with self-respect would wish to work for, and certainly not anyone with financial qualifications or banking experience.

THE RISE OF THE ARAB BANK

Without doubt the 1920s marked the start of a period of great banking opportunities for local Arab citizens, although initially it was only in the context of the Bank Misr group that progress seemed to be occurring. The local moneychangers and moneylenders seemed ill-equipped to expand outside their traditional business areas at the time, and were reluctant to take on new, unknown clients, or indeed back any modern economic activity. Thus when the initiative came to found the first wholly Arab-owned bank outside the Bank Misr group, it came not from a traditional moneychanging family, but from an Arab entrepreneur whose previous interests were completely unconnected with finance. Interestingly, the initiative came not in the bazaars of Damascus or Beirut, but in Jerusalem, which in comparison had hitherto been rather unimportant as a financial centre, especially from an Arab point of view.

The founder of the first Arab commercial bank in Asia was Abdul Hameed Shoman whose institution, the Arab Bank, opened its doors in Jerusalem in 1929. Shoman, a Palestinian Arab, had virtually no formal education himself, and at the early age of six, was already working in the family quarry business near Jerusalem.[3] He later moved into livestock trading, buying and selling sheep and goats, the main grazing animals on the rocky hills of the West Bank of the Jordan. However, not content with the limited economic horizons of Arab Palestine, and eager to get away from the constraints of his family, Shoman emigrated to the United States, taking only $80 with him. There he went into textiles, establishing his own business in a sector dominated by Jewish businesses, especially in New York, where he operated from. Shoman prospered in America, but he yearned to return to his native Palestine after a few years, and live near his family again.

Fortunately just before the great Wall Street crash Shoman was able to sell off his New York textile interests at an appreciable profit, and he returned to Jerusalem in 1929 with what was a considerable sum of capital by the Arab standards of the day, $30,000. He used the money to found a new bank, not based on the practices of the traditional Arab moneychangers and moneylenders, but on the practices of the various American banks he had experience of during his time in New York. Annual reports were issued from the start, and the accounts were kept up-to-date and subject to external audit. The lending policy corresponded to that of many small-town United States banks, and Shoman was interested not only in the security his clients could offer, but also how profitably they could utilise their loans. The emphasis was on loans to small businessmen such as traders, or those who owned small manufacturing establishments.[4] The Palestinian Arab community in Jerusalem was one of the most educated and widely travelled in the Arab world at the time, and Shoman lent to the new Arab business and professional classes rather than the large landowners who constituted the old Palestinian elite. These new middle-class clients did not object to Shoman asking them about their financial affairs in detail, and advising them how their money could be best deployed. In contrast the conservative landlords would have regarded such questions from moneylenders as unwarranted interference.

This new style of Arab banking proved popular with the growing middle classes, and the combination of an ownership which could appeal to nationalists, with American financial practice, seemed a recipe for success. The European banks were resented to some extent, not only because they were foreign, but also because as conservative institutions they tended to favour the old landed Arab classes themselves rather than the new businessmen. In some respects their pattern of granting credits was not much different from that of the traditional moneylenders. Shoman in contrast was much more venturesome; but yet he avoided being reckless, and his new bank soon gained a reputation as a safe place to deposit funds as well as to borrow money. As the bank's entire initial capital was Shoman's own money, he had clearly as much at stake as his clients if problems arose. This the clients realised and it increased their confidence in the new institution. In addition nationalistic pressures helped Shoman, as the growing Palestinian middle classes had good reason not to be well disposed towards British banks such as Barclays given the policy of the London government during the mandate period. Nor were Palestinian Arabs keen to bank with the newly-established Jewish institutions, whose intrusion into what they regarded as their homeland was scarcely welcome even in the 1920s and 1930s.[5]

By 1940 the Arab Bank had opened branches in all the main Arab centres of urban population in Palestine, including not only Jerusalem where it had two branches, but also Jaffa and Haifa. In addition the bank had branches in Cairo, Beirut and Damascus, which served local nationals as well as Palestinians.[6] Through its Cairo office it was competing with Bank Misr on its own home territory, although admittedly its impact on Egypt at that time was only slight. In Palestine however the bank prospered during the period of the Second World War, as the area developed as an important supply base for the Allied troops in North Africa through the Middle East Supply Centre. Many Palestinian Arab businessmen who were Shoman's clients made considerable fortunes in this period through clothing, footwear, and food supplies.

With the foundation of the state of Israel in 1948 the bank suffered serious losses, however, and it closed down all its former Palestine operations which were located within Israel's borders, including the Jaffa, Haifa and West Jerusalem branches. There was no compensation for the land and premises it lost, yet the bank managed to stay solvent unlike some of the Palestinian moneylenders and moneychangers who were forced out of business completely. Throughout the difficult post-1948 period the bank managed to meet all withdrawals, unlike these other institutions, and this enhanced Shoman's reputation still further. Supposedly one client who was sceptical about the bank's position during this period asked to withdraw $80,000 which he had deposited, largely in order to test the bank's creditworthiness. When told that he could have his money immediately, he proclaimed his complete confidence in the bank, and did not proceed with the withdrawal.[7]

The Arab Bank was the sole Palestinian financial institution to emerge largely unscathed from the remnants of that region after the creation of Israel. It actually expanded its operations in the West Bank during the 1948–67 period, opening offices in most of the major centres, including Ramallah, Nablus, Hebron and Bethlehem, while it increased its number of offices in East Jerusalem to three. Although East Jerusalem remained the centre for the West Bank, however, it was cut off from the rest of Palestine, and it was out on a limb as far as the rest of the Arab world was concerned. As a kind of frontier town, with its main communications links gone, it could scarcely be considered as a financial centre, or an appropriate place for an aspiring pan-Arab bank to have its headquarters. Accordingly the headquarters was moved to Amman, which was the new capital of both the East and West Banks of the Jordan after 1948.[8]

In Amman the Arab Bank prospered, winning the business not only of expatriate Palestinians, but also that of the traditional residents of the East Bank. Admittedly until 1956 there was no local competition apart from the moneylenders and moneychangers, as the only bank established in Amman was the foreign-owned British Bank of the Middle East. Most of the businessmen on the East Bank were Palestinians in any case, as the indigenous inhabitants had mainly been Bedouin Arabs, many of whom continued their nomadic lifestyle rather than settling in urban areas where they were more likely to use banks. It was the Palestinian element which comprised the modern sector of the Jordanian economy, while the traditional Bedouin sector was largely unmonetised, and did not even need moneychangers. Thus it is not surprising in these circumstances that the Arab Bank, a Palestinian institution, dominated the local banking system, and by 1960 had four branches in Amman alone, as well as other East Bank branches at Irbid and Zarqa north of the capital, and at Aqaba, Jordan's outlet to the sea and sole port.

Jordan's small size was undoubtedly a constraining factor for an institution as ambitious to expand as the Arab Bank, however, and its main opportunities were to lie in other Arab countries. At the same time it tried not to neglect its new home base, and it increased to six its number of branches in Amman by the mid-1970s. The loss of its branches on the West Bank with the Israeli invasion of 1967 was a serious blow, nevertheless, and cut the bank completely off from its original base in Jerusalem. The build-up of operations on the East Bank only partly compensated for this loss, which was not only a loss of premises, but also represented a continual financial drain. The bank was reluctant to move its staff from the West Bank, as politically this would have meant appearing to have given up a right to remain in Palestine, and it continued to pay salaries to its staff, even though they were in effect retired.[9] As the years have passed without an end to the Israeli occupation some of these staff have officially retired and are now on pensions, but it seems unlikely that many of those in unofficial forced retirement will ever return to banking again. The latter have forgotten much of their financial training, and are out of the routine of working the regular hours which banking demands. Within Jordan the Arab Bank has now been overtaken in terms of branch banking by both the Jordan National Bank, founded in 1956, and the Bank of Jordan, founded in 1960. While the Arab Bank has only nine branches on the East Bank in operation, the Jordan National Bank has sixteen and the Bank of Jordan seventeen. Both these banks have received some official encouragement and favouritism on the East Bank at the expense of the originally West-Bank-dominated Arab Bank, although all are privately owned commercial banks without government participation. The Jordan National Bank even has Lebanese and Gulf institutions represented amongst its shareholders, although private East Bank shareholders own most of its equity. Overall, however, the Arab Bank remains the largest in terms of paid-up capital, and its total network of 35 branches throughout the Arab world and beyond far exceeds that of the other banks. Its paid-up capital amounted to 11 million Jordanian dinars in 1978 ($37 million), compared to only 3 million dinar for the Jordan National Bank, and a mere 1.5 million dinar for the Bank of Jordan.[10]

By the 1960s the Arab Bank had become the largest bank in the Arab Middle East in terms of deposits and lending, and even the loss of the West Bank branches did not upset its position. It was only in the late 1970s that the Rafidain Bank of Iraq, the National Commercial Bank of Saudi Arabia, and the National Bank of Abu Dhabi, overtook it, but it has a strong home base which accounts for most of its business, and it is not surprising that the leading banks in the world's major petroleum exporting countries should assume a dominant position. In contrast the Arab Bank does not even get much governmental favouritism in Jordan, as already pointed out, and Amman in any case is the capital of a poor and vulnerable country with few resources of its own. Furthermore the success of the Arab Bank is even more remarkable when it is realised that its expansion plans in many of the largest Arab states, particularly Egypt, Iraq and Syria, were thwarted by the socialist policies pursued in those countries, and the nationalisation measures of the 1960s which were directed at banks specifically.

The bank has also suffered along with its Palestinian customers in those Arab states where large numbers of Palestinians reside. The Jordanian civil war of September 1970 curbed activities, and proved disastrous for some of its borrowers. [11] The bank was well represented in Lebanon before the civil war, where it served local citizens as well as the Palestinian community. The civil war badly affected business in Beirut, however, and most bank activity has been concentrated in the Ras Beirut branch only, and the three branches in Palestinian dominated Tripoli, Lebanon's main base for the exiles. To the bank's credit it was the only financial institution to keep its Ras Beirut branch open throughout the civil war, which has enhanced the bank's reputation still further. Customers believe they can depend on it whatever disturbances the future brings, given its long record of operating under troubled conditions, and in the aftermath of the Lebanese civil war it was attracting five thousand new customers a month. Its staff are willing to stay while other banks have closed and their staff quitted at the first sign of political disturbances.

Apart from its nine branches in Jordan, by 1980 the Arab Bank had 35 other branches throughout the Arab world, from Oman and North Yemen in the east and south to Morocco in the west. In addition, it has overseas branches in London, Paris and Athens, and owns subsidiary companies in Switzerland and Nigeria. [12] The fastest-growing region for business since 1974 has of course been the Gulf and Saudi Arabia. The Arab Bank was the first non-Saudi Arab financial institution to be allowed to establish itself within the kingdom, and its links there date back to 1949. Ten years earlier Bank Misr had tried to gain a foothold in Jeddah but failed, and it was only much later that Banque du Caire opened its first office in Saudi Arabia. The bank has undoubtedly benefited from its Arabness or ethnicism in Saudi Arabia, and even before the bank's Jeddah and Riyadh branches were Saudi-ised, the Saudi government took a small stake in the capital of the bank as a whole of around 10 per cent. The Kuwait government took a similar stake of 10 per cent, and the government of Qatar a smaller share. Saudi Arabia alone accounts for around 30 per cent of the bank's business, and the Gulf region a further 20 per cent.

Although it was necessary to raise outside capital to finance expansion, the Shoman family still own around 20 per cent of the Arab Bank's capital, and Palestinians retain a majority stake, despite the institution's growing pan-Arab ownership diversity. Abdul Hameed Shoman died in 1974, but his two sons, Abdul Majeed and Khalid, continue to run the bank, which is entirely staffed by Arabs, most of whom are Palestinians, usually with Jordanian or Lebanese passports. The major business remains ordinary branch banking, and the bank has been slow to diversify its range of financial activity. To some extent this was due to staff constraints, as it lacked experienced foreign exchange dealers, for example, and was relatively late in becoming involved in the Bahrain inter-bank money market. The bank's somewhat conservative financial policies may have helped it gain respectability in Saudi Arabia, where many are suspicious of sharp financial practices in general, and speculative dealing in particular. Nevertheless the bank is broadening its range of financial services, and guarantees and acceptances are becoming increasingly important, while it is also participating to a greater extent in syndicated loan business.[13] The bank's main contribution to the development of Middle Eastern finance however was to show that Arabs could run a modern bank, and many of its ex-employees are among the most senior personnel in the newer Arab banks in the Gulf and elsewhere.

STATE-OWNED COMMERCIAL BANKS

Unlike the Arab Bank which is under majority private ownership, and is a pan-Arab institution, most of the major Arab banks are under state ownership, which is usually exclusive to one country. Thus the largest bank in the Arab world in 1979, the Rafidain Bank, is wholly owned by the Iraqi state, while the Arab world's oldest financial institution, the National Bank of Egypt, has long had the Cairo government as its sole shareholder. Even the National Bank of Abu Dhabi is 100 per cent state-owned, although the National Bank of Kuwait is private, while Qatar's National Bank is a semi-public institution, with the state owning half its capital and private citizens the remainder.[14] These ownership arrangements reflect the present political ideology, or past political ideologies, of individual Arab states, with some favouring free enterprise and private capital, while others favour government intervention and state ownership of key sectors of the economy.

The reasons for nationalisation in general, and a public takeover of the banking sector in particular, vary from state to state in the Arab world, but a few common benefits are usually cited in most of the countries which have adopted such measures. Firstly there is the realisation that the objectives and practices of the private banks may conflict with those of the state, particularly with respect to lending policy. Arab governments have been keen in recent years to provide financial encouragement to industrial ventures and other directly productive undertakings which it is hoped will speed national economic development and diversification. Private banks, it is alleged, are more concerned with the interests of their own shareholders and management than the national interest, and often fail to back such ventures, either because the risks involved are deemed too great, or the period of credit needed is too long. Although this argument carries much conviction, the account of Bank Misr activities in Chapter 2 shows that not all private banks were reluctant to back industry. In addition, in so far as there was a gap with regard to industrial finance, specialised state institutions such as Industrial Development Funds are perhaps the best means of closing it, rather than commercial banks, whether private or state-owned.

A second criticism of the private commercial banks was that they concentrated their lending on real estate ventures which tended to raise land prices and cause unwanted and undesirable speculation. This often resulted in hardship in the rural areas as landlords raised the rents of their increasingly valuable land, and the poor peasants had difficulty in paying them. At the same time in the urban areas, income disparities worsened, as much of the bank credit was to finance the purchase of existing property and drove prices out of reach of middle-income citizens. In so far as new property development was financed it tended to be luxury housing and apartment buildings rather than accommodation for the urban industrial workers. There can be little doubt that there was some justification in this criticism, and the rapid appreciation of property values in Cairo, Damascus and elsewhere contributed little to the development of Egypt, Syria or any other state. However, it was the bank's borrowers who chose to use their credit for such purposes, not the banks themselves, which were not even keen usually on long-term lending.

A third cause of concern about bank lending was the preference which private commercial banks supposedly had for financing trade, especially imports, rather than helping domestic production. Such a bank policy is only natural, however, as importers and traders generally have concrete security to offer in the form of the goods which they hope to sell. Finance of stockholdings is one of the main functions of banks in most western countries, and in so far as the stocks consist of imported goods in the Arab world, this may only reflect deficiencies in domestic production, not discriminatory bank policy. Foreign trade finance is often more profitable for the banks than domestic credit, as the banks providing the credit usually also carry out the foreign exchange transactions on which they earn commission. Forward transactions may be involved, another source of revenue, while where trade is financed through bills, as is often the case, the bank may provide the acceptances and guarantees, resulting in yet more business.

All these criticisms of private commercial bank policy are at the micro level of the individual borrower, but at the macro level the case for state control of the banking system is also argued in the Arab world. There is a belief that state participation in commercial banking will ensure control over domestic resource allocation between consumption and investment at the aggregate level, as well as control over which type of investment gets undertaken. The financial structure can be adapted to the needs of economic planning, and the commercial banks are merely instruments to implement state planning decisions. It is thought it is not sufficient to send out directives to private commercial banks, as obedience to the letter does not always mean obedience in spirit, and institutions with independent discretionary powers can thwart government policy. The evidence from the Arab world certainly suggests that where governments have nationalised their banking systems they have enjoyed greater success in steering their economies, although the extent to which that steering has always been in the most appropriate direction remains a matter of controversy. Whether private or public decision-makers are the more successful is inevitably a question for political debate.

Arguments for state control do not necessarily imply of course that state ownership is the only way of exercising such direction; indeed the creation of a strong central bank may be a more relevant means of acquiring government control than public ownership. Yet, as actual experience shows, central banks and currency boards are often far from being effective in the Middle East. Unlike in western economies there has been little attempt to control the money supply by varying reserve requirements, introduction of "corsets" on banking lending, or even large-scale, open market operations.[15] Nevertheless nationalisation is not a prerequisite for such policies in any case, as they are often pursued in essentially free-enterprise-orientated economies. Nationalisation was however seen as a way of keeping interest rates low, and controlling financial flows, especially in Nasser's Egypt. It was believed that low interest rates would mean cheap credit for industry and encourage its development. At the same time it was necessary to control capital outflows to ensure that investors did not seek higher interest abroad. The elimination of all private competing banks domestically meant that funds would not flow from state banks offering low interest to private commercial banks offering higher returns.

When the first nationalisation measures were discussed in the Arab world in the late 1950s however, the arguments just outlined were not the prime factors considered. Rather nationalisation of the banking sector was seen as part of the nationalistic process under which foreign interests, including economic influences, were to be eliminated. In the debate there was some confusion between socialisation, and nationalisation, as in theory it would have been possible to have "nationalised" the foreign-owned banks without taking them into public ownership. When Saudi Arabia for example Saudi-ised its banking system in the 1970s, it merely ensured that some foreign-owned capital shares, usually 60 per cent of the total, were sold off to private local nationals. Similarly in Kuwait, where the curb on foreign banking came even earlier in the 1960s, most of the local banks are in private ownership, although the Kuwait government owns a 49 per cent stake in the Bank of Kuwait and the Middle East, which took over the former interests of the British Bank of the Middle East in Kuwait.[16]

In the revolutionary or socialistic states of the Arab world such as Nasser's Egypt, Baathist Syria and Iraq, and Gadaffi's Libya, the governments wanted to overthrow the old economic order completely, and it was deemed inappropriate to merely replace the foreign ownership interests with ownership by wealthy local citizens. These often consisted of the former ruling classes who were against the revolutions in any case so it was not seen why they should profit. In addition, in Egypt so much private capital fled the country in the 1950s that there would probably have been insufficient funds to take over the former foreign ownership shares, even if the private capitalists had been inclined to take such action. Thus the state saw little alternative but to acquire the shares itself. In many cases the former bank directors were in exile, and hence the state saw an opportunity to substitute its own nominees. From the government's point of view this had the merit of increasing its powers of patronage in the financial field, in the same way as it was doing in other areas of domestic economic activity. The new regimes not only wanted to take over the existing levers of power, but were also ambitious to extend the power of government, not so much because of socialist principles, but in order to increase their popular influence. In the financial world, not only would their new nominees on the boards of the bank owe the government allegiance, but also all those bank employees and others who aspired to such positions.

Nationalisation in the Middle East, as elsewhere, has tended to be an irreversible process and, although in Egypt Sadat's government moved away from the socialist policies of the Nasser era, there was no attempt to return the state-owned banks to private ownership, or even allow foreign private banks to play much of a role in the domestic financial system despite the open-door policy.[17] In Syria, Iraq and Libya there is even less sign of any change in the state-controlled system, nor does there appear to be much pressure from the banking community for a return to the former ownership status. As a result of more than two decades of state ownership in some cases, new vested interests have been created, and the systems have established their own built-in inertias as is usual in bureaucracies.

When the nationalisation measures were introduced, however, little time was wasted over their implementation. To some extent this was helped by the concentration of banking business in the hands of a few institutions which simplified the takeover. In Egypt, for instance, at the time of the revolution the six largest banks accounted for 78 per cent of all advances and 85 per cent of deposits, while the two largest, Bank Misr and Barclays Bank, together were responsible for 46 per cent of advances and 56 per cent of deposits.[18] A second factor in Egypt's case was that the local assets of Barclays Bank were sequestrated in 1956 following the Anglo-French invasion of Suez, thus setting a precedent for the other banks.[19] A third factor of significance in Egypt was the dissatisfaction with the National Bank's role as central banker, especially after it was given the power to undertake open-market operations in 1957. The conflict between its role as central bank and as a commercial institution was becoming more apparent, and in 1960 a central bank was established independently. This nevertheless did not end the dissatisfaction entirely. Finally there was the realisation in Cairo that state control of Bank Misr would not only give the government influence over finance, but also over large amounts of Egypt's industry, especially the textile factories, which the Misr group owned.[20] Therefore there was little surprise when Bank Misr was nationalised in 1960.

The remaining Egyptian banks were nationalised in 1961, but the measures were not applied in Syria, even though at the time, both countries were part of a United Arab Republic with Nasser at its head. Of course the task was easier in Egypt with Barclays Bank and Bank Misr already under state ownership, and the British share of the National Bank also having been sequestrated in 1956. Although in theory Law 117 of 1961 nationalised all banks and insurance companies in both regions of the United Arab Republic, in Syria the groundwork had not been laid, and the measures were not implemented. It was only after the Baathist takeover in 1963, which came after the dissolution of the United Arab Republic, that ironically similar measures were taken to those in Nasser's Egypt. All that happened in Syria before the Baathist revolution was that foreign participation in the banking system was reduced to 25 per cent, but this meant little in practice as leading French institutions such as Crédit Foncier d'Algérie et de Tunisie had already transformed themselves into autonomous Arab companies, renamed, in the case of Credit Foncier, Banque de l'Orient Arabe.[21]

Iraq was the last of the major Arab states to nationalise its banking system, as its measures were not taken until 1964. As in Syria, it was decided to merge all the former commercial banks into one large bank, called in Iraq's case the Rafidain Bank and in Syria's case simply the Commercial Bank of Syria. In this way it was hoped to rationalise operations, overcome indivisibilities in the provision of financial services, and provide organisations which would be large enough to deal with foreign financial institutions on equal terms. In addition it was thought that the new larger organisations could provide a more attractive career structure to local citizens entering banking, and hence better recruits would be attracted. The limited extent of commercial banking in both Syria and Iraq even in the early 1960s meant that if the former foreign-owned banks were kept as separate financial institutions, they would be so small in size without their parent bank that their viability would be open to question. Both governments believed that, even with state-owned institutions, sheer size would help confidence.

In Egypt in contrast, as commercial bank operations were much larger in scale prior to nationalisation, and as branch banking was more extensive, there was not the same need to merely establish one large bank. Indeed in Egypt's case it was thought such an organisation would be excessively cumbersome, and would introduce an unnecessary monopolistic element into financial activity. Therefore it was decided to rationalise the system around the four major banks operating in the country before nationalisation, while keeping them essentially intact as institutions. Thus both the National Bank and Bank Misr continued to operate under their own names although state-owned, while Barclays Bank became the Bank of Alexandria as it was in that port where much of its activity had been concentrated. The interests of Crédit Lyonnais and other French institutions were incorporated in the newly-formed Banque du Caire, which of course was also state-owned.[22]

It was hoped that keeping four independent commercial banking units would prevent the worst features of a centralised bureaucracy developing, but there was little thought of the institutions competing against each other, as the government ministers at the time believed competition was wasteful in terms of resources, and unnecessary in the Egyptian context. Formerly only the middle and upper classes in Egypt had banked anyway, and it was mainly the more affluent amongst this limited group who found it worthwhile to switch loyalties from one bank to another in response to competitive pressures. The aim of Arab socialists in Egypt was to ensure that banking services reached a wider spectrum of society, including the less affluent, and small businesses, who had hitherto relied on expensive credit from traditional moneylenders. Larger businesses were also being taken into state ownership, and it was inconceivable that they would need to shop around the different state commercial banks to seek a price advantage. The emphasis was on state enterprises moving ahead in partnership, and the tensions of competition would certainly have been against the spirit of the time, even if the new state-owned organisations had been flexible enough to switch allegiances, which seems doubtful, given the customary inertia of Egyptian bureaucracy.

Instead of competing with each other, Egypt's four state-owned banks were encouraged to specialise in a particular field of financial activity. Hence the National Bank, which was formerly the central bank and handled the country's foreign exchange dealings and reserves, was given a monopoly of foreign trade finance because of its expertise in this field. To some extent, however, the National Bank was granted this monopoly in 1961 as compensation when it lost its central bank status to the new organisation set up for that purpose. Bank Misr was encouraged to specialise in development banking, providing venture capital for new enterprises, especially in those areas of activity where the Misr group had always been active such as textiles.[23] In contrast the Bank of Alexandria was assigned the role of assisting the new public sector industries, especially consumer durables such as electrical goods, the Nasr car assembly plant and other heavy industrial undertakings. It had a core of specialised staff retained from the old undertakings of Barclays who had gained some expertise in industrial finance with the former parent bank in England. Meanwhile the Banque du Caire was allowed to continue concentrating on the finance of services and construction, as it was in these fields that its former French parent companies had been most active, at least as far as Egypt was concerned.

In practice the specialisation was less than complete within Egyptian banking, and there was a considerable degree of overlap in the range of services which the four state-owned banks provided. Rather than building on the foundations laid down by their privately-owned predecessors, the state-owned banks gradually extended their general consumer and business banking activities, but without any particular dynamism. They grew with the market, rather than seeking to create new markets and opportunities, and they were rather sluggish to modernise their banking methods. The main growth of business was with the new state-sector industries, but these were scarcely vigorous themselves. Over-manning became the rule in banking, as the banks were virtually forced to accept secondary school-leavers and university graduates from the expanding educational system, under a government policy that guaranteed every person with higher education a job.[24] Remuneration in banking was low, however, and there was little incentive within the banks. A general lethargy gradually decended over the whole financial system and, although Cairo under Nasser may have aspired to have become the political and cultural capital of the Arab world, it was certainly far from being a financial capital, or even a banking centre of any international consequence.

THE BEIRUT BANKS AND ARAB FINANCE

With the nationalisation of the banking systems of Egypt, Syria and Iraq, many of the more able and ambitious bankers in these countries decided to leave and seek employment elsewhere. Although Jordan attracted a few of these expatriates, both Arab and European, its main banking institutions, especially the Arab Bank, were predominantly Palestinian rather than being multinational Arab institutions, in which Egyptians, Syrians and Iraqis could feel more comfortable. Meanwhile banking in the Gulf remained in its infancy, with the higher positions mostly monopolised by Europeans. Beirut therefore seemed the only centre in the Arab world where opportunities remained, especially as its role had already grown substantially in the 1950s, and it no longer merely catered for the financial needs of Lebanon's somewhat limited economy.

In contrast to the major Arab states where free enterprise was in retreat, in Lebanon private initiative was being encouraged, and the government's philosophy of *laissez-faire* meant there was little worry about future state interference in banking activity. During the 1950s the free enterprise environment was strengthened, in the realisation that Lebanon could never hope to become a major industrial state in the region with government-sponsored heavy industry, and instead its future lay in smaller-scale private industrial concerns, handicraft production and the numerous trading and commercial activities within the service sector in which it had so long specialised. As Beirut had been the most important financial centre in the Ottoman Empire after Constantinople, and as after the demise of the Empire it had continued to serve the Syrian hinterland, it was not surprising that efforts were made to maintain and enhance its status. Its comparative advantage lay in fields such as banking and moneychanging, and it had a local pool of expertise which was unrivalled in the Middle East at that time.

The government took several measures to enhance Beirut's position, some of the most important of which concerned the country's currency. First, unlike the other Arab states, Lebanon maintained a liberal foreign exchange policy, and allowed free convertibility which is essential to the success of any financial centre. Secondly, the authorities sought to maintain a stable parity for the Lebanese pound by pursuing only modest government spending programmes, in order to maintain and build up foreign exchange reserves. Spending was kept well within the means of the economy to sustain it. Thirdly, a large portion of the reserve assets themselves were converted into gold to further boost confidence in the country's currency. Fourthly, and perhaps of paramount importance, the government on 3 September 1956 enacted a law on banking secrecy, modelled on the Swiss legislation, which prevented the disclosure of the names of depositors to any authorities or investigators.[25] This law in fact went further than that in Switzerland, as even Lebanese government ministries could not demand disclosures, whereas the Berne government could request information on depositors in certain legally defined circumstances.

Lebanon's bank secrecy law was well timed, as it came when substantial funds from the major Arab revolutionary states were seeking a safe haven, either from newly imposed taxes, or from outright sequestration of the assets of wealthy individuals such as former landowners. Beirut became a base not only for Syrian funds, but also for those of the wealthy of Cairo and Alexandria, especially the Christians and Egypt's foreign community, many of whom had family connections with Beirut in any case. The 1958 revolution in Iraq caused a further outflow of funds, while in addition the absence of developed international banking on the Arabian peninsula meant that some funds also started to flow in from these less populous oil-exporting states. It was not until the mid-1960s however that the latter started to replace the Arab socialist states as the major source of external finance for the Beirut banks, as both oil prices and production remained at modest levels, and to an extent the expatriate banks in the Gulf, such as the British Bank of the Middle East, handled at least some of this early recycling.

Beirut's attraction as a financial centre of course partly reflected the city's other amenities, not least its appeal as a tourist centre. Business in Beirut was often combined with pleasure, and the city became increasingly important as a stop-over between Iraq, the Gulf and Europe. With the advent of jet aircraft of course there was less need to touch down in Beirut, and even in the early 1960s it was not needed as a refuelling stop. Rather travellers actually chose to spend some time in Beirut, although the development of Lebanon's own airline, Middle Eastern Airlines, as a carrier for the whole region, undoubtedly contributed to Beirut's business success. Other communications facilities also favoured Beirut, as its post and telephones functioned efficiently, and it was the first centre in the Middle East to have telex equipment installed. In contrast the telephone system in Cairo got worse rather than better during the 1960s, and postal deliveries were often unreliable, and at best, infrequent.

Most of the deposits within the Beirut banking system were of a short-term demand nature as Table 3.1 shows, and even before the civil war the proportion of time deposits declined from over 14 per cent in 1964 to under 4 per cent by 1973. A major portion of the demand deposits were not in chequing accounts, on which cheques could be drawn, but in so-called "savings" deposits, which could be withdrawn on request at the bank where the deposit was held, either by calling in

TABLE 3.1 *Commercial bank deposits in the Lebanon, 1964–74*

	Total deposits (millions of Lebanese pounds)	Demand deposits as proportion of total (%)	Foreign currency deposits as a proportion of total (%)
1964	2,277	81.2	35.1
1965	2,606	87.5	45.8
1966	3,061	86.8	50.7
1967	2,894	89.1	58.0
1968	2,835	90.0	59.8
1969	3,186	90.7	51.5
1970	3,441	96.0	60.1
1971	4,222	96.3	62.3
1972	5,304	96.0	63.1
1973	6,386	96.8	66.8
1974	7,819	96.3	68.4

NOTE Figures are average for first quarter of each year, except for proportions of foreign currency deposits for 1964 which refers to second quarter. $1 = 2.3 Lebanese pounds during this period.

SOURCE John N. Bridge, "Financial Growth and Economic Development: A Case Study of Lebanon", Ph.D. thesis, University of Durham, 1975, Tables 7.1–7.4, pp. 205–7, 212 and 214–15.

person, or by letter, or even by telex in some cases. These savings accounts were not time deposits, however, as they were payable immediately on demand, but in practice the funds in them tended to be held for much longer periods than was usually the case with chequing deposits. As a result of this stability, interest was paid on these accounts, although it was generally below the level on time accounts.

Over the 1964–74 period the proportion of foreign currency deposits in relation to deposits in local Lebanese pounds steadily increased as Table 3.1 shows, rising from approximately one-third of total deposits to over two-thirds. This partly reflected the increased significance of the multinational banks in the Beirut market as the 1960s progressed, as these institutions preferred to run their accounts in dollars, and to a lesser extent other western currencies. It also however resulted from the growth of deposits in the system from the Gulf oil-producing states and Saudi Arabia, where businessmen were accustomed to dealing in dollars, the currency in which most oil revenues were paid. A further factor dictating the growing preference for foreign currency deposits may have been the reluctance of the banks to take in deposits in local currency, which they could not hope to loan out profitably in Lebanon. Domestic demand for loans was extremely limited, and there was no international loan market in Lebanese pounds or even much of a local bond or securities market in local currency. If the banks had taken in deposits in local currency, and lent them out in other currencies, then the banks themselves would have borne the exchange risks. [26]

A final factor causing the preference for foreign currency deposits was undoubtedly the higher interest that could be earned. Interest rates on deposits in Lebanese pounds were generally two or three percentage points below the rates on the dollar and other western currencies throughout the period. Nevertheless there was no run on the Lebanese pound at any stage, as it tended to appreciate slightly *vis-à-vis* the dollar and most other major currencies owing to the conservative monetary policies of the Beirut authorities. [27] Even during the civil war confidence in the Lebanese pound remained, and the authorities did not need to suspend convertibility at any time. [28] Despite this confidence, however, and the chance of making a capital gain to offset any interest losses, there was no rush into Lebanese pounds. This was possibly because of the relatively higher exchange conversion costs when moving funds in and out of the currency which were levied in Beirut, compared with the charges in western financial centres for conversion of dollars into European currencies.

Beirut was the first centre in the Arab world to attract a wide range of western banks, as in the two decades prior to its civil war many American and European banks which would otherwise have gone to Cairo or possibly Damascus, established their main Middle Eastern base in Lebanon. Western banks with a strong regional interest such as the British Bank of the Middle East already had a presence in Beirut of course, as did some of the French banks in view of the strong Franco-Lebanese ties, but the 1960s and early 1970s saw the arrival of a large number of North American banks such as the Bankers Trust Company of New York, American Express, the Chemical Bank, Citibank, Continental Development of Chicago, Fidelity Bank of Philadelphia, First National of Boston, Manufacturers Hanover

Trust, Morgan Guaranty and Republican National of New York.

Banks were also attracted from Canada and Western Europe, especially Switzerland, whose banks hoped to benefit from their own experience of banking secrecy following the enactment of similar legislation in Lebanon. Active Swiss banks included Crédit Suisse, the Swiss Banking Corporation, the Union Bank of Switzerland and Bank Leu of Zurich. Japanese banks also chose Beirut as their Middle Eastern base in view of the city's importance as a communications centre and a transit stop for their own airline, although Bahrain has now attracted the leading Japanese institutions. In addition banks from the communist world selected Beirut as their centre for Arab finance, partly because of the city's geographcal proximity to Eastern Europe, but also because of Lebanon's undoubted neutrality both in inter-Arab politics and with regard to East–West conflict. [29] Eastern European financial institutions represented include Ceskoslovenska Obchodni Banka, Litex Bank of Bulgaria, Ljubljanska Banka of Yugoslavia, the Moscow Narodny Bank as well as Oesterreichische Laenderbank of Vienna which has numerous Eastern European connections. Interestingly, all the Eastern European institutions still remain active in Beirut despite the civil war, although Oesterreichische Laenderbank temporarily moved its office to Amman.

For the United States and Western European banks however the civil war of 1975–76 and the subsequent "no war, no peace" situation had a devastating effect. Expatriate staff to work in Beirut could only be recruited with difficulty, or transferred with reluctance, and even many of the more able or ambitious Lebanese had left the country for posts elsewhere. Personal callers from other Arab states rarely visited, and the volume of new business declined substantially. Confidence had of course been shaken before with the Intra Bank crash of 1968. Then one of Beirut's largest local banks collapsed after a liquidity crisis, a result of lending on long-term, high-risk ventures but accepting mainly short-term deposits. This crisis mainly affected the Lebanese banks, however, and not the foreign banks, unlike the civil war which affected all institutions.

Lebanon's own banks have nevertheless proved remarkably resilient in spite of the many problems of recent years. These included not only the Intra Bank collapse but also the two wars with Israel in 1967 and 1973, which affected the whole region even though Lebanon was not directly involved, and of course the civil war itself. Branch banking has spread rapidly, and the banks attracted many deposits from the Gulf, especially before 1975. Since the Intra Bank collapse, from the Gulf, especially before 1975. Since the Intra Bank collapse, the central bank has played a more active role in regulating the local banking system, especially its reserve requirements, and confidence in domestic institutions was reinforced.[30] In addition the central bank is in a sufficiently strong position to act as lender of the last resort, unlike some of the currency boards elsewhere in the region. Furthermore the Lebanese banks were able to meet all withdrawals, and stayed open for most of the civil war and its uncertain aftermath.

Undoubtedly the willingness of the Lebanese banks to continue business strengthened their position *b is-à-vis* the foreign banks and even banks from other Arab countries, which, apart from the Arab Bank, suspended operations with the outbreak of hostilities during the civil war. Those still engaged in trade and commerce in Lebanon had little choice but to use the domestically-owned banks. In addition, as the number of Lebanese emigrants abroad increased, in Europe, America and especially the Gulf, the amounts of remittances flowing into the Beirut banking system grew, and to some extent made up for the loss of foreign deposits. The 200,000 Lebanese working abroad were sending back an estimated $200 million a month by 1980.[31] With the boom in Saudi Arabia and the Gulf, many Lebanese and Palestinians from Lebanon found their career prospects enhanced, and their salaries steadily increased, which aided further the flow of nds. As a consequence the Lebanese domestic banking system has continued to expand despite the country's internal problems, and many local moneychangers are starting to reconstitute themselves as full commercial banks.

Around six new baks were opening each year by the late 1970s and early 1980s, and by 1981 the number of banks operating in Lebanon was 91, compared to 73 prior to the civil war.[32] Although many of the forty banks included in this figure only operated an extremely restricted domestic service after the civil war, the resurgence of local banking has kept activity buoyant, if less internationalised than in pre-civil war days. Inflation has ironically encouraged the formation of new banks, as under Lebanese law, a new bank must have a minimum capital of 30 million Lebanese pounds ($9 million), but this figure has remained fixed in money terms since the late 1960s. Thus the threshold for moneylenders reconstituting themselves as fully fledged banks has been progressively lowered in real terms, tempting many to improve their status through official registration and publication of accounts. By 1981 deposits within the expanded banking system had risen to 25 billion Lebanese pounds ($18.6 billion), and 18 new banks had been formed, yet there were no bank failures despite the difficulties formed, yet there were no bank failures despite the difficulties prevailing in contrast to the more favourable environment in the 1960s when the Intra Bank collapsed. Certainly Lebanon's troubles illustrate the strength of the country's comparative advantage in banking and financial activity.

CREATION OF AN ARAB MULTINATIONAL

Traditionally the Lebanese banks have been regarded as more outward-looking than those of other Arab countries, partly because of Lebanon's small size, but also as a reflection of the cosmopolitan nature of Beirut's society and its strong links with Europe and the Mediterranean region generally. However, the emphasis of the Lebanese banks was on attracting funds into Beirut, and recycling them from there, rather than branching out abroad. Only one institution, the Lebanese Arab Bank had more branches abroad than within the country as by 1980 it had eleven foreign branches, but only six within Lebanon. Its foreign branches however mainly served Lebanese citizens, and even its distant Buenos Aires office primarily catered for Lebanese expatriates. Other Beirut banks were established with funds from such Lebanese expatriates, but essentially to cater for the domestic market. Banque Libano-Brasilienne, for example, was partly funded from Brazil, but all its ten branches are within Lebanon.[33]

None of the Lebanese banks has sufficient capital to aspire to become a multinational institution, however, despite the surprising wealth that many Lebanese at home and abroad have been able to acquire through their commercial skills. Nor has there been much incentive to spread operations outside Lebanon, given the profitability of the local market and the favourable banking environment. No Lebanese bank even became as large as the Arab Bank, or as pan-Arab in operations. Hence there has always been something of a paradox in Lebanese banking as, although the country's financial institutions were outward-looking, at the same time their operations were essentially parochial. Perhaps one explanation is that only market limitations favoured outward expansion, but domestic comparative advantage favoured expansion at home, or at least within the Lebanese commercial community, even if non-resident.

In contrast to Lebanon, other centres in the Arab world, with the possible exceptions of Bahrain and Dubai, lack any comparative advantage in banking or other financial activity. They either do not have the human resources, as in the Gulf where expatriates have been hired in large numbers for senior and even junior banking posts, or else have environments where state interference precludes expansionist commercial banking activity, which seems to thrive best under free enterprise conditions. At first sight Abu Dhabi would appear to be an extremely unpromising location for the emergence of the Arab World's first multinational bank, as it fulfils neither condition for successful commercial banking, lacking both indigenous personnel with banking skills, and having an economy which is firmly state-directed, even compared to the neighbouring Emirate of Dubai.

Abu Dhabi is the main base however of a unique institution, the Bank of Credit and Commerce International, which claims with some justification to be the first Arab multinational commercial bank. Several differences from the Arab Bank, and other potential Arab multinationals, should be noted. First, whereas the Arab Bank is pan-Arab in its operations, its branch network beyond the Arab world is limited, unlike BCC which by 1980 had 194 offices in 40 different countries, both Arab and non-Arab. Secondly the staff of the Arab Bank is predominantly Palestinian as already noted, but the staff of BCC·is drawn from virtually every country in which it operates, and, although a high proportion still come from the Indian sub-continent, this proportion is declining. Thirdly, although the majority ownership of the Arab Bank remains Palestinian, the ownership of BCC is diverse, yet predominantly Arab. Finally it is worth mentioning that BCC, like the Arab Bank, provides a full range of commercial banking functions, but has most of its activity centred on ordinary branch banking activities. In contrast aspiring multinationals such as the Gulf International Bank and the Arab Banking Corporation of Bahrain are essentially banker's banks, whose main activities are at the wholesale rather than at the retail level. Neither needs extensive branch networks to carry out their syndicated loan activities on behalf of governments and other major borrowers. In addition both Gulf International and the Arab Banking Corporation are inter-governmental joint venture undertakings, which puts them in a different category from wholly privately-owned commercial banks such as BCC and the Arab Bank.

BCC is usually regarded as an Arab institution because of its ownership, although the actual structure of the ownership is complex, and not easily disentangled, even by bank officials. The BCC group is owned through a Luxembourg-based holding company established in

1972, with capital funds of over $220 million by 1980 as Table 3.2 shows. Middle Eastern interests directly own 49 per cent of this capital, with leading shareholders including Sheikh Sultan Al-Nahyan, Crown Prince of Abu Dhabi, other members of the Abu Dhabi ruling family, Sheikh Kamal Adham, former Chief of Intelligence in Saudi

TABLE 3.2   *Growth of the Bank of Credit and Commerce*

	Total assets ($000s)	Capital fund ($000s)	No. of offices	No. of countries
1973	200,833	5,206	19	5
1974	610,167	11,105	27	7
1975	1,206,371	23,982	64	13
1976	1,656,439	50,071	108	21
1977	2,205,505	113,887	146	32
1978	2,801,186	171,374	181	38
1979	3,700,000	220,000	194	40

NOTE   Figures for 31 December each year; 1979 figures provisional.
SOURCE   BCC.

Arabia, and other Saudi princes, members of the ruling families of Bahrain, and some of the former Shah's relatives from Iran. The remainder of the capital, the 51 per cent majority share, is owned by a further company, the International Credit and Investment Company (Overseas) Limited. Approximately 35 per cent of this company is in turn owned by a charitable foundation, again largely under Arab ownership, but eligible for tax exemption because of its special status, although of course non-residents of Luxembourg are exempt from local taxes in any case, but they may be liable for tax elsewhere. A further 30 per cent is owned by a business promotions corporation, which is largely fed by profits and dividends generated from within BCC,[34] but not taken out by the main shareholders, sometimes for tax reasons. The final 35 per cent of the International Credit and Investment Company represents a staff benefit trust, in which members of the bank's staff receive share options as part of a bonus scheme, or in some cases in lieu of part of their salaries, which again may bring tax advantages for employees in certain courtries.

The ownership structure of BCC has proved controversial on several grounds, and has been the subject of much discussion in Arab and international banking circles. First, the principle of financing capital with borrowed funds, which will eventually be paid back out of future bank profits and dividends, gives rise to concern, as it seems reasonable to ask what would happen if future profits or dividends fall, or the original investors want more distributed. Secondly, the thinly disguised schemes for tax avoidance, although legal, cause much disquiet, especially with European central bankers. A third worry is that so far the bank's ultimate owners do not seem concerned that they have in effect lost control to the management through the complicated ownership arrangement which gives them only a 49 per cent direct equity stake. What would happen if they became discontented with the management, and sought to exercise their influence through the 51 per cent stake owned by the International Credit and Investment Company. If they found themselves unable to exert influence, they might sell out completely. Finally, the staff benefit fund, although having the laudable objective of ensuring worker participation, is far from popular with the bank employee trade unions in some of the countries in which BCC operates, as the unions feel that many of their members are already too tied to the institutions in which they work without introducing these further ties. The unions prefer higher salaries, rather than share options.

BCC has nevertheless proved an outstandingly successful financial institution, but this success owes much to the dynamism of its founder, Agha Hasan Abedi, the organisation's president.[35] Originally an employee of the Habib Bank in India, he later resigned to help found the United Bank of Pakistan. Prior to the nationalisation of the Pakistan banks, he left, with a number of senior colleagues from the United Bank, to found a new institution, BCC. Drawing some of the most able bankers from Pakistan's financial community, and combining their expertise with Muslim capital from the oil-rich Gulf, proved a recipe for profits, most of which were ploughed back to finance expansion, which was extremely rapid as Table 3.2 shows. By 1980 both the ownership and the personnel had become more internationalised, but there is little doubt that those originally involved from the Gulf and Pakistan have benefited substantially.

The bank was of course founded at a fortunate time, in 1972, just before the oil price rises, and at a time when oil production in the Gulf, and in Abu Dhabi in particular, was reaching its peak. Deposits flowed in initially from relatives and friends of the original investors, but soon from a much wider circle of Gulf Arabs. The bank could offer interest only half a per cent below inter-bank rates,[36] as it had the skill to deploy the funds in international financial market in a way that no other private institution in the Gulf could at that time. It had the resources, the manpower and the contacts that rival banks in the Gulf were unable to match, and certainly not the traditional European banks involved in the region who were finding difficulty in adapting to a post-colonial situation. BCC soon expanded into financial markets as far apart as Canada, the United States,[37] Hong Kong and West Africa[38] through the acquisition of finance houses and even other banks. Its dealings in the United States however caused some controversy with the Securities and Exchange Commission, and its much publicised involvement with Bert Lance, former President Carter's one-time budget director, was probably counter-productive.

Connections with the United States have always been important for BCC, as at its inception California's Bank of America owned one quarter of the equity. Bank of America provided some specialised staff through a secondment arrangement, and acted as a correspondent in major European and American financial markets while BCC was building up its operations. There is little doubt that the connection with a much respected institution such as Bank of America also brought the new bank considerable prestige, and that the goodwill generated was extremely valuable. As time progressed, however, as is often the case where an established institution and a new bank are concerned, the relationship became uneasy. Bank of America was unhappy about BCC's rapid pace of expansion, and some of its banking methods. As a major shareholder, Bank of America tried to dictate balance sheet ratios which BCC was not allowed to exceed, and imposed a two-year moratorium on the raising of new capital between 1975 and 1977. This caution naturally displeased members of the BCC board, as it meant other institutions in the Gulf would profit from the buoyant trading conditions rather than the new bank. As Table 3.2 shows, BCC did not adhere to the Bank of America moratorium, however, and it must be a matter for debate whether it had much effect.

Finally, late in 1977, Bank of America bowed to pressure and allowed BCC to expand again, as it had been doing in any case, but Bank of America did not increase its own equity stake, which declined proportionally as a result. This marked the parting of the ways nevertheless, as other tensions between the two institutions were arising. Bank of America wanted to expand its own direct operations in the Gulf, but found it had to go through BCC as an intermediary. Meanwhile BCC wanted to establish branches in the United States, but found it was precluded from doing so under the Federal Reserve Authority's anti-monopoly regulations on banking, as it was part-owned by Bank of America. Therefore the decision was taken to separate. By 1979 the Bank of America's stake in BCC was already reduced to 12 per cent, and by July 1980 it had sold off its remaining shares.

The new Arab multinational since then has been on its own, but there is little doubt that it has matured sufficiently to survive. It has its own training academy in central London for its staff,[39] and has opened branches in most major European capitals. BCC has been particularly active in the United Kingdom where it has branched out in all the areas with large immigrant communities from the Indian sub-continent, and it has competed successfully with the Pakistani banks for "ethnic" business, although the bank is far from being a Pakistani institution. Branches are located even in relatively small towns and cities such as Blackburn, Rochdale, Slough and Wolverhampton. Within London its expansion has been phenomenal, and by 1980 it had 26 branches located on most areas of the city. There much of its retail business consists of moneychanging, and it specialises in the exchange of currencies from the Gulf states into sterling and dollars. The favourable rates it quotes attracts a large number of Arab customers from the Gulf and Saudi Arabia, many of whom are relatively long-stay tourists throughout the summer season.

BCC management structure is geographically decentralised, as, although the bank has two registered headquarters, one in Luxembourg, and the other in the Cayman Islands for its overseas division, these are not centres of control or decision-making. The Luxembourg branch does handle many accounts, including those of European expatriates working in the Gulf who do not wish to remit their earnings to their native countries for tax reasons,[40] but the bank's president, Agha Hasan Abedi, and members of the central management committee rarely visit Luxembourg. In practice most top-level decisions are made either in the Abu Dhabi main office on the Corniche, where BCC owns perhaps the most imposing building in the Gulf, or at the Leadenhall Street office in London. Abedi himself does much commuting between the two, as Leadenhall Street controls and co-ordinates most non-Arab business, while Abu Dhabi is the nerve centre for the 29 branches in the Emirates, and the 12 branches in Oman. Other Arab countries where BCC is strongly represented include Egypt, where it has six branches, Lebanon, where it also has six, and Jordan, where it only has three, but plans further expansion.

In the longer run, like other multinationals, BCC may lose any national identity, and its Arab connections may become relatively less important. Agha Hasan Abedi may want to encourage such a disassociation, and there are already some indications that the focus of operations is moving more towards London at the expense of Abu Dhabi. The bank would clearly like to expand further in the United Kingdom, and was only prevented from such expansion by the Bank of England in the late 1970s. The ownership remains predominantly Arab, however, despite the complex restructuring, and the original investors show little inclination to divest themselves of their holdings, even though they have lost majority control, as already indicated, and profitability has been sacrificed to expansion. In its practice the bank also remains more oriental than western, as more weight is given to experience and less to short-term results than is the case with western institutions. The members of the central management committee all have over 25 years of banking experience, and are older than their contemporaries in many western multinationals, despite the relative youth of the institution.[41] For this reason alone BCC should remain a more durable institution than many of its critics in rival banks claim, and even if it becomes less Arabised over time, it should retain some oriental character.

4 Islamic Banking in Principle and Practice

The Koran, like the Bible, is not only concerned with spiritual matters of an abstract nature, but also with how believers should conduct their everyday lives. Unlike the Bible, however, which concentrates its temporal teaching on social relations, the Koran explicitly deals with economic questions such as the distribution of property on inheritance, hoarding, usury and the utilisation of financial resources. Mohammed was not just a prophet, but also a law maker, and the Sharia or Islamic law has to be followed by all believers. It would be incorrect to suggest of course that Christian scholars were never concerned with economic matters, since for example Thomas Aquinas and the scholastic philosophers deliberated on the notion of a just price and the morality of interest charges. Nevertheless these concerns are not given much emphasis in the Bible itself, and they are far from being central issues in modern Christian debate. In contrast the revival of interest in fundamentalism in the Muslim world has resulted in greater attention being paid to Koranic teaching and the Sharia law on economic issues. At the same time given the new financial wealth of parts of the Muslim world, it is only natural that believers are particularly interested in those parts of the Prophet's teaching offering economic guidance, perhaps even to the exclusion of other matters.

Mohammed's home city, Mecca, was a major centre for banking and commerce during the Prophet's lifetime, and it was no doubt partly this that prompted his interest in financial affairs. While not condemning the moneychangers, moneylenders and traders of the city out of hand, he witnessed for himself the hardship which both usury and hoarding caused, as well as inequalities resulting from the inheritance system. As far as the financial community was concerned, it was not their activities which Mohammed abhorred, but their methods. The Prophet saw how sharp financial practices caused division and antagonisms in the community, which internally lowered

70

moral values and led to weakness, while externally it meant constant feuding amongst the tribes and cities of the Hijaz. In such circumstances any advance of civilisation was constrained, as a substantial proportion of the population lived in indebtedness from which there was little hope of escape, yet meanwhile the payments collected by the creditors were hoarded for personal use and security, rather than recirculated for the benefit of the community. It is this practice the Koran condemns, not the accumulation of wealth, but the failure to use it to help others.

> Proclaim a woeful punishment to those that hoard up gold and silver and do not spend it in Allah's cause. The day will surely come when their treasures shall be heated in the fire of Hell, and their foreheads, sides and backs branded with them. Their tormentors will say to them: "These are the riches which you hoarded. Taste then the punishment which is your due."[1]

The practice of usury was singled out for particular attention because of the misery it caused.

> Those that live on usury shall rise up before Allah like men whom Satan has demented by his touch; for they claim that usury is like trading. But Allah has permitted trading and forbidden usury.[2]

Usurers are to be given every chance to reform their financial practices, but those who do not take advantage of Allah's mercy stand condemned.

> He that receives an admonition from his Lord and mends his ways may keep what he has already earned; his fate is in the hands of Allah. But he that pays no heed shall be consigned to Hell-fire and shall remain in it for ever.[3]

Both creditors and debtors are given direct advice by the Prophet. Those advancing credit are urged to be understanding to debtors who get into difficulty with repayments, and to be at least lenient with rescheduling.

> If your debtor be in straits, grant him a delay until he can discharge his debt; but if you waive the sum as alms it will be better for you, if you but knew it.[4]

Those seeking credit are advised to have the terms of the loan put in writing, and the contract with their creditor witnessed by two neutral parties.

> Believers, when you contract a debt for a fixed period, put it in writing. Let a scribe write it down for you with fairness . . . and let the debtor dictate, not diminishing the sum he owes. If the debtor be a feeble-minded or ignorant person, or one who cannot dictate, let his guardian dictate for him in fairness. Call in two male (or female) witnesses from among you . . . so that if either of them commit an error, the other will remember. Witnesses must not refuse to give evidence if called upon to do so.[5]

Thus the interests of both parties are protected, and the risk of fraudulent dealings considerably reduced. Those who attempt to interfere with the independence of the scribes or witnesses are condemned.

Where it is not practicable to have legally written contracts, then pledges may be taken, but this is a second-best solution. If a pledge is in force, borrowers should not seek further loans from other parties until the first loan is repaid, but this does not apply with written legal contracts. With the latter there is clearly less danger of the borrower overcommitting himself, as a creditor can easily find out who is in debt to whom, and the sums involved. In the early tight-knit Muslim communities scribes were limited in number, and often senior men from the tribe or village acted as witnesses. Creditors would clearly know where to seek information, and there were no penalties for disclosure, indeed it was in the borrower's interest that his financial situation should be revealed. From this it is clear that much of the Prophet's concern was with protecting debtors, and the condemnation of usury has to be seen in this context. It was not the so-called unearned income as such that was seen as unjust, but the unwarranted hardship placed on the borrowers. Most of those seeking credit, especially poor peasant cultivators or herdsmen, lacked financial resources, which was their reason for wanting a loan in the first place, and it was seen as unfair that the usually richer creditors should benefit from this hardship. Benefits would be transitory in any case, and if the rich merely indulge in conspicuous consumption this is pointless. The ostentatious find no lasting rewards in their material possessions.

Such men are like a rock covered with earth: a shower falls upon it and leaves it hard and bare. They shall gain nothing from their works.[6]

If the believer is not to hoard or consume in a conspicuous fashion, how are any finances accumulated to be utilised? It is clear that the Koran does not assume that all citizens in an Islamic state should consume on the same level, it is only that the adverse demonstration effects of lavish consumption on social harmony are seen as undesirable. There is no objection to pecuniary incentives, but the richer members of a community have to manage their financial resources in a socially responsible manner, and, as wealth increases, the responsibility becomes greater, as well as perhaps the temptation to misuse funds for dubious pleasures. At the same time wealth can bring opportunities for pleasing Allah, as it enables the believer to give alms to the poor and needy generally and to pay the Zakat, a religious tax levied annually at 2 per cent of the total value of a person's wealth. The proceeds of this also help the poor. In summary,

A person should not find enjoyment and prestige in wealth but in right-doing and beneficence. He should not find security in treasures, but in the solidarity of the Islamic society, a society which fills its responsibilities by neglecting and rejecting none.[7]

Nevertheless in giving the believer must also be discreet, as donations are not made to impress others, but as an expression of the donor's social responsibility.

To be charitable in public is good, but to give alms to the poor in private is better and will atone for some of your sins. Allah has knowledge of all your actions.[8]

FUNDAMENTALISM IN A MODERN SETTING

Obviously the financial system and commercial relations of Mecca and Medina fourteen centuries ago were very different from those prevailing today in the Arabian peninsula or elsewhere in the Islamic world. The question arises how the believer should best treat the Prophet's message in a modern context or indeed, for the less devout, whether the message has any relevance at all, at least in the sphere of financial activity. Should the prohibition of usury apply in complex money and financial markets, and if so, how should it be interpreted? Do the reservations about hoarding mean that savings are undesirable, especially as even to Keynesian economists they are often viewed as a leakage out of the circular flow of money as Mohammed suggested? Clearly in the Hijaz of the Prophet's time, there was little emphasis on savings to finance investment, as there simply was so little investment, and concepts such as capital formation and technical change were certainly not of critical importance, although that does not imply that they were completely absent.

In the modern Muslim world, at first sight Koranic ideas appear to have had relatively little effect on financial development, although this may have been because most of the first banks established were European rather than indigenous, as pointed out in Chapter 2, and they primarily served the numerous expatriate communities. To a large extent the advent of modern banking bypassed the majority of local Muslims in the Middle East, and it tended to be in the more remote areas in any case where the most conservative believers lived. These areas had no banks, and even the Agricultural Bank established in the Ottoman Empire, which charged interest, mostly served the richer landowners who lived near cosmopolitan settlements, and who were far from being fundamentalists. There was always some unease of course in states throughout the Middle East about the spread of western banking practices, but, apart from in Saudi Arabia, most governments until the 1950s at least, were prepared to drop any reservations they had for the sake of modernisation. At the same time there was an unhappy feeling that economic advance, and the institutional framework and practice that implied, was somehow incompatible with literal interpretations of the Koran, but most governments tried to push the issue aside, and sought to avoid conflict by ignoring Muslim teaching. No attempt was made to try to re-interpret the Koran, or to study how it should be applied in the contemporary world.

The fundamentalists were not very vociferous for the most part, and their influence seemed to be in decline until the last decade, especially in the urban areas. Some states, especially Turkey, were so keen to westernise that there was a drive to secularise the society generally, and a strong anti-clerical movement.[9] Others, such as pre-revolutionary Egypt, Syria and Iraq, were so locked in a virtual colonial relationship with European powers that they were concerned to do nothing to offend. When the revolutions came in these countries, however, the emphasis was on nationalisation or socialisation of the financial sector, as the last chapter showed, and on Arabisation. The application of fundamental Islamic principles was far from the minds of most revolutionaries, who were more influenced by European socialism, or even Marxism than by the Prophet's teaching. The quest was to find an Arab socialist path of economic development, not to try to reconcile Islam with socialism or anything else.

The only real debate about the application of Islamic principles to commerce in the l950s took place not in the Middle East, but in Pakistan, where it had been the sense of a separate religious identity that had resulted in the formation of the state in the first place. The merits of inserting a clause in the 1956 constitution banning interest was discussed, [10] but the issue was put aside because of commercial considerations, although the question of interest was subsequently raised time after time in the national assembly in Islamabad. Despite the failure to get a ban on usury enforced at the national level, an experimental local Islamic bank was founded in the late 1950s in a rural area of Pakistan which charged no interest on its lending. The institution was backed by a small number of pious landowners who were prepared to deposit funds without interest rewards, and the credit was advanced to other poorer landowners for agricultural improvements. No interest was charged for the credit, but a small fixed administrative fee was levied to cover the operating expenses of the bank. However, although there was no shortage of borrowers, the depositors tended to view their payments into the institution as a once-and-for-all effort, and the institution soon ran short of funds. In addition the depositors took a considerable interest in how their deposits were loaned out, and the bank officials enjoyed little autonomy. With no new deposits forthcoming and problems over the recruitment of bank staff, who were unwilling to give up lucrative and secure careers in city commercial banking for an uncertain venture in the countryside, the institution soon foundered. Enthusiasm waned and, once the small staff was disbanded, existing loans were merely handled as bilateral arrangements between landlords, without any financial intermediation. They were mostly repaid by the early 1960s.

Just as the Pakistan venture was being ended a new experiment was being tried in Egypt, the first recorded in modern times in the Middle East or the Arab World. Like the Islamic bank in Pakistan, the Egyptian institution was in a rural area, in this case a small provincial town in the Nile Delta. The main instigator of this institution was

Ahmad El Nagar, who later became secretary-general of the International Association of Islamic Banks.[11] On 25 July 1963 the Mitr Ghams Savings Bank, as the institution was known, opened for business, with El Nagar as the manager, and a carefully selected staff of Muslim enthusiasts who had some banking experience with commercial institutions, although El Nagar himself was primarily an academic. The staff soon gained the confidence of the conservative country community, who saw they were devout Muslims like themselves, as they worshipped locally with their potential customers. The region's peasants were suspicious of outsiders, and few had ever used commercial banks, which were seen as alien institutions, belonging to the cities, and mainly to serve westernised Egyptians. These new bankers were viewed as different, however, as they shared the same views and moral values as the peasants themselves, despite their education.

The Mitr Ghams Savings Bank soon prospered, and within three years the 1000 founding depositors had been joined by a further 59,000. No interest was paid on deposits but, in order to receive an interest free loan, a borrower had to have a certain minimum sum in a savings account for at least a year. Thus there was some financial motivation to deposit funds, as depositors and borrowers belonged to the same group, unlike in Pakistan. Loans were used for a variety of purposes, including house building and repairs, the purchase of simple machinery for handicrafts industries, such as hand looms for weaving textiles, or even simple sewing machines. Some loans helped finance the purchase of farm animals and basic improvements to the irrigation systems as efficient water provision was essential in a community based on agriculture. Usually loans were of short-term duration, one to three years, but some medium-term lending of up to five years was allowed, although there were no grace periods on repayments. The emphasis was on keeping the funds circulating, following the Prophet's teaching on the evils of hoarding.

The success of the bank was commented on in a glowing Ford Foundation report in June 1967 which noted how the institution had won the personal support of a large number of farmers and villagers who regarded the bank as their own.[12] Problems of rural indebtedness were reduced, as borrowers no longer had to depend on the local moneylenders, many of whom charged high interest rates. The poorer peasants who had not sufficient funds to become depositors were unable to become beneficiaries of the bank, however, and in general it tended to be the middle-income earners who were most enthusiastic about the institution, although arguably it was this group which were the backbone of the local rural economy. The loans generated welcome income for those borrowers who deployed their funds for investment purposes, and there is little doubt the bank made a useful contribution to development.

Despite the popularity of the Mitr Ghams Savings Bank, and its initial success, it eventually got into difficulty, as it did not share in the profits which the borrowers made. As in Pakistan the bank only charged borrowers a small administrative fee, which was fixed at the time the loan was made regardless of the purpose for which the credit was to be utilised. Borrowers were not required to pay back more even if their financial position improved substantially. The amounts to cover administrative expenses were therefore limited, and bank salaries remained unattractive. With expansion it was difficult to recruit extra staff and, as in Pakistan, the bank's rural location was a disincentive, even though the distance to the amenities of Cairo and Alexandria was not great. A further problem was that some of the initial staff started to drift away, as their initial enthusiasm inevitably waned, as it was difficult to maintain this over time. Many had increasing family commitments which drew them back to the cities and more remunerative employment, for which they could hardly be criticised.

Far from the experience with the Mitr Ghams Savings Bank being a deterrent to future endeavours, Ahmad El Nagar was encouraged to widen the experiment, and in 1972 he helped found a new institution, the Nasser Social Bank, in which he was to become a deputy general manager. By this time El Nagar had won the support of some close associates of the late President Nasser, who agreed that the institution should be given state funding, which Sadat's new government agreed to, and an initial 1,400,020 Egyptian pounds was paid in (over $2 million). This meant the institution was on a much firmer financial footing from its inception, as it had substantial resources to fall back upon. Obviously El Nagar had learned the lesson from the Mitr Ghams Savings Bank experience. The latter was in fact taken over by the new bank, which thereby gained some initial popular goodwill, and the Nasser Social Bank agreed to honour all the outstanding commitments of its predecessor. Unlike the former local bank however it was based in Cairo, where the senior staff worked, and they enjoyed the same job security which was found elsewhere in the Egyptian state sector.[13]

The Nasser Social Bank is authorised only to operate under strict

Islamic principles and, as with the Mitr Ghams Savings Bank, all loans are interest-free, but only depositors can borrow funds in this privileged way. In general the emphasis is on short-term lending to ensure rotation of funds, and preference is given to those who want to borrow for social purposes, although these can be very broadly defined. Loans are often used for housing, but borrowing for speculative purposes such as real estate acquisition for capital gains is frowned upon. Credit is not allowed to be re-deposited with other banks for interest, or re-loaned for interest of course, and, although the purposes for which loans are utilised are not closely supervised, the onus is put on borrowers to ensure that funds are deployed in accordance with Islamic principles. Given the trust which exists between bank and borrowers, and the strict moral conduct of most believers who obtain credit, it is unlikely that there is much abuse. Indeed the quality of the clients is such that they would be given an extremely good credit rating by any financial institution. In this sense there is little doubt that Islamic banks in general are at an advantage, as they are unlikely to attract dubious borrowers, and believers know that it is not the bank they must fear if they squander the funds which the depositors have placed on trust, but Allah.

The functions of the Nasser Social Bank are much wider than deposit taking and the provision of interest-free loans. It also offers a full range of normal banking services from its Cairo head office, although its foreign exchange dealings are fairly restricted and it still refers clients to other banks for such purposes. The bank has been keen to build up its investment activities through direct participation in projects, and it takes an equity share in suitable ventures. Profit sharing is seen as fully consistent with Islamic principles, indeed it is thought to be socially desirable, as it is a way that risks can be shared between those being funded and those providing funds. By such means the bank can fully participate in the community it is designed to help, and no hardship is imposed on the borrowers if their plans go wrong. The bank as their partner shares in their gains, but also shares any losses. Interestingly there have been few losses, which perhaps reflects the calibre of those seeking bank support.

Although the Nasser Social Bank has diversified its activities, and helped pioneer new Islamic banking methods, the main thrust of its activity remains in branch banking. It aims to provide deposit facilities for believers in as many locations as possible, and to grant a large number of small interest-free loans which benefit those who have not used banks in the past. By 1979 it had 25 branches throughout Egypt, and its total deposits had reached 240 million Egyptian pounds ($345 million). [14] Its profits were also healthy, if unspectacular, as they rose to 12 million Egyptian pounds ($17.3 million) in 1978–79, and have maintained a steady upward trend since the bank's inception. The increase in deposits and activity generally has resulted in the paid up capital being raised to the authorised limit of 4 million Egyptian pounds ($5.8 million), and further increases are expected in the future.

The evidence from Egypt appears to suggest that the established banks do not appear to object to the competition which Islamic banks provide, although ultimately in any Muslim society they must pose a serious threat to the conventional banks which follow western methods. To some extent this is because the Nasser Social Bank has attracted a new kind of customer who hitherto did not use the commercial banking system but relied on traditional moneylenders. It is the latter whose business is threatened, but this disturbs nobody in influential circles given the alleged exploitation which moneylenders are charged with having carried out in the past. This extension of the banking net to attract non-banking clients was also the case with the Mitr Ghams Savings Bank as already indicated. Furthermore, in so far as the Islamic banks directly invest in ventures themselves, they are providing a financial service which complements rather than threatens the conventional banks, who have little interest in exposure of this type.

As Egypt's main commercial banks are nationalised in any case, they do not worry unduly about competition, as they always have the state to fall back on, and they have specialised roles, which arguably they have a first claim to perform as indicated in the previous chapter. In addition although the paid-up capital of the Nasser Social Bank is half that of the National Bank of Egypt, and as large as that of Bank Misr, the amount of deposits is only a small fraction of those in these banks, reflecting the limited size of each deposit with the Islamic institution. Furthermore the Nasser Social Bank is regarded as a charitable institution in many quarters, which bankers are loath to criticise. The bank has done much to revive the Zakat in Egypt, the charitable tax levied on wealth, the proceeds from which help the needy. It has helped establish over 700 special committees throughout the country, which take charge of the collection of the tax on a voluntary basis, and supervise the distribution of funds for worthy causes. [15]

TAKE-OFF FOR ISLAMIC BANKING

Although the Nasser Social Bank was a purely internal Egyptian venture, its experience and objectives attracted the attention of many in the Gulf and Saudi Arabia who believed it was highly desirable to found similar institutions elsewhere in the Islamic world. In particular Ahmed El Nagar interested the influential Saudi, Prince Mohammad bin Faisal, son of the late King Faisal, in his ideas about banking, as well as leaders of the Dubai merchant community. Characteristically it was the Dubai merchants who acted fastest, as they saw the opportunity which the new type of organisation would bring to harness the wealth of those in the Emirates who refused on religious grounds to have dealings with conventional banks. The oil boom had created considerable personal fortunes, but many of those who benefited were extremely conservative, yet they had to utilise their funds in some way. At the same time there were those who did not object to deploying some of their fortunes through western banks, but their consciences dictated that at least a portion of their assets should be used in strict accordance with Islamic principles.

The Dubai Islamic Bank commenced operations in September 1975 and, as Table 4.1 shows, it was soon to be followed by a significant number of similar institutions across the Islamic world. Unlike the state-owned Nasser Social Bank, four-fifths of the equity was in private hands, the investors mostly being Dubai merchants, but a small equity stake was taken by the governments of Dubai and Kuwait, largely as an indication of official goodwill towards the new venture. Like the Nasser Social Bank the Dubai Islamic Bank offers a full range of banking services, including interest-free loans in accordance with the Sharia. However, it puts a greater emphasis on direct investment than on lending, and it has taken a major stake in several major industrial projects, including the Dubai aluminium smelter and the construction of residential housing complexes in the Gulf,[16] to provide rented accommodation for expatriate labour. Its profits from these investments have been considerable already, even though many of the projects are long-term in nature and have yet to yield a return. Profits rose from $1.3 million in 1976 to over $3 million by 1978, and overall the bank hopes for a return of around 15 per cent on its investments.

Two types of accounts are provided for depositors by the Dubai Islamic Bank, savings accounts and investment accounts. No interest is earned on savings accounts, but depositors qualify for interest-free

TABLE 4.1 *Local Islamic banks*

Institution	Head office	Founded	Ownership status	Paid-up capital ($ million) 1979
Nasser Social Bank	Cairo	1972	Egyptian state-owned (100%)	5.8
Dubai Islamic Bank	Dubai	1975	Joint stock company with 10% Dubai government share and 10% Kuwait government share	13.2
Kuwait Finance House	Kuwait	1977	Kuwait government 49%, private investors 51%	8.6
Faisal Islamic Bank of Sudan	Khartoum	1977	Sudanese citizens and state institutions 40%, Saudi private citizens 40%, other nationals 20%	1.9
Faisal Islamic Bank of Egypt	Cairo	1977	Egyptian citizens and state institutions 51%, Saudi and other Arab nationals 49%	10.0
Jordan Islamic Bank for Finance and Investment	Amman	1978	Jordanian private investors 98.7%, Housing Bank 1.3%	3.4
Bahrain Islamic Bank	Manama	1979	Bahrain citizens, government, and social security fund 30%, Kuwaiti interests 30%, Dubai Islamic Bank 5%, Saudi investors 35%	1.3
Iran Islamic Bank	Tehran	1979	Iranian merchants 100%	N/A

Non-Middle Eastern Islamic institutions:
    Pakistan — Muslim Commercial Bank, National Investment Trust, Investment Corporation of Pakistan, House Building Finance Corporation.
    Bahamas — Islamic Investment Company, Nassau (Saudi-owned).

SOURCES Islamic Development Bank, *Fourth Annual Report,* Jeddah, 1979, pp. 36–8; *Middle Eastern Financial Directory* (London: MEED, 1980).

loans, as is the case with the Nasser Social Bank, and many depositors who have not made use of this loan facility nevertheless regard it as worthwhile to maintain funds in such an account as it offers them security. Those who open investment accounts are entitled to a share in the profits from the bank's investments, but funds have to be maintained in such accounts for a certain minimum period to qualify, normally a year. Funds cannot be withdrawn from investment term accounts on demand, as notice must be given in advance, but the bank is fairly flexible about this, and usually one month is the notice stipulated for small amounts, and three months for larger sums. If a client needs funds urgently and is in financial difficulties, the bank is always understanding, especially as it is aware of its religious obligations. Debtors will never be squeezed under any circumstances; the bank will instead offer advice about how their financial affairs should be reorganised. Obviously the record and moral standing of the client is taken into account when help is offered, and this will play a part in determining the conditions attached to the help given.

A committee of religious advisers is consulted by the Dubai Islamic Bank on all issues of policy, and sometimes even on matters concerning particular clients. This committee is composed of religious authorities, including those with a detailed knowledge of Sharia law, so that they can ensure that all bank practices conform with the letter, as well as the spirit of Islamic teaching. Their advice is taken very seriously by all the bank staff, who are of course practising Muslims themselves, although many have extensive banking experience throughout the Arab world, and in Pakistan and Iran in a few cases. The bank has tried to build up its pool of expertise so that it can advise its clients about all aspects of their financial affairs, and help them to ensure that they conduct their financial dealings in accordance with the Sharia law. A full investment advisory service is provided, and clients in particular fields of activity are often put in touch with other clients of the bank who are likely to be of use to them. In this way the bank performs a kind of merchant banking activity. [17]

Clients can also obtain assistance with foreign exchange dealings from the overseas department, and an Arab Islamic Insurance Company has been set up under the Dubai Islamic Bank's auspices. Believers are forbidden from taking part in forward foreign exchange transactions, and must trade in spot markets, as it is believed that taking forward cover amounts to a kind of speculative activity that is out of keeping with the intent of Sharia law. Obtaining insurance cover with conventional insurance companies is also discouraged, as these companies hold substantial portfolios of interest bearing securities, and in any case it is thought inappropriate for believers to seek protection through organisations involving Infidels against what Allah decrees for the future.[18] The Arab Islamic Insurance Company is organised as a type of mutual society, in which premium income is invested in accordance with Sharia principles, but in which cash assets are held in strictly limited amounts. Participants agree to help other members out by increasing their subscriptions if there are a large number of clients putting in claims at the same time, but they are reimbursed by the company eventually, as those receiving assistance are expected to repay at least some of the compensation they obtain, unlike the practice with conventional insurance companies. This last proviso is justified, on the grounds that it keeps down premium levels, but it also serves to give all participants a sense of solidarity with the others involved as the Prophet might wish. The identification and the commitment are with the other members rather than an impersonal corporate entity, and the emphasis is on mutual sharing.

As Table 4.1 shows, the Dubai Islamic Bank has become the largest in the world of its type, with paid-up capital valued at over $13 million. Over $26 million was deposited in the first year of operations alone, and by 1980 deposits exceeded $100 million. The lack of profitable investment opportunities in the Emirates has encouraged it to expand its overseas interests, and in 1978 it obtained permission to open a branch in Cairo, mainly with the intention of deploying some of its funds within Egypt's economy. It has also taken a small stake in the Bahrain Islamic Bank, and hopes to do the same in Qatar and other Gulf states where Islamic banks are also being planned. As the Dubai Islamic Bank has built up a substantial specialist staff at its headquarters, the intention is that it will be able to provide some of the services on behalf of the smaller Islamic banks elsewhere in the Gulf which they themselves have not the capacity to undertake.

The Kuwait Finance House, founded in 1977, functions in much the same fashion as the Dubai Islamic Bank, and differs mainly in its 49 per cent government ownership share held by the Ministry of Aqwaf and Islamic Affairs and the Ministries of Justice and Finance. Unlike the Dubai Islamic Bank, it has a minimum deposit amount, set at one thousand Kuwaiti dinar ($3600), in order to curtail the administrative expenses which are high in relation to the size of smaller accounts. This minimum limit on account size does not seem to have hindered its expansion, as within one year of opening its deposits were worth $96 million, and by 1980 their value was worth $332 million. The number of account holders grew to over 23,000 over the same period, which gave an average deposit value of $14,560, over four times the legal minimum.[19] Most of these deposits were in savings and investment accounts. No overdrafts are available on current accounts as according to the Sharia borrowers should agree to the extent of their debt contractually as already indicated, and not merely run up debts accidentally, as those that squander funds on instant pleasures tend to do. The emphasis is on financial planning to increase certainty, and reckless spending behaviour is discouraged because of the burdens it ultimately imposes on others. In an Islamic society believers are expected to conduct their financial affairs in a socially responsible way. There is little doubt however that some of the Kuwait Finance House's customers are maintaining current account facilities with other banks and running up overdrafts with them.

Profits are distributed to depositors at the Kuwait Finance House in accordance with the type of account, determined by a fixed formula based on utilisation rates, which allow for the amount of funds that have to be held in liquid form to meet withdrawals. A 100 per cent utilisation rate for shareholders' capital is assumed, while for investment deposits which are subject to a year's withdrawal notice a ratio of 90 per cent is assumed. For fixed-term deposits subject to a six-month notification period 80 per cent is assumed, and for savings deposits where only short-term notice of a month or less is required, 60 per cent is assumed. In 1979 investment account holders got a return of 9.18 per cent, fixed-term deposit holders 8.18 per cent, and short-run savings deposit holders 6.18 per cent. Shareholders received a dividend of 20 per cent, having forgone any payments in the previous year.[20] Such returns on Kuwaiti dinar deposits compare favourably with those from other conventional Kuwaiti financial institutions, and the demand for the bank's facilities has been such that its network in Kuwait extended to five branches by 1980.

As with the Dubai Islamic Bank, much of the investment funding of the Kuwait Finance House has been in large-scale projects, and one of its larger undertakings is providing $89 million for a low-cost housing scheme which will benefit many low- and middle-income Kuwaiti families as well as expatriate labour. Its short-term credit has often been for trade finance, and it has introduced some innovatory practices to conform with Sharia law. When the bank for example provides credit for imports, it opens the letter of credit itself in favour of the overseas supplier. Once the goods are received in the usual manner by the importer they are in fact the property of the bank. The bank however sells back the goods to the importer at a slight profit, and in this way interest is avoided, and the claims are on real goods, without the importer needing to have recourse to financial instruments for their own sake. This practice of profit-taking with respect to letters of credit is referred to as *murabahah*. [21]

Two largely Saudi-inspired Islamic banks were founded in 1977, the Faisal Islamic Bank of Sudan and the Faisal Islamic Bank of Egypt, in both cases Prince Mohammad bin Faisal playing a leading role in their formation. Private Saudi citizens, including the Prince himself, provided 40 per cent of the capital for the Sudanese venture and 49 per cent of capital for the Egyptian bank. The intention is for the banks to concentrate on direct investment activities and participate in project financing, especially small-scale industries and handicraft activities. The Faisal Islamic Bank of the Sudan started operations in an extremely promising way, and by the end of its second year had two additional branches as well as its head office in Khartoum. The Faisal Bank in Egypt is not seeking to expand as rapidly as a domestic, deposit-taking institution, as there is already the Nasser Social Bank in the country which functions on Islamic lines. Unlike the other Islamic banks, however, it aims to attract foreign deposits, especially from Muslims from outside Egypt, but including Egyptian expatriates working in the Gulf and Saudi Arabia. Deposits were coming in at the rate of $2 million a month during its first year of operation, so its future seems assured.

Saudi interests, including Prince Mohammad, also subscribed 35 per cent of the capital of the Bahrain Islamic Bank opened in 1979, which is run by former Arab Bank employees in Manama, the island's capital. The bank participates in Bahrain's international financial markets, but does not of course undertake forward foreign exchange transactions. It is however keen to collaborate with other Islamic banks in investment projects, and sees its function as receiving deposits in Bahrain, but recycling at least a portion of them to other Muslim states, perhaps in association with the Kuwait Finance House and the Dubai Islamic Bank, both of which have small stakes in the bank's equity as already indicated in the case of the Dubai Islamic Bank. Unlike the Bahrain Islamic Bank, the Jordan Islamic Bank is entirely domestically owned, and intends to invest mainly within Jordan. It nevertheless collaborates with the other institutions which are members of the International Association of Islamic Banks, and seeks advice from the association concerning the application of Koranic principles to modern finance, although, like the other Islamic banks, it has its own committee of religious advisers as well.

Prince Mohammad bin Faisal is chairman of the International Association of Islamic Banks, and Professor Ahmed El Nagar of the Nasser Social Bank is the organisation's secretary general.[22] The association maintains an office in Jeddah where the chairman is generally present and an office in Heliopolis, Cairo, which the secretary-general uses as his base, although both travel extensively. The aim of the association is to encourage the formation of more Islamic banks, and to arrange meetings for its members, as well as generally trying to co-ordinate their activities. One of the association's major tasks has been to organise the research, writing and religious approval of what is intended to be a definitive account of Islamic economics. Seventy people are working on this task, and the work is being published in Arabic in several volumes. The first volume appeared in 1981, three years after the task began, but it is expected to take more than a decade to complete the work.[23] The association's only disappointment so far is that the Iran Islamic Bank has not joined, but there have been major organisational problems with getting the Tehran bank started, and its objective of merely seeking to break even financially, rather than be profit making, like the other Islamic banks, has not encouraged investors.[24]

FINANCIAL IMPLICATIONS OF INTEREST RESTRAINT

Despite Saudi Arabia being the centre for Islamic civilisation, and the nation where Islamic principles are most rigorously enforced, there is surprisingly no Islamic commercial bank within the kingdom. The Jeddah-based Islamic Development Bank, whose activities are reviewed in the concluding section of this chapter, is a development assistance agency, not a deposit-taking institution to serve local customers. Sudan's Faisal Islamic Bank has a small office in Jeddah which accepts deposits from Saudi citizens, but they are immediately recycled to Khartoum where its activities are centred, and it has no authorisation to lend or carry out other financial activity within the kingdom. Yet many Muslims regard Saudi handling of commercial banking activity as exemplary, as interest rate charges have been constrained considerably within the kingdom, and there is little of the speculative activity that is found in the Gulf, at least as far as financial instruments are concerned. At the same time Saudi Arabia has done much to further Islamic practices in the banking field, one instance of which has been the encouragement given to the provision of separate banking facilities for women.

Modern banking first came to Saudi Arabia in 1925 when the National Handelsbank (eventually absorbed into Algemene Bank Nederland) set up an office in Jeddah to serve Muslim pilgrims from the Dutch East Indies (later Indonesia). [25] However, it largely provided moneychanging facilities, and did not take deposits or grant loans, so the question of interest did not arise. Other European financial institutions were forbidden access to the new kingdom by King Saud himself who mistrusted western commercial banks, so traditional moneylenders and moneychangers served the needs of the local community as Chapter 1 explains. Only Jeddah's small community of foreign residents deplored the absence of conventional commercial banks, but they largely relied on the trading concern Gellatly Hankey. Although the latter was mainly involved in shipping, and was not a registered bank, it gradually extended its financial activities beyond import cover to provide wider services for Jeddah's resident expatriates, but it was careful to avoid any activity involving interest payments to, or receipts from, local citizens.

Even banks from other Arab states were not encouraged into Saudi Arabia, as Egypt's Bank Misr sought permission to open a branch in Jeddah in 1936 but was refused. The following year, however, after much lobbying within the royal family, the Bin-Mahfouz family, in association with two other moneychanging families from Jeddah, the Abdel-Aziz Kakis and Musa Kakis, was finally given permission to establish a bank. After further delays while the details of its operations were worked out, the resultant institution, the National Commercial Bank, first started conducting business in 1938. Later, after the kingdom's oil boom, it was to become the second largest bank in the Middle East or Arab world as a whole, but initially its expansion in the largely feudal and backward Saudi economy of the 1940s was extremely modest. It catered largely for the financial needs of Jeddah's merchant community, providing deposit-taking facilities, and limited foreign exchange services, although the moneychangers of the souks continued to dominate in this field. Most depositors kept their funds in current accounts on which no interest was payable, and there was no attempt to introduce savings schemes. Overdraft facilities were available, but the amounts had to be agreed in advance and to this extent the bank complied with the Sharia. A charge was levied for overdrafts, which was fixed at a percentage rate like interest, but which was sometimes referred to as a fee. Whether this conformed to the Sharia is debatable, but as the amount levied was modest in view of how cheaply the bank obtained its funds, and as most borrowers were relatively wealthy in any case, few worried about these charges for credit.

The National Commercial Bank had a complete monopoly of banking in the kingdom until the 1950s, but its expansion was slow, although its lack of vigour probably suited the Saudi social climate of the time. However, by arguing that the principle of allowing banking had already been conceded, the British Bank of the Middle East was allowed to open offices in Jeddah and Al Khobar in 1950, and other foreign banks soon followed including the French Banque de l'Indochine et de Suez. Nevertheless like the National Handelsbank they largely catered for the needs of expatriates, although in the case of the British and French banks it was the new foreign oil workers and not pilgrims who were to become the clients. Surprisingly it was only in 1957 that a second local bank was founded to challenge the National Commercial Bank's dominance of the domestic market, and the institution established, the Riyadh Bank, had great teething problems. It nearly went bankrupt in 1964,[26] justifying some of the worst fears of Islamic critics of banking, and was only saved when the Saudi Arabian Monetary Agency intervened, reformed the management, and took a 38 per cent stake in the bank's equity.

It would be erroneous however to regard the Saudi Arabian Monetary Agency as a great defender of Islam, although it does try to curb interest rates, or their proxy, service charges, from rising too high within the kingdom. The agency's original problem was that its own resources were severely limited, and it had difficulty in even rescuing the Riyadh Bank at its time of crisis. In recent years its resources have naturally increased with the enormous growth of Saudi Arabia's foreign exchange reserves, but of course, in so far as these are converted into riyals to support local banks, this can have inflationary consequences for the domestic money supply. Therefore there remain financial constraints on its ability to act as a lender of the last resort, while in addition the Islamic fundamentalists have objected to the agency's power being extended too far in any case, and to its being turned into a fully-fledged central bank. Even names matter in Saudi Arabia, and it is felt inappropriate that the state acting as the guardian of Islam's holiest places should have a governmental institution calling itself a central bank.

The reluctance to permit banking activity in Saudi Arabia has resulted in several unfortunate consequences for the financial and monetary development of the kingdom, although many may regard these as a price worth paying for the preservation of what they see as Islamic values. In particular the banking structure is a virtual duopoly, with deposit data for 1979 revealing that the National Commercial Bank alone accounts for 60 per cent of deposits in the kingdom, while the Riyadh Bank accounts for a further 20 per cent. Clearly the Saudi banking market is far from being competitive, and the monopoly power of the "big two" has resulted in them having a fairly quiet time, and being far from dynamic. The range of banking services offered is extremely restricted, with customers with an account at one branch being unable to withdraw money from another branch of the same bank, except by special arrangement. Chequing remains in its infancy, and most everyday transactions in Saudi Arabia, including payment of salaries, are carried out on a strictly cash basis with the inefficiencies that implies. There are no cash or credit cards; if the latter work on an interest charging principle this would obviously conflict with the Sharia law. All account records are manually operated, and there has been no computerisation, while cash dispensers are non-existent. There is no reason why such innovations should be precluded in an Islamic community, and their absence merely reflects the constraints that have been put on competitive forces.

As the foreign banks were not allowed to expand their branch networks, the "big two" accounted for virtually all banking outlets until 1975, and even in 1980 they still accounted for over 70 per cent of all bank branches in the kingdom. Complaints about high bank charges and poor service forced the authorities to take some action in the mid-1970s, however, as it was thought undesirable that the world's leading petroleum exporter, and the only Third World state with a permanent seat on the International Monetary Fund's board of governors, should have such a backward domestic banking system. At the same time both fundamentalist Muslim and nationalistic elements were criticising the authorities for permitting foreign banks to operate at all on Saudi Arabian soil. Therefore the authorities decided to try to satisfy all critics by Saudi-ising the foreign banks, but at the same time permitting them to expand their branch networks to create a more competitive banking environment. The Saudi-isation was carried out by offering 60 per cent of the shareholdings of the domestic operations of the foreign banks, such as Algemene Bank Nederland, the British Bank of the Middle East etc., to local private citizens, and

letting the parent company retain the remainder.[27] Middle Eastern
banks which served the lower grades of expatriate labour in Saudi
Arabia, such as the Banque du Cairo and the Arab Bank, were also
Saudi-ised. Since this change there are signs of increasing competition,
and the Saudi American Bank (formerly Citibank) in particular has
been vigorously promoting new banking schemes, such as a small
business lending programme, and an account record card system
whereby a client can make a withdrawal at any branch on production
of his record card, a major advance by Saudi standards.[28]

The restraint on interest in Saudi Arabia, or even proxies for
interest such as percentage service charges, has serious implications
for the control of the domestic money supply. Rather than deposit
funds domestically in accounts which earn no interest, and at most a 2
to 3 per cent commission, many Saudis, especially the richer members
of the society, transfer their funds abroad where internationally
competitive rates can be earned. Most keep some funds with the
National Commercial or Riyadh Banks but, after a certain point, the
opportunity cost of maintaining such deposits becomes too great and,
in the absence of exchange controls, the temptation to export capital
to Bahrain, London or New York becomes irresistible. Those involved
can clear their consciences by pointing out that they have some funds
deposited in accordance with Islamic principles, and their surplus
deposits are mainly with non-Muslim institutions in any case, which
scarcely harms believers. At the same time it is argued that the
domestic banks have not the capacity to handle the deposits
themselves, which was certainly true in the past given the inefficiency
of the "big two" and their slowness in identifying lending
opportunities. Meanwhile the foreign banks operating locally were not
allowed to increase their capital bases, and hence could not expand
deposit facilities or their volume of lending.

There would have been no problem of course if there had been a
lack of domestic demand for credit, but this was far from being the
case as, with only small charges levied on borrowed funds, there was
great incentive to ask for loans. The National Commercial Bank and
the Riyadh Bank rationed credit as best they could amongst their
depositors, with the social status of the client, rather than the purpose
for which the loan was to be utilised, determining who got credit and
the amount provided. Without interest there could be no pricing
mechanism to control the market. Some even borrowed so that they
could re-deposit funds abroad, thus making a large profit, but the
banks were reluctant to enquire too closely into their clients' affairs

given the emphasis which is placed on personal privacy in Saudi Arabia. At the same time the need for investment funds and credit generally within the domestic economy was rising rapidly. The enormous increase in imports in the mid-to-late 1970s created a large demand for trade credit, while simultaneously the ambitious development plans generated a large demand for credit from the private sector. Even the loans from the Saudi Industrial Development Fund required that borrowers should finance half their capital needs from commercial sources, and the government was keen for the Fund to deploy funds as rapidly as possible, subject only to the projects being viable. This has, of course, increased the demand for commercial bank credit.

With the general rise in international interest rates in the late 1970s, and a greater awareness amongst Saudi citizens, especially the widely travelled more affluent sections of the society, the export of funds increased rapidly. The differential between returns on deposits within the kingdom and those in nearby Bahrain exceeded 10 per cent. However, just as a supply shortage was starting to become apparent, the demand for funds was also increasing owing to rising income factors, and as a consequence interest rates on freely available riyal borrowing rose as high as 18 per cent during the 1978–80 period. Favoured clients of the "big two" domestic banks could still obtain some cheap credit at 2 to 3 per cent, but many borrowers had to resort to the expensive offshore riyal market in Bahrain, or the foreign or newly Saudi-ised banks which were only able to supply funds at a high price, comparable to international levels. The whole financial system seemed to near collapse, with the Islamic constraints ironically resulting in usury becoming worse.

By 1980 it is estimated that almost half the money supply had left the country, with the Saudi Arabian Monetary Agency uncertain of the best method to ease the domestic liquidity shortage.[29] Foreign exchange controls were ruled out, partly because it was doubtful if they could have been effectively enforced given the large role played by unregulated moneychangers in exchange dealings. In addition, as a member of the governing board of the International Monetary Fund, a body which is against such controls, it would have been embarrassing for the state with the world's largest surplus to curtail capital movements. As some of the exported funds were deposited in Bahrain in riyals in any case, exchange controls would have been irrelevant to at least this type of offshore placement. The Riyadh authorities therefore tried three alternative methods, the first of which was to stop denominating large contracts in riyals, which would mean major western contractors would no longer take foreign exchange cover in Saudi currency through Bahrain. This would reduce the offshore demand for riyals, and would, it was hoped, mean there was less incentive for Bahrain banks to seek riyal deposits. As a substantial part of the riyal borrowing in Bahrain is by Saudi citizens themselves rather than foreigners, this move had only marginal impact.

The second measure, a riyal revaluation, was tried in March 1980. Those who had converted riyals into dollars, largely because of higher interest rates, but also owing to the dollar strength at that time, made a slight capital loss rather than a gain. Interest rate differentials were so marked however that such moves were a relatively minor irritant. The third measure adopted was for the Saudi Arabian Monetary Agency to reduce the liquid assets ratios for the domestic banks, to enable more funds to be made available for lending. The ratio on demand deposit was reduced from 15 per cent to 12 per cent in 1979, and even further to 7 per cent the following year, while that on the minute amount of time and savings deposits was reduced to a mere 2 per cent. This provided some temporary relief from the liquidity shortage, but the problem with such measures is that they are of a once-and-for-all nature. Too great a reduction would threaten sound banking practice, and the monetary stability seen as essential in an Islamic society. The basic problem has yet to be resolved, and the only long-term solution would be to introduce new domestic savings instruments which were in harmony with the Sharia laws. As the foreign banks are unlikely to move in this direction despite their Saudi-isation, the onus must lie with the National Commercial and Riyadh Banks, or any future local Islamic banks founded within the kingdom.

INTRODUCTION OF WOMEN'S BANKING

The main pioneering effort by the domestic banks in Saudi Arabia to conform with Sharia principles has been through the introduction of women's banking. Apart from the United States, Saudi Arabia is the first country to open banks run exclusively by women for women.[30] This is not, of course, because of any pressure from women's movements in the United States or anywhere else, but rather because of the sexual segregation of finance which Muslim law provides. A woman's inheritance under the Sharia remains her own, and is not shared, or transferred to her husband's management on marriage. In an Islamic society there is no provision for joint bank accounts, and what a woman inherits, she keeps in her own account. Conservative Saudi women do not want to go into male dominated banks personally, yet at the same time, because of the emphasis on privacy in financial affairs, many do not even want their husbands to conduct their business on their behalf. Hence the demand for women's banks.

Many Saudi women have substantial fortunes because of the workings of the inheritance system, and some of these funds have been untapped in the past by the banks because of the reluctance of women to participate in what was seen as a male sphere of activity. Although males inherit twice as much as females, the division of a parent's wealth on death does at least mean that all children get a share, and there is no male primogeniture, as there was in most of feudal Europe in the middle ages.[31] In addition, women inherit at an early age, as, when a parent dies, most of the wealth passes directly to the children, including the daughters, as a wife only inherits one quarter of her husband's estates if he dies first, and a husband only half of his wife's estate if she dies first.

As more Saudi women enter the workforce, there is no doubt their financial significance will increase, and the growing number of Saudi women company directors already indicates their importance. Although both sexes do not usually work alongside each other in Saudi Arabia, office equipment innovations are aiding the sexual segregation of workers, and presenting more opportunities for women to work in completely female environments, which the dominant Wahhabi sect of Islam believes is desirable for the kingdom. There is little doubt that banks which can harness the increasingly significant earnings of Saudi women as a result of these changes will profit handsomely. In 1979 the National Commercial Bank, the Saudi Cairo Bank and Bank Al-Jazira (formerly the National Bank of Pakistan) all opened women's branches, and in 1980 Saudi American and Saudi-British (formerly British Bank of the Middle East) followed suit. The initial experience indicates that finding staff presents few problems, as although most in the first instance are expatriate women, mainly Palestinians and Pakistanis, it seems many Saudi girls are keen to learn the necessary skills to serve in such branches, and are enthusiastic that a new career channel has been opened up for them.

THE ISLAMIC DEVELOPMENT BANK

Saudi Arabia's main contribution to Islamic banking has been to provide the largest equity share in the Islamic Development Bank and to act as host nation for this new Muslim institution.[32] This Jeddah-based organisation, founded in 1975, is essentially a development assistance agency and plays little part in the Saudi Arabian domestic economy apart from providing some employment. Few of its staff are Saudi citizens, however, as most are specialists in various financial fields drawn from the 38 participating states of the Islamic conference which finances the bank. The purpose of the bank is to promote economic advance and social progress in its member states, but its assistance is given in accordance with the principles of the Sharia. Unlike agencies such as the Kuwait Fund for Arab Economic Development which provide credit on which interest is payable, the Islamic Development Bank is required to provide interest-free loans and participate in the equity capital of the ventures it supports.

Not all of the broad objectives of the Islamic Development Bank's charter have yet been realised, as one is to provide a fund for assistance to Islamic communities in non-member countries, including presumably the Soviet republics of central Asia where Muslims are in a majority, as well as Albania, which according to the bank has a Muslim majority. Another, as yet unrealised, aim is to accept deposits from governments, companies and even individuals, who will be able to share in the profits from the projects supported by the bank. Only member states' paid-in capital has so far been deployed by the bank, and no attempt has been made to raise outside funding from any source, although plans are being drawn up for this. The institution is also charged with responsibility for assisting in the promotion of foreign trade, amongst member countries, especially in capital goods. It provides technical assistance, and extends training facilities for personnel engaged in development activities and undertakes research for enabling economic, financial and banking activities in Muslim countries to conform to the Sharia.

All these activities remain in their infancy, as trade amongst Muslim states is minimal, and most of the countries trade mainly with the western world, exporting their primary products and importing manufactured goods. Less than 5 per cent of the average trade of subscribers in the Islamic Development Bank is with other Muslim states, and most of this is in oil and related commodities.[33] Only Jordan, Lebanon and Somalia have over half their exports destined for other Islamic states according to the bank's statistics, while, apart from Bahrain which imports 47 per cent of its goods from the Islamic World (mostly re-exports), all other states import less than 20 per cent.[34] The Islamic Development Bank is nevertheless trying to increase the volume of inter-Muslim trade by giving balance of payments support to the poorer Muslim countries in order to increase their import capacity. Assistance is tied to specific categories of imports from other Muslim states, and is provided free of interest but subject to a small mark-up of 2 per cent. This charge is justified not only to cover existing administrative overheads, but also because it is the bank's intention to raise funds in the future in international financial markets in order to augment its resources. It is planned to eventually finance all balance of payments support in this way, as this will free capital resources which can be used instead for project assistance. The bank's role will be to act as a financial guarantor, while at the same time providing a degree of subsidy, so that the country receiving support will obtain more favourable terms than would be the case if it borrowed directly in international financial markets itself.

Over the 1977–80 period, during the first three years of the foreign trade financing scheme's operation, almost 60 per cent of total Islamic Development Bank funds were tied up in the scheme. Assistance was generally for short- to medium-term periods, three to five years being the usual time. Most of the assistance was to meet the cost of crude oil imports and refined petroleum products, with Turkey the largest single beneficiary thanks to a $30 million dollar loan agreed to finance crude oil imports from Iraq. The refined petroleum products supplied have come from Kuwait, Algeria and Libya. Several loans have been organised for the importation of urea fertilisers with the beneficiaries including Pakistan and Mali, and supplies coming from Kuwait, Saudi Arabia and, in one exceptional case, Europe. In some instances loans have been arranged to finance trade amongst the poorer Islamic countries which might otherwise not have been possible, such as the export of jute finished goods worth $16.5 million from Bangladesh to the Sudan in 1979, or the export of cotton yarn worth $5.3 million from Pakistan to Somalia the same year.[35]

Originally when the Islamic Development Bank instigated its foreign trade financing, the intention was that the bank would organise the trade itself, including the necessary transportation arrangements, and eventually it would even acquire its own shipping fleet. Owing to a shortage of personnel with the relevant experience, however, the bank's role has been largely that of a financier,[36] but in the long run its aim is to act as a trader, handling the goods itself. There is also an intention to link trade with development by promoting trade in capital goods although, as few Islamic countries supply capital goods, there may be a conflict between this aim and that of promoting inter-Muslim trade. Shortage of personnel has also hampered the bank's project appraisal role when granting project finance, but it has tried to overcome this deficiency by collaborating with the other Middle Eastern development assistance agencies whose activities are described in Chapter 7. The Kuwait Fund in particular has considerable experience in project appraisal.

One of the Islamic Development Bank's main contributions has been to pioneer new forms of project support distinct from those offered by the other Middle Eastern aid agencies, but conforming in full with Sharia law. A profile of the bank's assistance is given in Table 4.2, from which it is apparent that, although interest-free lending constitutes the most significant item under project financing,

TABLE 4.2   *Islamic Development Bank finance (total 1975 – 79)*

	Millions of Islamic dinar	
Trade financing	445.68	
Project financing	313.85	
of which: Loans		127.11
Equity		124.82
Leasing		54.27
Profit sharing		4.27
Technical assistance		3.38

NOTE   1 Islamic dinar = 1 Special Drawing Right = $1.3 approximately at 1979 values.

SOURCE   Islamic Development Bank, *Fourth Annual Report,* Jeddah, 1979, p. 55.

equity financing is almost as important. The Islamic Development Bank under its charter has to satisfy itself that any project in which it takes an equity stake is well managed, but it is not allowed to take a majority or controlling interest, except where it is necessary in order to protect the bank's investment.[37] In view of staffing deficiencies, and possible resentment from the host country, the bank does not want to assume responsibility for managing any project, and has not done so, although it has the power to take over itself if a scheme is seriousiy mismanaged. The bank can also sell off its investment when it is appropriate to do so, [38] and the objective in any case is not to provide permanent equity participation, but to provide start-up assistance of a transitory type, although the period of involvement may last a decade or more, given the teething problems infant industries often have in developing counties. Although the Islamic Development Bank in accordance with the Sharia law shares in both the profits and losses of the companies in which it invests, it naturally will, in taking its decision regarding when to sell shares, ensure both that the interests of the company being financed are served, and that market conditions are opportune from the point of view of share prices. In practice there is unlikely to be a conflict, as share prices will be high, and buyers plentiful, when the company has finally taken off.

It is unlikely that the Islamic Development Bank will be selling off any of its equity shares before the late 1980s as its buying only started in 1977. Its early investments were varied, including a poultry project in North Yemen, a cement plant in the United Arab Emirates, a textile company in Pakistan and an iron ore extraction project in Mauritania. Rather than build up a portfolio in too many fields where its own staff expertise is limited, however, the bank is starting to concentrate on taking equity shares in other financial organisations, which themselves back industrial projects. In a sense it is moving one step back, from a retail to a wholesale financial capacity. It invested almost £4 million in the Bahrain Islamic Bank, and it has bought shares in national development banks in Jordan, Tunisia and Turkey. Under its charter the Islamic Development Bank does not provide loans to an enterprise in whose equity it has participated except in special cases approved by not less than two-thirds of the total voting of the members. [39] By 1981 no such cases had arisen. It should be noted that equity participation is classified differently from profit sharing by the bank, which as Table 4.2 shows, has been relatively insignificant. Profit sharing is where the bank provides a loan, but instead of charging interest, as is the practice with non-Islamic banks, or levying a fixed service charge, as the bank usually does as an Islamic institution, it receives a share in the future profits of the enterprise being financed. This method of finance is thought to be appropriate where a venture is of a risky kind, and a commitment to a fixed charge would be undesirable, but where there is an excellent chance of a good profit if the plans proceed smoothly. In some ways the profit-sharing finance is similar to the purchase of preference shares which are without voting rights.

Leasing is of growing significance for the Islamic Development

Bank, and the institution is unique amongst the Middle Eastern development assistance agencies in providing this type of support. Under this method of finance, the bank purchases a particular piece of equipment on behalf of the company it is helping and the company then pays the bank rent for use of the equipment. The bank has leased rolling stock to the railway system of Morocco, purchased two ships which Somalia is renting, bought machinery which is being hired by the Turkish electrical industry under a long-term contract, and is leasing refining equipment to a Pakistani oil company.[40] Such assistance means that the Islamic Development Bank ties up its capital rather than the developing country which may want to invest in other items. As the leasing contracts are for long periods, usually seven to ten years, with the terms fixed in advance according to Sharia principles, there is complete certainty for all parties to the agreement, unlike many commercial rental contracts. This type of assistance demonstrates the extent to which Islamic institutions are being innovative in trying to apply the ideas put forward by the Prophet in a socially useful way. The application of Sharia principles to commercial law and economic development is being carried out completely in the spirit of Koranic teaching.

5 Financial Specialisation in the Gulf

During the 1970s the focal point of Arab banking moved from Lebanon to the Gulf. There were of course two obvious reasons for this move, firstly the civil war in Lebanon, and secondly the quadrupling of oil prices in 1974 which resulted in a correspondingly increased need for financial institutions in the oil surplus Gulf states. In the late 1960s, Beirut served as an important intermediary for Arab funds from the Gulf, but even then confidence was shaken by the Intra Bank collapse, details of which are given in Chapter 3. In addition long before the civil war, many bankers doubted the prospects for long-term stability in Beirut as a financial centre, in view of the continuing uncertainty resulting from Lebanon's close proximity to Israel and the presence of large numbers of Palestinian refugees, who virtually ran their own state within a state.

No single Arab state in the Gulf took over the whole of Beirut's role, however, in the sense that none performed such diverse financial functions.[1] It would be wrong to conclude from this nevertheless that none is as important as Beirut was during its heyday. Both the scale of and scope for financial activity in the Middle East increased so enormously during the 1970s that today Kuwait, Bahrain, and Dubai are all more significant than Beirut ever was, at least in terms of the absolute amount of banking business. Beirut's tragedy was that its eclipse as a financial centre coincided with the greatest period of banking opportunities in the modern history of the Middle East. The Gulf was at the centre of this financial boom, with the smaller Arab states along the Gulf developing institutions to serve not only their own needs, but also some of those of their larger, and richer, neighbours. Thus Kuwaiti institutions served Saudi Arabia and to a lesser extent Iraq, as well as Kuwaiti investors themselves. The banks of Bahrain mainly served interests outside the island altogether, and their role in the Saudi banking system was, and continues to be, highly significant. Meanwhile further down the Gulf in Dubai, the banks there serve not only businesses and private clients from the neighbouring Emirates, but also non-Arab interests from across the Gulf in Iran.

Overall it seems that the main financial centres in the Gulf are starting to specialise, as, although the funds generated in the region are vast, it makes some sense for each centre to try to carve out a special role for itself, rather than for all to attempt to provide the same services. Duplication is to some extent avoided with such a differentiation of role, yet fortunately the differentiation has not been sufficient to curb competition, which the clients of the financial institutions obviously want. The market for financial services is being increasingly compartmentalised, but each compartment cannot be viewed entirely in isolation, and if any became less competitive, spill-over would inevitably occur. Specialisation however implies the build-up of pools of expertise in particular fields in each centre, which must be beneficial from the client's point of view. In economic terms it means that sufficient business is generated to overcome the indivisibilities which exist in the financial field below a certain minimum scale of operations as in other fields of business activity. Externalities are generated in terms of a supportive financial structure, while in addition further specialisations are encouraged which enhance the reputation of the centre. Together these internal and external factors are sufficient to result in economies of scale being realised with financial specialisation even over a short time span. In the longer period, however, as the scale of operations increases, such economies are further strengthened and the environment itself becomes conducive to the emergence of further economies as part of a dynamic process. The 1980s should undoubtedly witness such favourable developments in Gulf banking and finance.

In broad terms it seems reasonable to categorise Kuwait as an investment centre, Bahrain as a money market centre, and Dubai as a merchant banking centre. The reasons for such a categorisation will be given in each of the sections of this chapter where the role of the particular centre is outlined. An investment centre is one in which private individuals and institutions such as pension funds can go for specialist advice on investments, and where a range of specialised financial institutions exist to provide such advice on short-term and, to some extent, long-term options. Such a centre will normally possess a bond market and a stock exchange, where shares are traded. Kuwait has both these prerequisites, as well as the necessary ancillary institutions. A money market centre needs a wide range of banks represented in it, with properly equipped dealer rooms where money and short-term securities can be traded, denominated in a variety of major international and regional currencies. It is essentially a wholesale market to serve banks and other financial institutions rather than private individuals or even governments. Bahrain, with over one hundred banks and financial institutions represented on the island and an officially decreed status as an offshore centre, seems well placed to play such a role. Finally a merchant banking centre is one where corporate clients can go for financial advice, and where trade credit can be easily arranged, especially for external trade including re-exports. It would probably be an exaggeration to say that Dubai already plays such a role to any significant degree as yet, but this appears to be its chosen field for specialisation. Given its background, and its buoyant trading environment, it seems uniquely placed to succeed in this role in the Gulf.

KUWAIT AS AN INVESTMENT CENTRE

By the late 1950s it was realised in Kuwait that the country was in the fortunate position of having more revenue resulting from oil exports than could usefully be invested locally, as the absorptive capacity of the small desert kingdom was strictly limited. Some industrialisation and domestic diversification was seen as desirable, but the size of the local workforce meant that this would imply reliance on imported labour, which would have worrying social and political repercussions. Therefore overseas investment was viewed as a preferable alternative — a way of securing an income for future generations of Kuwaitis once the oil revenue ran out. Even before the country's independence the groundwork was being prepared to establish appropriate institutions to channel the country's actual and potential investment funds and, in 1961 following the formal relinquishment of direct ties with Britain, the Kuwait Investment Company (SAK) was established.[2]

The government of Kuwait itself took most of the initiative in establishing this new institution, the details of its initial operation being worked out by officials at the Ministry of Finance. At the time Kuwait was in a unique situation in the Arabian Peninsula, as it had a properly organised government, and the finances of the state were kept completely separate from those of the ruling family. Therefore when the state itself offered to raise half of the initial capital for the new investment company, it had little problem in finding private partners to participate. A group of leading Kuwaiti families put up most of the rest of the remaining 50 per cent of the equity individually, while a minor share was held by smaller investors, who had to be Kuwaiti citizens according to the terms under which the company was established. The leading private shareholders included the Al-Rifais, Al-Shalfans, Al-Shayas, Al-Mousas, Al-Bahars, Al-Kharafis and Al-Sayers, all of whom retain representatives on the board of directors. [3]

The Kuwait Investment Company was authorised to sponsor domestic as well as foreign projects, and its initial activities included funding for a local refinery and pipe manufacturing plant to serve the domestic petroleum industry. It took an equity shareholding in the companies concerned, and provided the underwriting for the entire share issue. In addition it took responsibility for the selling of the remaining shares, a task it still performs for many Kuwaiti companies. It has a significant stake in such well-known companies as Gulf Fisheries, one of the world's largest shrimping companies, and the Kuwait Real Estate Investment Consortium, the largest property finance company in the Gulf, which was established in 1975. Unlike the Saudi Industrial Development Fund however, which awards interest-free loans, the Kuwait Investment Company only invests according to strict commercial principles and in no sense can be regarded as an arm of government providing subsidised funds. Kuwait in any case has a separate Industrial Bank established in 1973 with a capital of 10 million dinar, as well as a wholly government-owned Real Estate Bank, established at the same time, which provides subsidised funds for housing.

Like any other finance company, the Kuwait Investment Company has sought to diversify its portfolio holdings as much as possible in order to spread its risks. Nevertheless some degree of specialisation is necessary, as through this the company has built up a considerable amount of knowledge of particular areas. When making investment decisions it is more important to know a lot about a little than a little about a lot. Obviously the Kuwait Investment Company knows the Kuwait market itself best, but as this market is limited, its policy has been to build up close, long-term associations with other investment institutions and banks, both inside and outside the Arab world. Then when these associate institutions see an investment opportunity which they feel might interest the Kuwait Investment Company, an approach can be made. The Kuwait Investment Company's response depends of course on their own view of the scheme's prospects, but they will also take account of how valuable their associate's advice has been in the past. Associates within the Arab world include the Banque de Développement Economique de Tunisie, Banque Nationale pour le Développement Economique de Tunisie, Banque Nationale pour le Développement (Morocco), the Jordan National Bank, and Rifbank (Lebanon).[4] The longest established overseas associate is the United Bank of Kuwait in London, a 100 per cent Kuwaiti-owned institution, in which the Kuwait Investment Company has a 14.3 per cent stake, dating from 1966. Its Paris listening post is FRAB (French–Arab) Bank, in which it, together with the Kuwait Foreign Trading, Contracting and Investment Company, owns an important stake through a Luxembourg holding company.

In recent years the Kuwait Investment Company has spread its activities worldwide outside traditional Arab lending markets. Together with its sister Kuwaiti institutions, the Kuwait Foreign Trading, Contracting and Investment Company and, in some cases, the Kuwait International Investment Company, it has sought partners in countries hitherto beyond Arab interest. There is no doubt Kuwaiti institutions have played a pioneering role in extending Arab financial activity, and Kuwait has wider investment links than any other Middle Eastern centre. The Kuwait Investment Company, for example, has a 35 per cent stake in the Kuwait Pacific Finance Company of Hong Kong, in which the Industrial Bank of Japan owns a 32 per cent share. This merchant banking institution has already advanced over $50 million to companies in Hong Kong and elsewhere in South East Asia, although it was only founded in 1975. Other diverse associates of the Kuwait Investment Company include the Industrialisation Fund for Finland, the International Investment Corporation for Yugoslavia, the Arab Brazilian Investments Company and the Arab Turkish Bank.

Although there have been times when the Kuwait Investment Company, the Kuwait Foreign Trading, Contracting and Investment Company and the Kuwait International Investment Company have competed with each other, it would be a mistake to regard the so-called "Three Ks" as business rivals. Collaboration is more significant than competition, and the companies freely swap information about potential investments, which soon spreads around Kuwait's close-knit financial community. In spite of all its modernity and sophistication, in some ways the atmosphere of Kuwait's business community still resembles that of an Arab coffee shop, where rumours abound and the latest gossip determines general thinking. In such an environment deals can be concluded extremely quickly on a personal basis, and there is little doubt that direct contacts are extremely important for both insiders and outsiders. Any outsider would certainly be ill-advised to attempt to play one Kuwaiti institution off against another, as he may be unaware of the depth of the underlying relationships, and the complexities of the community which date back to its tribal history.

The Kuwait Foreign Trading, Contracting and Investment Company was founded in 1964, three years after the Kuwait Investment Company. The government subscribed 80 per cent of the capital, giving it a controlling interest unlike that in the Kuwait Investment Company, and local citizens subscribed the remaining 20 per cent. Although established as a merchant banking company to provide trade credit for the country's importers, a role the Kuwait Investment Company was not designed to perform, the Foreign Trading, Contracting and Investment Company soon diversified into direct investment activity.[5] Today, therefore, its role has become virtually indistinguishable from that of the Kuwait Investment Company, although that was not the original intention. As the organisation grew, however, it found merely providing trade credit generated insufficient business, as the banks provided this as well. Its clients, many of whom were in the process of acquiring substantial fortunes, expected it to play an advisory role regarding overseas investment, a function into which it launched itself with enthusiasm.

Clearly market forces above all else have determined the pattern in which Kuwait's financial institutions have evolved, and it is the presence of hundreds of wealthy local investors which has resulted in Kuwait's evolution into the leading investment centre in the Arab world. The petroleum riches have filtered down to a large number of local citizens through the government's land purchase programme and state contracts, and this dispersal of wealth has caused a market to arise for investment funds. Elsewhere in the Gulf the local populations are smaller in size, and the total wealth, even in Abu Dhabi, is on a much more limited scale. Meanwhile in Saudi Arabia, much of the oil wealth has remained in the hands of the government, and the handful of individuals who have benefited substantially do not constitute a market. This may of course change in the future as the size of the private sector grows in Saudi Arabia, but for the moment the Saudi middle class seems content to invest in their own housing or land, rather than outside the country entirely as is the case with the Kuwaiti middle class. American and European financial journals sell many more copies in Kuwait than in Saudi Arabia.[6] Only a few extremely wealthy Saudis invest abroad and read such publications, whereas in Kuwait most of the middle class are interested in stock market developments which affect them personally.

The so-called "Three Ks" still dominate the Kuwait investment scene, but their dominance is undoubtedly less than it was in the mid-1970s as the number of investment institutions has proliferated in recent years. The largest institution in terms of capital resources remains the Kuwait Foreign Trading, Contracting and Investment Company, with paid-up capital of around $100 million and deposits of more than double that amount. However, although the Kuwait Investment Company has a smaller paid-up capital, worth approximately $50 million, its deposits are over ten times that amount, and therefore well in excess of those of the Kuwait Foreign Trading, Contracting and Investment Company. The financial impact of the Kuwait Investment Company is certainly greater, with the size of its lending and investment activity closely related to deposits, and there can be little doubt about its paramount importance despite the greater publicity surrounding the activities of its sister institution. The Kuwait Foreign Trading, Contracting and Investment Company seems to be more concerned with image building, which is perhaps only slightly hampered by the Company's rather lengthy name.

The third of the "Ks", the Kuwait International Investment Company, is smaller than its two sisters as, although its authorised capital at $50 million corresponds to that of the Kuwait Investment Company, its paid-up capital is believed to be considerably less. Its total assets and liabilities only amount to one quarter of those of the Kuwait Investment Company. Nevertheless, as the newest of the three institutions, only founded in 1973, this is not surprising. One of the main strengths of the Kuwait International Investment Company appears to be the outward looking stance that it has taken since its inception, and the closeness of its connections with Swiss finance. It is the main Arab participant in the Arab International Finance Company of Zug, near Zurich, and it has an interest in a Geneva registered investment company, Overseas Princeton Placements.

As well as the three major investment companies in Kuwait, there are over thirty smaller concerns which describe themselves as investment companies, more than in any other single centre in the Middle East. About two-thirds of these are family businesses or partnerships which were originally trading concerns, but which have subsequently established themselves as investment companies, or established offshoots run by some member of the family or families. Typical of these are concerns located in the commercial centre of Kuwait such as the Abdel-Aziz and Ali Yousef Al-Muzaini Company, Abdel-Rahman Mohamed Al-Bahar and Sons, the Al-Hadi United Company, Hamoud Zaid Al-Khalid Company and the Khalifa Investment and Trading Company.[7] Others, such as the Al-Ahlia Industrial and Trading Investment Company and Zaid Al-Kazemi and Sons Trading Company, are located in Safat where rents are higher, but proximity to the stock exchange and the financial centre where bonds are traded is seen as an advantage.

Another group of investment companies are under a more diversified public ownership, although they are not necessarily larger in size than the family concerns and partnerships. These include firms such as the Arab Company for Trading Securities, the Arab Finance Corporation of Kuwait, the Arab Trust Company, the Financial Group of Kuwait, the Kuwait Development Company, the Joint Investment Company, the National Investment Company, the United Gulf Company and many others. In addition there is a group of companies in which there is direct foreign involvement such as the Arab European Financial Management Company, the International Financial Advisor and the Kuwait International Finance Company, in which the Bank of Credit and Commerce of Luxembourg owns a majority stake. Other companies, although entirely, or almost wholly, Kuwaiti-owned, have a specific investment focus. These include Arab Investments for Asia, the Afro-Arab Company for Investment and Foreign Trade and the Joint Investment Company (which specialises in Pakistan). Such a diversity of investment companies illustrates Kuwait's growing sophistication as an investment centre.

The emergence of Kuwait as an investment centre has been encouraged by the government, which has done much to create favourable business conditions. In particular since the late 1960s the government of Kuwait has bought from the local investment companies securities denominated in dinars as well as dollars and European currencies.[8] Initially most of these purchases were from the Kuwait Investment Company, which sold securities worth 130 million dinar ($ 455 million) to the government over the 1968–73 period, but the National, Commercial and Gulf Banks were also involved. Then in June 1974, the Kuwait International Investment Company launched the first publicly quoted issue, which marked the start of a long series of issues in dinar and Euro-currencies which were to be managed by the investment companies. Usually one of the "Three Ks" would act as lead manager for dinar bond issues, either singly, or jointly with some foreign investment broker or bank. The other smaller Kuwaiti investment companies would then be invited to take up the issue, together with any Arab or foreign companies or banks which were interested.

For the Kuwaiti investor, the creation of such a market was an extremely welcome development, as it was gratifying to see large international borrowers coming to Kuwait for funds, and being prepared to take up loans denominated in local dinar. This eliminated the exchange risk for the Kuwaiti investor, many of whom had vivid memories of the exchange losses they faced with sterling investments in the 1960s, and dollar investments in the early 1970s, as these currencies fell in value. At the same time the rates offered were low enough to attract a wide range of international borrowers, often 2 or 3 per cent below Euro-market rates in London for dollar issues. By 1979 several triple-A borrowers entered the market, giving it added prestige. Mitsubishi Heavy Industries, the Japanese multinational for example, borrowed ten million dinar in July of that year over a five year period at 7 per cent, with the lead management carried out by the Kuwait Investment Company and Morgan Stanley.[9] The month previously Banque Nationale de Paris had sought a similar loan, also managed by the Kuwait Investment Company, with the bonds running for ten years at 7 per cent. By 1979 major new issues were being offered denominated in dinar at a rate of around eighteen to twenty a year, an impressive rate for such a small country as Kuwait. Significantly not only Kuwaiti investors were taking up the issues, but also those from other Gulf states and Saudi Arabia.

Bonds of course provide an extremely safe form of long-term investment, especially if the bond is held to maturity, as there is no risk of a capital loss, at least in monetary terms. Usually rates are fixed for the whole term period, with the price varying inversely in relation to current interest rate movement with respect to the fixed rate. As most bonds carry government guarantees from the country of the borrower, repayment failure on maturity is extremely unlikely. The only exception prior to 1980 not requiring a government guarantee was Occidental International Finance, a major United States company, which obtained a 7 million dinar loan for 12 years at 8 per cent. Growth of the Kuwait bond market has been extremely rapid in the late 1970s as, although there were only 31 million dinar worth of bonds issued in 1977, in 1978 the figure reached 122 million dinar for international borrowers alone, and 32 million dinar for local borrowers.[10] In 1979, however, after bonds worth 106 million dinars had been issued, the government was forced to declare a temporary moratorium on further new issues in order to protect the market as, with interest rates very high elsewhere, money was leaving Kuwait, and there was a fear of prices collapsing if bonds were left unsold.[11] Clearly too rapid an expansion can be disastrous if confidence becomes undermined.

Initially, as already indicated, the Kuwait government was the main purchaser of the bonds issued by the Kuwaiti investment companies on behalf of western clients as, without this state initiative, the bond market would not have developed. By the mid-1970s however a growing number of local institutions were investing in bonds, including pension funds, the banks, insurance companies and state sector organisations, following the government's lead, which gave them confidence in the market. In addition even private individuals participated, and this participation grew once a secondary market developed. Finally by the late 1970s, the buyers in the market included not only Kuwaitis, but also purchasers from elsewhere in the Gulf and Saudi Arabia. As Kuwait was the only regional centre with a developed market, it seemed natural to channel some of their bond purchasing activity through it, especially if they wanted bonds denominated in a currency whose parity only varied slightly against their own, such as the Kuwaiti dinar. However, it was these foreign purchases which proved to be first to be curtailed in 1979 when interest rates elsewhere became more attractive, and this speculative element is undoubtedly a worry to the Kuwaiti authorities.

In the long term nevertheless prospects look encouraging for the Kuwait bond market, especially with the development and diversification of the secondary market which enables bond holders to sell at any time, and others to purchase existing bonds and not merely new issues. The specialist company formed in 1977 to run the secondary market, the Arab Company for Trading Securities, dominates most of the business, especially that in dinar-denominated securities.[12] In 1980 it extended its own capital base from one million to three million dinar by bringing in three domestic commercial banks as additional shareholders, the Al-Ahli, Burgan and Commercial Banks. This move makes it more securely placed to handle most buying and selling operations. To some extent it felt it had to act quickly, as other companies have also started to handle some secondary market trading in bond issues which they led or co-managed. Merrill Lynch started such activity in Kuwait in November

1978, and each of the "Three Ks" are planning similar moves. Wisely the Kuwait government refused to give the Arab Company for Trading Securities an exclusive monopoly, and more competition in the market must be a welcome development for those involved. This is particularly the case as the bond market develops from being just a wholesale market serving banks and other financial institutions with considerable power and resources, to being a retail market catering also for private individuals who, even if wealthy, cannot easily compete with institutions.

Of course the bond market in Kuwait, like bond markets elsewhere, will inevitably remain largely in the hands of institutional investors, even if more wealthy individuals participate on a personal basis, or on behalf of their businesses. Individuals tend to be more attracted to stock markets than bond markets, and Kuwaitis appear to conform to this universal preference. Shares can be purchased normally in much smaller quantities than bonds, and the long-term capital gains can be much greater, although of course there is no interest rate return. From modest beginnings in the early 1970s when the Ministry of Commerce and Industry assisted the formation of a small stock market on which a few local stocks were floated, Kuwait has now emerged as the leading stock exchange centre for the entire Middle East. This is perhaps not surprising however in view of the large number of wealthy middle-class families and the high level of financial awareness already mentioned. Even before the Kuwait market was formed, in the 1960s many Kuwaitis invested in the London market and gained much valuable experience.[13]

By 1980 Kuwait's stock market had become the eighth largest in the world in turnover terms with some 18,000 people owning shares.[14] The total market capitalisation of companies traded on the stock exchange was 4.5 billion dinar. This extremely high daily turnover in relation to the size of the companies quoted reflects the buoyancy of trading activity, and the keen interest in buying and selling. Over forty companies are listed in the market, but not as yet the "Three Ks", nor many of Kuwait's smaller, family-run investment companies. This is expected to change, however, as the "Three Ks" increase their capitalisation, and as the family investment companies seek to expand beyond the capacity of family resources. As the width of the market has increased, it has become more stable, and the sudden flurries of speculative activity that caused price chaos in early days no longer occur. The government in any case set up a securities commission to supervise dealings, and in any panic the government itself has shown a willingness to intervene to iron out sudden fluctuations, without affecting the basic trends.[15]

The securities commission is composed of only eight members which makes it a tightly knit and highly effective body. Three members are drawn from the Ministry of Commerce, including the chairman, while there is one member each representing the investment companies, the central bank, the brokers, the chamber of commerce, the commercial banks and the general public. The commission is therefore a representative body, and no group involved with the exchange is excluded. Stockbrokers are accredited by the commission, and by 1980 there were fourteen brokers, all of whom were Kuwaiti companies or individuals. Foremost amongst the broking companies were Abdel-Rahim Ahmad Akhbar and Company, Fahd Al-Aqari and Company and Euro-Kuwaiti Securities, all of which were organised as partnerships. Investors normally deal through their brokers, some of whom can also handle deals in overseas stockmarkets, including London, through associate companies. An increasing proportion of the broker's business is with non-Kuwaitis, however, especially Saudis, but also Iraqis and citizens of the Emirates, Qatar and Bahrain. This foreign business obviously produces favourable spin-offs for Kuwait, especially as it is their nationals who are acquiring the financial skills, and have the promise of lucrative careers as investment analysts, as well as in other similar prestigious fields.

BAHRAIN AS A MONEY MARKET CENTRE

The promise of favourable economic spin-offs was undoubtedly the major factor which prompted the government of Bahrain to encourage the island's development as a banking and service centre. Unlike its oil-rich neighbours, Bahrain's reserves of oil are extremely limited and petroleum production was already starting to decline by the early 1970s. The need for diversification was therefore viewed as imperative, especially as Bahrainis were perhaps more conscious of the dangers of over-dependence on a single source of revenue after their disastrous experience with pearling in the 1930s.[16] Industrialisation was seen as one means of diversification, but the costs of creating a heavy industrial base are high, and Bahrain can really only be competitive internationally in energy-related fields such as aluminium smelting, which increasingly the major petroleum producers want to invest in themselves. Service activities such as ship repairing were also encouraged through the building of a massive dry dock, and this generated some useful local employment. However, it is in the financial service field that Bahrain's greatest potential lies, a field that has the merit of requiring relatively little capital expenditure on the part of government, whose main role is to create an appropriate legislative background.

Bahrain undoubtedly offers some advantages as a banking centre compared to other locations in the Gulf, not least of which is the aptitude and skills of its labour force.[17] Unlike Kuwait and Abu Dhabi where many school-leavers are keen to find state sector employment, either as civil servants, or in some government institution, in Bahrain there seems to be a marked preference for private sector business. Of course the government in Bahrain is not in a position to offer employment to all secondary school-leavers and those with college certificates, as is the case elsewhere in the Gulf, but it is noticeable that even the best-qualified local citizens, who probably could find government employment, prefer private services instead. At the same time there is a tradition of clerical activity in some local families, dating back to the time of the British presence in the 1960s, when to some extent the United Kingdom used Bahrain as the unofficial administrative capital for the Gulf. Even the British military facilities employed many Bahrainis in a civilian capacity.

Traditionally banking has been highly regarded as a career in Bahrain, and although the National Bank of Bahrain only dates back to 1957, United Kingdom banks such as the British Bank of the Middle East have been represented on the island since 1944. In fact the British Bank of the Middle East increasingly regarded its Bahrain office as its regional headquarters, especially as the Kuwait offices were run under a 30-year lease which expired in 1971. Its Kuwaiti operations were then nationalised, and a new bank formed, the Bank of Kuwait and the Middle East, but no similar action was taken or threatened in Bahrain against it, or Grindlays, the other main British bank on the island.

In general there is little doubt that the absence of nationalistic pressures has aided Bahrain's emergence as a leading banking centre, as foreign banks which were unable to establish themselves in Saudi Arabia or Kuwait found Bahrain the most conveniently placed alternative. Only Citibank, amongst the American majors, succeeded in gaining a foothold in Saudi Arabia for example. Even this was short-lived as now its operations there have been Saudi-ised, and a new bank formed, the Saudi American Bank, in which the New York parent only holds a minority stake. Only in Bahrain can major foreign banks operate branches which they fully own and control themselves. Citibank therefore runs much of its Gulf business from Bahrain rather than from Riyadh,[18] while Chase Manhattan, unable to establish itself in Kuwait or Saudi Arabia, has its regional office for the Gulf in Manama, Bahrain's capital. Other western banks with Gulf, or even Middle Eastern, operations centred in Bahrain include the Bank of New South Wales, the Bank of Tokyo, Bayerische Vereinsbank of Munich, the Canadian Imperial Bank of Commerce, Crédit Suisse, the Dresdner Bank, First National of Dallas, the National Bank of Greece, Société Générale and the Swiss Bank Corporation.

The list of Bahrain banks reads almost like a roll-call of the world's most famous institutions. By 1980 there were 21 different full commercial banks located in Bahrain, 35 representative offices, and 51 offshore banking units operating as well as a further six licensed to start.[19] In terms of the range of institutions with an interest on the island, Bahrain now rivals such other international banking centres as Singapore, Hong Kong, Luxembourg and Nassau, and its banking community is almost as diverse as that of Tokyo, London or New York, despite the obvious difference in the economic and financial environment compared to that found in a major western capital. There is little doubt that Bahrain has built up a significant lead over other Gulf states that might want to bid to become banking and financial centres, particularly those in the Emirates, where some view themselves as potential rivals. The national diversity of the Bahrain banking community makes it possible to obtain financial information locally on virtually any area of the world, as it can be guaranteed that someone will be on hand with the necessary knowledge and contacts. In addition the sheer number of banks increases the potential scope for inter-bank activity, and the range of interests which such activity can encompass.

Far from being antagonistic towards the foreign banks, the three locally owned Bahraini banks appear to welcome their presence because of the status it gives the island. Both the main domestic banks, the National Bank of Bahrain and the Bank of Bahrain and Kuwait, are under majority private ownership, with Bahraini citizens owning 51 per cent of the former and 50 per cent of the latter. A 49 per cent shareholding in the National Bank of Bahrain is held by the government, but the other 50 per cent in the Bank of Bahrain and Kuwait is held by Kuwaiti interests, including the "Three Ks" which collectively own almost 10 per cent of the total equity. Thus even the second-largest domestic bank is part foreign-owned, which makes it more outward-looking. The newest, and much smaller, exclusively Bahraini-owned institution, the Al-Ahli Commercial Bank, is partly run by Bank of America personnel under a management services contract. Hence it is far from being a nationalistic institution.

One of Bahrain's prime functions of course is as a money market centre, and in this regard the island has several distinct advantages. [20] Bahrain's time zone means it can be open for currency dealings after Singapore, the nearest money market to the east, closes, but before the European money markets open. Since most major currencies were floated in the early 1970s, there has been a much greater interest in exchange rates, and it is thought to be useful to have markets for some currencies such as the dollar, sterling and the yen open twenty-four hours a day. Bahrain helps in this effort, by completing a circle of money centres that runs from London to New York, San Francisco, Tokyo, Singapore and finally via Bahrain back to Europe. In addition the Bahrain market remains open on Saturdays and Sundays, unlike centres in Europe or the United States, as its weekend is Thursday afternoon and Friday. Thus dealers in Europe can see how the Bahrain market reacts to any important international developments over the Christian weekend before the markets in Frankfurt or London open. [21]

Bahrain is also fortunate in being in the same time zone as Saudi Arabia, as much of its financial business originates there. Dubai and Abu Dhabi, its main potential rivals, are one hour ahead of Riyadh's time, which is a distinct disadvantage. For foreign exchange operations this time zone factor is extremely important, especially given the volume of riyal exchange business, and this factor has undoubtedly been significant in attracting several well-established international money brokers to Bahrain. These specialist firms include Charles Fulton, Kirkland Whittaker, Marshalls, R. P. Martin and Tullett and Riley, all of which are active in the London foreign exchange market. The best-known firm that handles most of its Middle Eastern exchange business from Bahrain is Sarabex, a part-locally owned firm which maintains offices in Frankfurt and Zurich as well as London. Sarabex specialises in the exchange of Arab currencies for central European currencies, especially the mark, schilling and Swiss franc, but it also handles some sterling and dollar business through London. Bahrain is a much better base for foreign exchange business than Beirut ever was, even in its heyday, as there is a complete absence of exchange control, not only on the island, but also in all the adjacent oil-exporting states of the Gulf. Hence transactions can be conducted with speed and efficiency, free from official control.

As money market centre for the Gulf, Bahrain serves as regional headquarters for the two major international traveller's cheque companies, American Express and Thomas Cook. In addition many of the foreign banks issuing traveller's cheques, such as Britain's National Westminster and Barclays Bank, handle much of their Gulf business through Bahrain. The efficiency of the local postal and telecommunications system is an aid to this business, but another factor favouring the location of such operations on the island is the high level of demand for such facilities locally. Bahrain has the largest international airport in the Gulf, and handles large numbers of transit passengers many of whom want traveller's chequing facilities. American Express also runs its Middle East regional office for its credit card operations from the island, and as credit card business spreads in the Gulf, activity in this area is expected to grow. At present most credit card transactions are conducted through hotels, airlines and luxury goods stores in the Gulf, with visiting businessmen from North America and Europe accounting for most of the transactions. However, American Express is making a determined effort to market its cards from Kuwait to the Emirates, and Bahrain is sure to benefit from this in terms of both income and employment, even if on a fairly modest scale initially. [22]

The greatest boost to Bahrain becoming a banking centre came in 1975 when the government announced it was to pass legislation allowing offshore banking units to be established on the island. [23] These units, which were to be free from any reserve requirements or capital ratio requirements, were allowed only to take part in wholesale banking and money market operations, and were not to practise retail banking through taking domestic deposits from the general public. The legislation founding the offshore banking units was modelled on similar legislation elsewhere, particularly that which had proved successful in Singapore and the Cayman Islands. [24] Offshore operations established in Bahrain are exempt from all corporate and profits taxes as is the case in Singapore with the Asian Currency Units, but the banks have to put down an initial deposit to receive offshore banking unit status, and pay an annual licence fee. Initially the latter only amounted to $25,000 per annum, which is hardly a deterrent for a major international bank, and was levied only to cover the cost of the Bahrain Monetary Authority's bank inspection unit, which looks at the accounts of the offshore units, and monitors developments in the market. The fee now however generates modest profits for Bahrain, as it has subsequently been raised, and the number of offshore units paying the fee has dramatically increased.

Fee revenue only represents a small part of the benefit which Bahrain's emergence as a banking centre has brought to the island. It has been estimated that each of the offshore banking units brings over $2 million in revenue annually to the island, bringing the 1980 total to over $120 million, a considerable amount for such a small economy.[25] This sum represents the spending of the bank employees, as well as investment in buildings and other fixed assets by the banks. The local multiplier effect of this spending is undoubtedly positive, despite the high marginal propensity to import of such an open economy. By 1980 over 150 Bahraini citizens were employed in the offshore banking units alone, while over a thousand local citizens are engaged in the banking system as a whole, mostly in the foreign-owned banks. It seems likely that employment opportunities for local citizens in banking will expand rapidly in the 1980s, and overall the value of the specialist skills now being acquired by local citizens should not be under-rated. Bahrain will probably be chosen as the site for the proposed training centre for Middle Eastern bankers, which is already needed despite the high-quality training offered to Arab nationals from Citibank's Athens centre, which trains employees from other banks as well as its own staff.

Bahrain remains a relatively expensive location for banks to operate from, for with suitable buildings scarce in the mid 1970s, rents were extremely high, and the expatriate bankers demanded high levels of remuneration for working in the Gulf. Costs are already falling to some extent, however, as Bahrainis can be recruited for all but the most senior levels, and they do not demand displacement allowances. In addition the construction boom has left plenty of office accommodation available, and hotel occupancy has also fallen with the enormous increase in capacity. Against the initial high cost of operating, there must be set the benefit of having no reserve requirements, which means the offshore banking units can lend all their funds profitably apart from a small contingency amount, and there is no need to have funds tied up unprofitably with the monetary authority. Finally, as already indicated, many foreign banks are in Bahrain because they could not get into Saudi Arabia or Kuwait. As their main competitors are also in Bahrain now, they have to ask themselves if they can afford not to be there and give potential business to these competitors. There is undoubtedly a negative as well as a positive attraction factor which Bahrain can capitalise on.[26]

One of Bahrain's major roles in recent years has been as a centre for forward transactions. There are forward markets on the island for all Gulf currencies, and firms undertaking work on projects where contracts are evaluated in regional currencies often seek to cover their foreign exchange risks. A firm for example which knows it has to make a payment on a performance bond for a contract in Saudi Arabia in three months' time, may decide to purchase riyals forward in Bahrain in case the spot rate rises too far, resulting in significant exchange costs. Such forward transactions grew rapidly over the late 1970s, with outstanding amounts increasing from US$0.5 billion at the end of 1976, to $2.3 billion in 1977 and $3.7 billion in December 1978. The United States dollar had a 40 per cent share of total forward purchases, regional currencies 44 per cent, and other currencies 16 per cent. Corresponding shares in forward sales were 56 per cent, 27 per cent and 17 per cent respectively.[27] This indicates that the market is a major purchaser of Gulf currencies on a forward basis against United States dollars, thus meeting a commercial need previously unsatisfied.

There has been some concern in recent years in Saudi Arabia about the growth of the offshore riyal market in Bahrain, which is beyond the direct control of the Saudi Arabian Monetary Agency. The free transfer of funds to and from Bahrain makes control of the domestic money supply difficult, and removes from the Riyadh authorities one means of tackling inflation. In addition developments in the Bahrain money market influence the exchange rate for the riyal, and these can conflict with policy decisions in Riyadh. To curb the growth of the forward market in riyals therefore in late 1979 the Saudi government announced it would stop denominating major state contracts in riyals and use dollars instead, a move designed to bring stability.[28] Kuwait quickly followed suit, as it was also concerned about the rapid growth of the forward dinar market in Bahrain, and the potential for currency speculation that it might bring. Despite such moves, however, the other states in the Gulf are sympathetic to Bahrain's plan to become a leading financial centre, as they recognise its need to diversify is greatest. Saudi Arabia's attitude is basically protective, as it wants the island to remain economically and politically stable, and to stay under its patronage as at present.

In practice the Bahrain Monetary Authority and the Saudi Arabian Monetary Authority collaborate closely, and a careful watch is kept on the maturity structure of the offshore banking units market by both bodies. As Table 5.1 shows there is some tendency for the

TABLE 5.1 *Maturity classification of Bahrain's offshore banks' assets and liabilities ($US million)*

	Up to 7 days	8 days to 3 months	3 months to 1 year	Over 1 year
Assets				
1976	1,059	2,462	1,609	1,120
1977	2,259	7,718	3,676	2,048
1978	2,793	12,444	5,382	2,822
1979	3,953	14,005	5,829	3,977
Liabilities				
1976	1,714	3,618	830	52
1977	3,344	9,730	2,477	150
1978	5,078	13,503	4,471	371
1979	6,212	15,485	5,444	623

SOURCE Bahrain Monetary Agency, *Quarterly Statistical Bulletin,* Vol. 5, No. 4, 1979, Tables 14–16, pp. 16–18.

offshore banks to borrow on a shorter-term basis than their lending, but the maturity structure itself has not changed much over the 1976–79 period. In comparison to the practice in other offshore centres, especially those in the Cayman Islands and Nassau, the maturity structure reveals just how cautious the banks themselves

TABLE 5.2 *Currency classification of Bahrain's offshore banks' assets and liabilities ($US million)*

	$US	Regional currencies	Marks	Swiss francs	Other
Assets					
1976	4,387	1,196	183	318	130
1977	11,594	3,242	319	389	157
1978	16,031	6,075	501	389	445
1979	18,216	7,440	524	637	947
Liabilities					
1976	4,471	1,168	175	258	142
1977	11,269	3,567	252	330	283
1978	15,459	6,720	383	295	584
1979	17,538	8,113	609	546	958

SOURCE Bahrain Monetary Agency, *Quarterly Statistical Bulletin,* Vol. 5, No. 4, 1979, Table 15, p. 17.

appear to be. Furthermore as Table 5.2 shows, most of the currency activity in the Bahrain market is in dollars, and although regional currencies dealings are increasing in relative importance, much of the market is likely to remain in the currency in which oil imports are usually paid for.

Although most of the assets and liabilities are in dollars, most deposits of course originate in Arab countries, which account for over 50 per cent of the total liabilities, the main non-Arab source being Western Europe, as it was responsible for deposits worth over $8000 million by 1980. This high level of deposits from outside the Gulf region indicates the growing confidence in Bahrain as a financial centre. Much of the funds in Bahrain are re-lent back to Western Europe through inter-bank markets, and a growing proportion is deployed in the Far East, especially in Hong Kong, Singapore and Tokyo. Specialised institutions such as the Arab Malaysian Development Bank and Bank Bumiputra Malaysia handle some of this business with the Far East through their Bahrain offices, but a major proportion is still carried out by the large western multinational banks.[29] Surprisingly, however, the major proportion of assets represent lending to Arab clients which belies the view that Bahrain is merely a centre for recycling oil revenues to the outside world. It seems Bahrain is an important centre for short-term finance for the Arab world as a whole, and the Gulf area in particular, a role which other states seem content to see Bahrain fulfilling.

There is little doubt that the 1980s will witness a continuing increase in the number of banks operating in the Bahrain money market, and establishing offshore units on the island. The Bahrain Monetary Authority has become stricter in recent years however about the banks to which it grants licences, and it has sought to avoid attracting fringe operators.[30] Only major western institutions are now welcome on the island, as there is a feeling that there are now sufficient western banks, and for a few months in 1980 there was a ban on new licences being issued to banks. There is a desire for some consolidation of activities, and a feeling that if too many institutions are attracted, the competitors will drive margins down so far that a possible crisis of confidence could arise. So far no offshore banker has left the island, but the departure of any institution could change expectations about the market.

The emphasis is now on attracting banks from areas of the world which are thinly represented in Bahrain, so as to diversify still further the geographic spread of institutions. Japanese banks are still under-represented in the island,[31] for example, although the Bank of Tokyo, Sumitomo Bank and the Nippon Credit Bank maintain representative offices. Recently Latin American banks have been attracted to Bahrain for the first time, and in 1979 the Banco de Brasil opened an offshore unit, while a new joint venture institution, the Arab Latin American Bank, plans to have Bahrain as its headquarters. The greatest financial coup for Bahrain was to be chosen as the headquarters for the massively funded Arab Banking Corporation, which was established in 1980 with an authorised capital of $1 billion of which $375 was paid up immediately. This inter-governmental joint venture, owned by Kuwait, the United Arab Emirates and Libya, plans to have 150 staff in Bahrain by early 1982, and assets worth over $2 billion.[32] Developments on this scale, with official foreign government support, illustrate the confidence which exists in Bahrain's future as a financial centre.

Bahrain of course needs the support of its Gulf neighbours if it is to continue to flourish, and there has been visible evidence in recent years that this support is increasing.[33] Both Saudi Arabia's main domestic commercial banks are represented in the island, the Riyadh Bank owning a 60 per cent holding in a joint venture in which Crédit Lyonnais owns 40 per cent, the Gulf Riyadh Bank. This was the first joint venture of its kind by one of Saudi Arabia's two major banks. The activity by the Gulf Riyadh Bank in Bahrain encouraged the National Commercial Bank, the largest bank in Saudi Arabia, to set up its own offshore banking operation there also. This was established in 1979, and there is little doubt the presence of this key Middle Eastern bank gave powerful support to the Bahrain offshore banking market. Other Gulf banks with offshore operations on the island now include the National Bank of Abu Dhabi and the Union Bank of Kuwait. A strong regional financial presence on the island undoubtedly strengthens Bahrain's position.

DUBAI AS A MERCHANT BANKING CENTRE

From an analytical point of view it seems both desirable and useful to categorise different types of financial centre, but there is inevitably some degree of overlap in practice. Thus Bahrain banks undertake some syndication business with respect to medium- and long-term bond issues, and institutions such as the Gulf International Bank and the Gulf Riyadh Bank to some extent compete with the Kuwaiti investment institutions. Nevertheless there is no official secondary market in bonds and securities in Bahrain, unlike in Kuwait, and much of the buying and selling takes place in the latter, even for institutions based on the island. The same applies in the case of Dubai and Abu Dhabi, and there is probably more overlap with regard to activities in these Emirates compared with Kuwait than there is between Bahrain and Kuwait. The distinction between merchant banking and investment finance is not easy to specify precisely, not least because most merchant banks would claim that a significant part of their business concerns investments. The concept of merchant banking comes from British financial parlance, and merchant banks do not exist as such in the United States or continental Europe. Nevertheless, as far as Dubai is concerned, the British term is probably the most apt description for the role which some of the financial institutions there actually play, or aspire to perform.

Merchant banks essentially aim to cater for business rather than personal customers, but yet provide services of a highly personalised nature. They not only take deposits and grant credits like other banks, but also give advice concerning business dealings and investments, provide introductions for clients which can help them in future dealings, and generally supply their customers with a wealth of information which may not otherwise be available. As Dubai in the past has served as a kind of listening post in the Gulf, and as an important point of contact with the world beyond, it would seem well qualified to perform as a merchant banking centre. Dhows from its creek sailed through the Indian Ocean from the shores of East Africa to the Indian sub-continent and beyond, long before European penetration in the area. In addition, historically Dubai has been an important centre for entrepôt trade, with its merchants re-exporting goods from the creek to the cities of southern Iran across the Gulf, and overland to the interior of Muscat and Oman.[34] As the finance of entrepôt trade was a prime function of the London merchant banks from the eighteenth century onwards, it would seem the British merchant banking concept has a special applicability in Dubai.

The merchants of Dubai have always to some extent been involved in trade credit, not only as recipients but also essentially providing for their own needs long before the advent of modern banking. Much of the financing for stocks held was generated within individual merchant families, but there was also a considerable amount of lending and borrowing amongst the main traders in Dubai's souk. The merchants have long been conversant with the complexities of foreign trade, as Dubai's creek was the market place not only for those from within the Emirate, but also those from neighbouring Emirates, the nomads of the hinterland, and seafaring traders from the Indian Ocean. Transactions involved considerable barter and consequent stock holding which had to be financed in some way, while in addition the merchants exchanged Maria Teresa thalers, for centuries the major medium of exchange of the Arabian interior, for gold from the East, and Iranian rials. So successful were the Dubai merchants in handling trade finance, there was little incentive to establish local banks to serve the local community. The two major banks represented in Dubai before 1960, the British Bank of the Middle East and Grindlays, essentially served the foreign community, especially the British residents, and to a lesser extent Asian immigrants who wanted to remit their earnings.

Nevertheless as the British banks expanded their activity and gained some local customers, the local merchant community in Dubai decided the time had come to found their own banks. The first of these, the National Bank of Dubai, was established in 1963, with foreign staff recruited from Grindlays Bank and the National Bank of Kuwait, which held a small minority stake. It was felt that experienced personnel were needed if the new institution was to be a success. This was the first experience with indigenous banking in the Emirates, and the private backers were keen that the venture should be profitable. Interestingly the bank was established five years before the National Bank of Abu Dhabi, indicating Dubai's earlier interest in modern commercial banking, and the finance was entirely private, unlike its Abu Dhabi equivalent, which was under majority state ownership. As in other fields of commercial activity, the merchants of Dubai seem to have been the first to take the initiative in the lower Gulf, as continues to be the case.

The main business of the National Bank of Dubai is ordinary branch banking, and merchant banking is only one aspect of its activity. Much of its lending, however, is to finance the trading establishments of the local merchants, and imports and re-exports generally, traditional activities for a merchant bank. Its lending to finance construction projects has been more modest than is the case with its rivals in Dubai, and much less than that of the Abu Dhabi-based banks.[35] The ending of the construction boom in the lower Gulf in the late 1970s did not cause the institution much alarm therefore, and it feels much more securely based than some of the banks in the other Emirates. The same concentration on trade finance is also expressed by the three other indigenously owned banks in Dubai, the Commercial Bank, the Dubai Bank Limited and the Bank of Oman, all of which are solidly based operations which have been running for over a decade.

Dubai's most distinct contribution in recent years in the financial field has been to attract a range of well-known foreign merchant banks, which no other centre in the Gulf has managed. These include Wardley Middle East Limited, the merchant banking subsidiary of the British Bank of the Middle East, which controls much of its regional operations from Dubai, and the County Bank, the merchant banking subsidiary of the National Westminster Group of London, which also uses Dubai as its headquarters for the Middle East. In addition Oryx Merchant Bank, a largely locally owned institution, but with its base in the Cayman Islands for tax reasons, does most of its Middle Eastern business from Dubai. It is associated closely with Arbuthnot Latham and Company, the old established London merchant bank, which owns a small share in the holding company. Leading Emirate citizens amongst the shareholders include Faraj bin Hamoudah.

Although American financial institutions rarely describe themselves as merchant banks, two whose activities clearly fall into this field are now well established in Dubai. The first is the New York firm, Merrill Lynch and Company, who describe themselves as stockbrokers and investment bankers. They established an office in Dubai in 1972, while in 1978 another New York investment services company, E. F. Hutton, moved into the Emirate. In addition, Citicorp, a project finance division of Citibank, but registered as a separate company, runs its main Arab business from Dubai. Apart from the reputation of Dubai as a free enterprise centre in the Gulf, and the high esteem in which Sheikh Rashid and the local merchant class are held abroad, there is little doubt that the congenial atmosphere in Dubai has attracted many expatriate banks and bankers. Dubai is not only a good business centre, but perhaps the most attractive location in the Gulf in which to reside.

Abu Dhabi, as the richest of the Emirates in terms of its oil resources, is of some significance as a financial centre, but it seems less clear about the role it should be playing than Dubai. It seems most likely to emerge as an investment centre, given its surplus revenues, and it has its own investment company, whose role corresponds to that of the "Three Ks" further up the Gulf, and which is in majority state-ownership through a 60 per cent holding by the Abu Dhabi Investment Authority. Although this investment company describes itself as a merchant bank,[36] its main client for advice is the Abu Dhabi government itself, and there is little outside private business.[37] For this reason, Abu Dhabi cannot really be regarded as a regional centre. It tries to recycle much of its own surplus earnings, but does not handle much external business, or even private investment from within the Emirate itself which often goes via Dubai or Bahrain. Activity in Abu Dhabi is to a much greater extent state directed than in the more private, business-orientated Emirate of Dubai, even though they are part of the same political and economic federation, and this inevitably affects the location of banking and finance. It would be an exaggeration to compare the Abu Dhabi–Dubai relationship in the same terms as the Saudi–Bahrain relationship, but some of the same differences and their consequences are manifest.

The resources of merchant banks are generally much smaller than those of major investment companies, so their role in lending and in providing equity finance is inevitably limited. For the client their value lies in the advice they can give about financing rather than the financing itself. This advice covers bond issues, syndications, acceptance credits and currency swaps. Acceptances are particularly important in the Dubai context, given its role as a trading centre. Much commerce relies on trade bills drawn against imports, which must be paid for before sale, or against exports or re-exports, shipped before payment is received. For many such self-liquidating transactions the trade bill is "accepted" by a merchant bank, which regards it as a short-term and highly liquid asset. In London trade bills which are accepted can be sold in the specialist discount market, but in Dubai there is no such market as yet. Nevertheless some bills accepted in Dubai can be sold privately, or even sold abroad in the London market, although most are held by the merchant banks as liquid assets against which loans can be made. There is little doubt however that the next few years will see the emergence of a fully fledged discount market in Dubai for acceptances.[38] Such a development would contribute more to creek's development as a financial centre than gimmicks such as restricted bank licences, which merely seek to duplicate Bahrain's offshore licences. Only five restricted bank licences were taken up in all the Emirates after their introduction in 1977, and by 1980 the scheme had fallen into disrepute. The creation of a discount market would attract a different type of financial institution however, at present not catered for in the Gulf region, or even in the Middle East as a whole. Dubai seems best advised to complement Bahrain and Kuwait as financial centres, not to compete with them directly. By creating a secondary market for acceptances it would be not only securing its unique position as a merchant banking centre, but also widening the range of financial activity to the benefit of the Gulf as a whole.

6   The Role of Commercial Banks in Recycling

In 1974 in the aftermath of the quadrupling of oil prices it became evident that the major oil exporters of the Arabian peninsula would emerge with substantial balance of payment surpluses. A surplus in one country of course implies a deficit in another, in this case the major Western oil importers, and to a lesser extent in absolute terms the oil importers of the developing world, including those in the Middle East itself. The problem for the international financial system was quite simply how to recycle the petro-currency earnings from those states in surplus to those in deficit. Despite the grandiose schemes proposed for collaboration between the OPEC surplus states and the OECD oil-importing countries in tackling the problem, in the end nothing was agreed, and most recycling has taken place on an *ad hoc* basis without any international supervision.[1]

Even the less ambitious scheme for dealing with the problem through the International Monetary Fund, of which all the countries concerned were members, was of limited significance in the end. Although the IMF introduced a special oil facility to complement the other lines of credit already available, the amount drawn on this account amounted to only $8 billion at the end of 1979, compared to the accumulated net surpluses of the OPEC countries which amounted to $200 billion.[2] Interestingly there has been little discussion about extending the oil facility beyond the limits agreed in 1974 and 1975, yet the oil price rises of l978–80 have further aggravated the payments imbalances in the international financial system.

DOMINANCE BY WESTERN MULTINATIONALS

Most of the recycling in practice has been carried out through the commercial banking system, with a few large American banks accounting for the major portion of the business. Of these banks, Citibank and Chase Manhattan of New York, and San Francisco's Bank of America would appear to dominate, with other lesser, if still important, institutions such as the First National Bank of Dallas following some distance behind. Their significance is perhaps surprising, as before 1970 none of these institutions had much Middle Eastern involvement, and even now their representation in the Middle East is usually confined to one office in Bahrain or to a lesser extent the Emirates.[3] Citibank alone was represented in Saudi Arabia, the largest surplus state. In the three other major surplus states, Kuwait, the UAE and Iran, which together with Saudi Arabia accounted for 88 per cent of the aggregate current account surplus over the 1974 to 1978 period, the banks now have at most a branch in Dubai, the Tehran branches being closed since the Iranian revolution and the suspension of American links with the new regime.

To their annoyance the role of the traditional European banks with a regional interest in the surplus states, such as the British Bank of the Middle East, appears to be less significant as far as recycling is concerned than that of the American majors, although it is greater than that of the United States secondary institutions such as the First National Bank of Dallas. It seems that a strong geographical presence is no longer a prerequisite for attracting business, indeed unless an institution has a successful record of local operations, it may even be a disadvantage. Nevertheless there is little doubt that the major United States banks, constrained by expanding their role as deposit-taking institutions outside their home state by Federal legislation,[4] were keen to seize the opportunity which the oil surpluses presented. Their wooing of depositors was much more aggressive than that of the more conservative-minded European banks, and the experience they built up through Euro-market dealings in the late 1960s and early 1970s gave them an edge over the regionally focused banks which were slow to become involved.

At the same time the sheer size of the major United States banks as institutions gave them financial muscle which the regionally specialised banks lacked, although the position of the British Bank of the Middle East had strengthened substantially in 1959 when it was taken over by the much larger Hongkong and Shanghai Banking Corporation. This placed the British Bank on a much stronger footing than its main French rival, the Banque de l'Indochine et de Suez, whose Far Eastern interests have steadily contracted since the ending of French involvement in the area, rather than expanded as

British interests in Hong Kong have done. In general the European overseas banks were in a rather dispirited state at the start of the 1970s, however, as many of their foreign branches had been nationalised, not only in the Middle East, but also in many parts of Africa, especially in the case of Grindlays.[5] The prevailing mood in the boardroom tended to favour consolidation or retrenchment rather than a desire to seek out new opportunities in what was seen as an unsettled and increasingly unpredictable world.

Given this malaise on the part of the traditional European overseas banks, by the early 1970s the leading British and French domestic banks were considering going into the Middle East themselves, rather than acting through their sister institutions. Thus in the case of the United Kingdom, Lloyds, the Midland and National Westminster all sought to establish a limited regional presence on their own account, even though these three main domestic clearing banks, unlike Barclays, had only slight overseas experience. Similarly the main French domestic clearers, Crédit Lyonnais, Banque Nationale de Paris and Société Générale also established a limited Middle Eastern presence, Cairo and Bahrain being the favoured locations by the late 1970s rather than Beirut. These European domestic clearers had little advantage over the main United States banks, however, as far as Middle Eastern knowledge was concerned, despite the long history of specialised British and French involvement in the Middle East. Admittedly there was some recruitment of experienced staff from the British Bank of the Middle East, Grindlays and Banque de l'Indochine et de Suez, but the American majors were in at least as good a position to recruit such staff as were the British and French banks. Indeed, in so far as there is more flexibility in American banks over employee remuneration, they may if anything have had the edge on recruitment.[6]

There is little doubt that currency considerations encouraged potential Middle East depositors to move towards American banks in the late 1960s, and to some extent away from British banks which dealt primarily in sterling. The devaluation of sterling in the mid-1960s, and the subsequent lack of confidence in the United Kingdom's ability to maintain its currency's value, were partly responsible for limiting the role of the British overseas banks. Of course the banks could have offered greater facilities for depositors in other currencies, including the dollar, as they have done subsequently. Until 1970 however their experience of Euro-markets was limited, and the main British domestic clearers had probably built up more expertise in this area because of the sheer scale of their operations. The French Banque de l'Indochine et de Suez for its part had even less experience, as Paris was not an international financial centre on the scale of London, and the franc was less significant than sterling as a reserve currency in any case, although arguably this should have encouraged more dealings in other currencies. [7]

The losses suffered by Kuwaiti investors on sterling deposits in the 1960s were undoubtedly a significant factor in prompting interest in Euro-dollar and other Euro-currency deposits in London amongst those from the oil-surplus states. As Kuwait has been a surplus state for a much longer period than other Arab oil producers, to some extent neighbouring states were guided by its experience. The impact of any Kuwaiti losses was therefore greater than the mere Kuwait currency withdrawals themselves as within the small Arab financial community of the late 1960s rumours spread quickly and a transfer of funds by investors from one state would quickly prompt others to follow. To some extent this remains the case in the Gulf, despite the much greater complexity of Arab finance as a result of developments in the 1970s.

Currency switching is only marginally important in explaining the enormous growth of dollar deposits by Middle Eastern oil producers. Indeed the major factor is simply the lack of alternatives which can play the role of the dollar in the face of the enormous surpluses which have arisen as a result of the oil price rises of 1974 and 1979–80. The oil exporters have little choice but to accept most payments in dollars, and the possibilities of switching the massive revenues involved to other currencies is severely limited by their availability. In recent years as Japan has moved into trade deficit, and the supply of deutschmarks has been augumented with record West German imports, alternatives have become available to the traditional reserve currencies, the dollar and sterling, but the overall dependence on the dollar still remains. [8]

The distribution of OPEC's identified financial surpluses is presented in Table 6.1. This of course tells us more about the geographical and currency dispersal of the surpluses than about the institutions they are channelled through, although information on the former does give some clue to the latter. From the table it appears that the United States itself accounted for between one fifth and one quarter of all recycled funds over the 1974–79 period, most of which was made up of short-term bank deposits. The largest proportion of these funds went through the New York banking system, with San Francisco, Chicago and Dallas playing more minor, if nevertheless

TABLE 6.1   *Distribution of OPEC's identified financial surpluses (1974 – June 1979, $ billion)*

	1974	1975	1976	1977	1978	Total 1974 –June 1979
United States	11.5	8.0	11.0	7.4	0.8	39.9
of which						
Dollar bank deposits	10.8	6.3	8.1	7.0	0.0	31.6
Direct investment	0.7	1.7	2.9	0.4	0.8	6.3
United Kingdom	7.2	0.2	−1.1	0.7	0.2	8.2
of which						
Sterling bank deposits	1.7	0.2	−1.4	0.3	0.2	1.3
Direct investment	5.5	0.0	0.3	0.4	0.0	6.9
Euro-markets	22.8	9.1	12.1	10.9	3.0	62.3
of which						
Euro-bank deposits in London	13.8	4.1	5.6	3.4	−2.0	28.2
Euro-bank deposits elsewhere	9.0	5.0	6.5	7.5	5.0	34.1
Investment and other direct funding outside US and UK	11.0	12.4	12.2	12.4	8.6	63.0
International organisations (IMF etc.)	3.5	4.0	2.0	0.3	0.1	9.6
Total	56.0	33.7	36.2	31.7	12.7	181.0

SOURCE Compiled by Sharif Ghalib, Vice President, Chase Manhattan Bank, New York, for *Euromoney,* London, April 1980, p. 121. Data from US treasury bulletins, Bank of England bulletins and BIS reports.

significant roles. Naturally it was American banks themselves which handled the bulk of these United States placements, the foreign banks represented in New York playing a relatively small role in dollar dealings until recently.

In the United Kingdom, unlike in the United States, most of the domestic currency business with OPEC funds has involved longer-term direct investments rather than bank deposits at call at short notice. The accumulated total of sterling business over the 1974–79 period was of course much smaller, and if 1974 is excluded the total amounts to only £1 billion of placements. There is little doubt the weakness of sterling in the mid-1970s prompted many Middle Eastern investors to look elsewhere, and although the relatively high interest rates in London may have made bank deposits slightly more attractive, they undoubtedly lowered the profitability of equity shares. Sterling's new-found strength as a petro-currency in the late 1970s has nevertheless resulted in renewed interest in United Kingdom domestic placements by Middle Eastern investors, and the situation seems to have reverted to that of 1974 *vis-à-vis* dollar holdings. It should be noted that the table refers to OPEC surpluses and not merely those of Middle Eastern producers. The latter as a group undoubtedly have a higher propensity than OPEC generally to channel funds through London, partly due to geographical proximity, but also because of custom.[9] Of the non-Middle Eastern major OPEC producers, Venezuela mainly uses New York, although Nigeria has traditionally made extensive use of London owing to its post-colonial links.

Most of the Middle Eastern funds deployed through the London banking system are not deposited in sterling, but in other Euro-currencies. Euro-dollars were the main unit of account in the past, but increasingly other currencies such as Euro-marks, Euro-yens and even Euro-riyals are playing a more significant role. Overall it appears from the table that over one-third of total OPEC surpluses are channelled through Euro-bank markets, with the London banks accounting for 40 to 45 per cent of the business. In London, as in other Euro-market centres, there is some tendency for national banks to handle deposits in their particular currency, with for example American banks handling Euro-dollar deposits, Japanese banks Euro-yen etc. This market characteristic is much less pronounced than in the 1960s as the financial community has become more internationalised generally, but it should not be ignored. There is little doubt that United States banks are still in the best position regarding knowledge of lending opportunities in dollars, and banks generally find it safer to match the currency in which their assets and liabilities are held.

Many of the North American banks use their London office as their base for Middle Eastern operations, and the specialised management team travel out to the region from England rather than residing in the Gulf or elsewhere. This practice is not surprising for banks handling significant Arab business, but without a representative office in the region, such as Wells Fargo of San Francisco or Kuhn Loeb Lehman Brothers of New York. Even those with offshore banking units in Bahrain or representative offices elsewhere in the Middle East still usually prefer to have London as their regional headquarters. This is the case for example with Bank of America, the Bank of Nova Scotia,

Chase Manhattan, Citibank, the Fidelity Bank of Philadelphia and the First National Bank of Chicago, as well as several others from the United States and Canada. These banks have found that London serves as a better communications base for the Middle East than any centre in the region itself,[10] while at the same time the range of financial services available in the city surpasses almost anything available elsewhere, with the possible exception of New York. The favourable experience of the North American banks with London has prompted other foreign banks to establish their Middle Eastern bases there as well in recent years. These include the Mitsubishi and Sanwa Banks of Japan, which formerly ran their operations from Beirut, the Sumitomo and Tokai Banks, also of Japan, and the Scandinavian Bank, which finds London preferable for Middle East communications and merchant banking generally to any Nordic centre.[11]

RISE OF EURO-ARAB JOINT VENTURE BANKS

The dominance of the western multinational banks in recycling was perhaps inevitable given their experience and expertise, but since the late 1960s there has been a desire in the Middle East that local institutions should play some role in the process.[12] As much of the activity was however concentrated in major international financial centres rather than within the region, it was difficult to see what role Middle Eastern institutions could play. Even if they established a presence in these centres, their more limited financial capability and lack of contacts would prevent them, at least in the short run, from being very effective. It seemed that, although financial nationalism might be easy to achieve in a Middle Eastern domestic context, abroad the issues were much more complex, and hasty moves could bring financial disaster.

With these potential pitfalls in mind, many Middle Eastern bankers, even in the more stridently nationalistic countries, decided one way to proceed would be to form some kind of joint venture consortium with western partners. Through such arrangements it was hoped that western expertise in financial management could be brought in to harness capital generated within the Middle East, but that interests from the area itself would maintain some degree of control. Middle Eastern bankers saw it as a means of getting access to international financial markets for a fairly modest outlay, enabling them to gain experience and contacts, and perhaps win new business which hitherto would have gone directly to the western multinationals. The advantages were seen not just in terms of control over the deployment of Middle Eastern funds, but as a way of tapping Euro-market lending for major national projects, thus gaining further new business for the banks from their own governments and local businesses, which otherwise they would not have been able to handle.

The first moves to found joint venture banks with Arab participation came in Paris in the late 1960s, and it was to be three years before similar moves were made in London. and then largely owing to the initiative of the French-based institutions. France's emergence as the main centre for these institutions was not surprising, despite the primacy of London for international finance, as the main Paris banks had a longer history of involvement in consortium banking generally, and with the growth of Euro-markets in the 1960s there was a proliferation of such institutions on the French banking scene. In addition France was closely involved economically with the Arab world, especially the Magreb states, while financial links between Paris and the partially French-speaking banking community of Beirut remained strong.[13] Finally the French government's support for the Arab governments in the aftermath of the 1967 war with Israel made Arab politicians more amenable to Paris than to other European capitals, and there was a desire to see the improved Franco-Arab relations produce concrete benefits in the economic and financial sphere.

The first institution, FRAB (French–Arab) Bank International, was founded in 1969 with the initiative on the French side being taken by Société Générale, one of the country's oldest and most respected banks. Société Générale brought in several major western banks including the Swiss Bank Corporation, the Amsterdam-Rotterdam Bank and the Industrial Bank of Japan. On the Arab side the main interests were from Kuwait, including the Foreign Trading Contracting, and Investment Company, the Kuwait Insurance Company and two banks, the National and Commercial. Other lesser interests included the National Bank of Bahrain, and the UAE based Bank of Oman, while Société Générale persuaded a range of institutions from the Magreb countries to participate, such as the Banque de Tunisie and Crédit Populaire d'Algérie. This initial ownership structure was to stay broadly similar until 1974 when it was decided to increase the bank's capital substantially in the aftermath of the oil revenue boom. For tax reasons this was done by establishing a new holding company in Luxembourg where no corporate taxes are payable, rather than by expanding the equity of the Paris bank. The capital of the Luxembourg company was set at $27 million, even greater than that of the French company with $17 million authorised and paid up. [14]

Personalities are particularly important in joint venture banks, as they need an able and diplomatic head who can satisfy all the diverse shareholder interests, as well as those of a multinational management team of greatly differing backgrounds and experience, many of whom are on secondment from the venture's parent banks. In the case of FRAB Bank International, Yves Bernard, the French chairman has steered the institution through its formative years, and built up a mixed European and Arab management team, in which French nationals figure prominently but not exclusively on the European side, and Lebanese dominate on the Arab side, but again not exclusively. There has been a desire to recruit staff independently of the parent banks, so as to stress the institution's identity in its own right. In this way it was hoped to counter the charges made initially that the formation of the consortium bank was merely a devious French scheme to attract Arab funds into the Paris financial market; some sort of new gimmick to challenge the dominance of London as an Arab deposit base. The role which the FRAB Bank has carved out for itself would seem to belie this assertion as, although most of its funds originate from the Arab world, rather than France, the bank has lent significant amounts back into the Arab world, and much of its non-Arab lending has been on a truly international basis, rather than just to French borrowers. [15]

FRAB's main rival, the Union de Banques Arabes et Françaises (UBAF) was founded just one year later in 1970, largely because Crédit Lyonnais did not want to see its major competitor, Société Générale, make all the running as far as Arab business was concerned. Initially the bank was under the dominance of Crédit Lyonnais to a much greater extent than was the case with FRAB Bank *vis-à-vis* its parent, as Crédit Lyonnais kept 30 per cent of the capital for itself, and did not invite other European banks to contribute. Most of the staff were on secondment from Crédit Lyonnais, and UBAF even operated from the same building as the headquarters of the French bank. The majority shareholding from the start was Arab, however, and included some of the leading Arab banks such as the Amman-based Arab Bank, the Commercial Bank of Syria, the Libyan Arab Foreign Bank, Banque Extérieure d'Algérie and the Central Bank of

Egypt. Unlike FRAB, UBAF was given an Arab director, an eminent Egyptian, Mohamed Alushadi, who had risen within Cairo's then state-owned banking system to be director of the National Bank.[16]

There is little doubt that having an Arab chairman increased regard in some Middle Eastern quarters for the institution and, although Alushadi originally envisaged the job being part-time only, it soon became full-time as business built up. Although private Arab depositors and banks may have been satisfied, or even have preferred to see European management in the early 1970s, the socialist states and institutions which were heavily represented in UBAF on nationalistic grounds welcomed the overall Arab control, by someone with an inside knowledge of the workings of their organisations. UBAF soon overtook its rival institution FRAB, and by 1979 its paid-up capital exceeded $60 million, with deposits amounting to over $3 billion. In comparison FRAB's capital at the same time was less than 60 per cent that of UBAF and its deposits were worth just under $1 billion. In addition, UBAF's French operations were only part of a much larger network, which encompassed other independent but associated companies, UBAF Bank (London) Ltd, UBAF Financial Services, also in London, UBAE Arab Italian Bank, UBAN Arab Japanese Finance Ltd, UBAF Arab American Bank, and Union des Banques Arabes et Européennes, based in Luxembourg. This last company operated in its own right, unlike the FRAB holding company in Luxembourg, as, when UBAF partially consolidated its ownership in 1978, this was done by forming a new company UBAC in the Netherlands to control the 60 per cent Arab shareholding in UBAF France.[17]

The third major Middle East consortium bank operating in Paris is Banque Arabe et Internationale d'Investissement (BAII), formed shortly before the oil price increases of 1973, and entirely owned by a Luxembourg-based holding company. Like FRAB and UBAF, BAII is backed by a major French bank, in its case Banque Nationale de Paris, but the Arab ownership majority is largely in the hands of investment companies rather than banks. These include the Kuwait Investment Company and the National Investment Company of Libya, although the Gulf Bank of Kuwait and the Bank of Kuwait and the Middle East also have important stakes. The institution professes to be primarily interested in long-term investment banking, and is keen to take an equity stake in the ventures it backs. This means it does not compete with Banque Nationale de Paris in underwriting syndicated loans in Euro-markets and, unlike FRAB and UBAF, is not trying to get its name on as many tombstones as possible.[18] It believes the Arab banks themselves are perfectly capable of taking part in subscribing to government-guaranteed loan issues without the need to resort to the consortium banks, and that the most valuable role it can play is as a broker for investments with higher risks involved.

Although Paris was the first centre in which consortium banks with Arab participation arose, and France remains the main focus of operations for these institutions, it was not long before they spread to other western financial centres. To some extent this was inevitable because of the limitations of Paris as a business centre, but it also reflected the obvious opportunities perceived elsewhere. UBAF has largely expanded on its own account as already indicated, its London operation opening as early as 1972. FRAB adopted a different strategy for expansion, however, as it backed a new institution, the European Arab Bank, rather than setting up offices elsewhere under its own name. The European Arab Bank first opened for business in Brussels in 1972, that city being chosen because of the range of pan-European institutions represented in what amounted to the capital of the European Community. As is now the case with FRAB, it was decided to vest majority ownership in a Luxembourg holding company for corporate tax reasons, and this holding company also owns the Frankfurt and London branches which were subsequently established, although each functions independently. The chairman of the European Arab Bank, Dr Abdel-Moneim Al-Qaissouni, a former Egyptian finance minister, sits on the board of each of the national companies, however, as do representatives of FRAB.

The relatively late emergence of the European Arab Bank enabled it to attract shareholders who had hitherto been reluctant to become involved in consortium banking. These included European banks such as the Midland of the United Kingdom, the Deutsche Bank and Banca Commerciale Italiana. On the Arab side Qaissouni was able to persuade old-established institutions such as the state-owned National Bank of Egypt to join, the latter becoming more outward-looking as a result of the changes in Cairo government policy.[19] Even more significantly, the National Commercial Bank of Saudi Arabia took a stake in the new institution, the first cautious step into international finance by the ultra-conservative Bin Mahfouz family who own what has become the largest private commercial bank in the Middle East and the Arab world as a whole.

Despite the attention which the Arab-European joint venture banks have attracted in the financial press, at no time have they accounted for more than 10 per cent of recycled funds,[20] and they have yet to expand out of their wholesale banking role; indeed most profess little desire to do this. With their main deposits coming from other banks and financial institutions, rather than the general public, they are inevitably vulnerable in times when liquidity is being squeezed. Naturally banks will look after their own interests and customers first, and other banks in which they own a small minority stake are likely to be of secondary importance. Initially of course the Arab participants in the consortium banks were keen to help their new offspring, and their deposits were certainly more stable than those held in the western banks. Thus if there was any shortage of funds, then it was the western banks which would experience the withdrawals first. In practice in the early 1970s, with their lack of international experience, the Arab banks were eager to place funds with the consortium banks. Then from the mid-1970s onwards those in the oil exporting states had a surplus of liquidity as their deposit base expanded much more rapidly than domestic lending opportunities. By the late 1970s the situation was starting to change however as the Arab banks began to place funds directly in international financial markets themselves.[21]

Since the late 1970s there has been considerable questioning about the role of consortium banks in general, and the place of the Euro-Arab joint venture institutions in particular.[22] Some even started to ask whether the consortium banks had outlived their usefulness, and what purpose their future continuance would serve. Once an institution is created, in banking as in other spheres of financial activity, it acquires a character and momentum of its own, and so far none of the Arab consortium banks look like disappearing or being merged with other institutions. Inevitably there will be a degree of re-structuring in the future nevertheless, with the European banks pulling out as they continue to build up their own operations in the Middle East, especially in Bahrain and to a lesser extent Cairo. The Arab banks are less likely to pull out, however, and may well increase their stake, as they have been expanding so fast that they are seeking as many outlets as possible in international financial centres. In addition even in the medium term, many Arab banks lack the trained staff to carry out all the operations in which they seek to be involved. A need is also felt by some individual Arab investors for consortium banks as institutions in which they can hedge their risks. The fortunes of national banks are inevitably tied up with individual governments and, in a politically turbulent region, many feel safer dealing with multinational institutions.

If the consortium banks are Arabised to an increasing degree, at least their role will become more clear-cut than it is at present. In so far as they have a distinctive contribution to make, as merchant bankers for example, a role most believe they can play, it can be through giving advice on funding in the Arab world, rather than in developing regions outside. It is there that their special expertise lies, and not in arranging Euro-loans for China or Latin America on thin margins that few European banks would accept, as some have done. In such markets they risk just gaining the left-overs. Another promising field would appear to be Euro-Arab trade finance, through which they could start to move out of wholesale banking into a wider retailing role. The institutions are well suited to this role, with their many contacts in both the west and the Arab world. Expansion of such activities would certainly compensate for any losses once Arab governments and state institutions eventually start to place most of their surplus funds through their own national banks, as seems likely in the late 1980s, if not earlier.

ENTRY OF MIDDLE EASTERN BANKS
INTO WESTERN FINANCIAL CENTRES

In the late 1960s there were only two individual Middle Eastern banks maintaining offices in London, Bank Melli of Iran and the Rafidain Bank of Iraq, the only other institution, the Ottoman Bank, being originally European rather than Turkish. Yet a decade later twenty-five Middle Eastern-based banks had established offices in London, some providing a full range of banking services, while others had representative status only.[23] In addition London is the headquarters for some Arab national joint venture banks such as the United Bank of Kuwait and the Saudi International Bank, which are entirely owned by financial institutions in single Arab countries, unlike the banks dealt with in the last section in which institutions from a number of Arab countries were involved. Back in 1966, nine leading Kuwaiti banks and investment companies decided that it would be wisest to pool their resources rather than go into London on their own, and it was this that led to the United Bank's establishment, initially as a kind of listening post to monitor developments in international markets.

In 1975 a number of Saudi institutions decided to follow the Kuwaiti example, including the Riyadh and National Commercial

Banks, although, as these banks were much more cautious than their Kuwaiti neighbours, it was the Saudi Arabian Monetary Agency which took the major 50 per cent stake in the new institution. The shares of the Riyadh and National Commercial Banks were a mere 2.5 per cent each, which gives some indication of their lack of interest in international operations even at this late stage. Unlike the United Bank of Kuwait, it was also decided to bring in Western partners to the Saudi International Bank, although to a much lesser degree than was the case with the Euro-Arab multinational consortium banks. Therefore the Bank of Tokyo, the Banque Nationale de Paris, the Deutsche Bank, the National Westminster Bank and the Union Bank of Switzerland were all allowed to take 5 per cent shares. This was to ensure that the new institution would have firm contacts which the Saudi banks lacked. In addition the lack of Saudi-trained banking personnel resulted in the management contract being awarded to Morgan Guaranty, one of Wall Street's oldest and most respected institutions, who agreed to take a 20 per cent stake in the new bank.[24]

To some extent these Arab national joint ventures may in their turn have outlived their usefulness like the Euro-Arab banks. One of the Kuwaiti banks which is represented in the United Bank, the Gulf Bank, now has an office of its own, while Saudi Arabia's National Commercial Bank established a full branch in the city of London in 1980. There is little doubt that some of the other partners in these institutions will follow these examples in the years ahead, as their scale of international operations expands sufficiently to justify separate representation. Some banks, such as those from Iran and Turkey, of necessity had to maintain separate representation in the absence of any joint national institution. This explains the proliferation of Iranian banks in London as, apart from the long-established Bank Melli, arrivals in the 1970s included Bank Bazargani, the Bank of Tehran, Bank Pars, Bank Saderat, Bank Sanaye and Bank Sepah. The Turkish Banks in London include Akbank Turkiye Cumhuriyet, Ziraat Bankasi, Turkiye is Bankasi and Yafi ve Kredi Bankasi, and in addition the country's central bank maintains a separate office.

Other Gulf states represented in the London financial market include Qatar, whose National Bank and Ministry of Finance and Petroleum Investment Office share the same building. The Emirates are as fragmented in their London representation as they are in domestic financial matters with the institutions which maintain offices including the Khalij Commercial Bank of Abu Dhabi, the Sharjah Investment Company, and the National Bank of Abu Dhabi. The latter has been one of the most expansionist Middle Eastern banks in international financial markets in recent years, as it now boasts, in addition to its city and West End branches in London, an office in Paris, and ten branches in the Middle East itself. Yet this young institution, which is 50 per cent owned by the government of Abu Dhabi, was only founded in 1968. The other major UAE-owned institution doing extensive business in London is the Bank of Credit and Commerce which is dealt with in detail in Chapter 3. Its headquarters are Luxembourg and the Cayman Islands, where the holding companies are based, and not the United Arab Emirates, although it does much of its domestic business in Abu Dhabi and Dubai. The bank nevertheless claims to be a wholly international institution, and prefers not to be classified with the other UAE-based banks.

Unlike the consortium banks, the Middle Eastern commercial banks represented in London and elsewhere usually provide a full range of retail banking services for their clients from the Gulf, many of whom are frequent visitors to Europe. Their business includes personal transfers, drafts and letters of credit, as well as ordinary traveller's chequing and other facilities.[25] On the company side they seek to play an active role in trade finance with the states which they represent, and provide credit to European exporters as well as to Middle Eastern importers. In addition the banks are also trying to develop their corporate advisory services, so that they can inform their Middle Eastern clients about potential sources of European supplies, although, given their limited Western experience, they are obviously at a disadvantage *vis-à-vis* the Western banks. The advice they can offer to European exporters and contractors regarding Middle Eastern contacts is probably more useful, although it is important to emphasise that some institutions are more able than others to provide this kind of service.

Retail banking and trade finance is nevertheless ancillary to the main activity of the Middle Eastern commercial banks represented in London, which is to provide a profitable outlet for funds which are normally deposited by the parent bank, and a few of its leading customers. Table 6.2 illustrates how such funds have been typically deployed in recent years by three important Arab institutions. It appears that most funds are still held either in cash or in deposit accounts with other banks through the inter-bank market, these being usually withdrawable at very short notice. There has been some tendency for the proportion of these highly liquid funds to decrease as

TABLE 6.2   *Asset structures of selected Arab banks in London, 1978*

	National Bank of Abu Dhabi (%)	Qatar National Bank (%)	Saudi International Bank (%)
Cash and short-term fund with bank	65	55	56
Advances and bills discounted	25	37	39
Investments	8	5	2
Other (prepayments, fixed assets, etc.)	12	13	3

SOURCES   Proportions estimated by author from published accounts of each of the institutions for 1978.

the banks have increased their lending, much of which is to firms involved in the Middle East in some way. It is this which accounts for the bulk of advances, bills discounted being of comparatively minor, if growing significance. Perhaps surprisingly, direct investments in equity or purchases of other types of long-term private security, which are included in investments, appear to be a relatively unimportant item. This would appear to belie the fact that these institutions are major investment bankers as some would claim.

THE ARAB BANKS IN THE EURO-MARKETS

Apart from their activity as depositors in the inter-bank market, the Arab banks have mainly devoted their efforts in international markets to participating in major Euro-loans, usually but not always on behalf of Arab companies. These loans are typically for amounts of at least $10 million, and most frequently of medium-term duration, five to ten years being the usual repayment period. As with Euro-market loans generally, they are either placed as fixed interest bonds, or else given a variable rate which is related to inter-bank official rates in some way. Spreads are often small, as low as ⅛ to ½ per cent in the late 1970s,[26] with the Middle Eastern institutions often prepared to accept lower margins in order to establish themselves in the market. There is usually little commercial risk involved regarding default, as the loans and bond issues are always fully guaranteed by government, and they are frequently to state-owned industries or the government itself in any case. The main risks tend to be political, but with at least twenty banks and investment funds usually participating in each loan, the degree of risk spreading is considerable.

The Middle Eastern commercial banks represented in London have been keen to lead-manage Euro-finance through loans and bond issues. This not only increases their prestige in the international financial community, but also gives the banks valuable experience, and means that frequently it is the Western banks which have to come to the Arab banks for business rather than vice versa, as has always been the case in the past. As the Arab banks are best placed to handle lending on behalf of Middle Eastern customers, not surprisingly this has been the activity in which many have specialised.[27] The National Bank of Abu Dhabi for example has lead-managed or arranged Euro-loans on behalf of its major domestic customers, including the Abu Dhabi Drilling Chemicals and Products Ltd ($14 million), the Abu Dhabi Gas Liquefaction Company ($25 million and $50 million) and the Emirates Telecommunications Corporation ($100 million). It is only recently that they have organised such loans on behalf of European companies, and most of these, including those on behalf of the Compagnie Française des Petroles, are to cover operations being undertaken within the United Arab Emirates rather than elsewhere.

Although most Middle Eastern commercial banks have been conservative in their Euro-market dealings, and in the business they have sought, there are some more venturesome exceptions, including the Libyan Arab Foreign Bank. Shortly after the start of their operations in 1973, the bank was already participating in loans to a diverse range of clients, including Lancashire County Council, the City of Nottingham who borrowed in dollars, the World Bank and Aéroport de Paris who borrowed in French francs, and the European Investment Bank and the Mortgage Bank of Denmark who borrowed in deutschmarks.[28] The Libyan Arab Foreign Bank's lead management role was also diverse, as it involved not only arranging Euro-market bond issues and loans for Arab clients such as Libyan Arab Airlines or Sonatrach of Algeria, but also others worldwide including Banco National Cuba, Jugobanka and the National Bank of Hungary. One of the largest loans it managed was a $100 million issue for the Sumed pipeline in Egypt, to mature four years after its issue at interest of 1 per cent over the inter-bank prevailing dollar rate.

Commercial criteria are of course paramount when the Arab commercial banks are deciding what loan and bond issues to support in the Euro-markets, but it would be naive to suggest political factors are irrelevant. For instance the strained relations between Egypt and its Arab neighbours in the aftermath of the peace treaty with Israel has made Arab banks reluctant to take part in financing on behalf of the

Sadat government or Cairo-based state corporations, although existing commitments are being honoured and private lending is unaffected. Not surprisingly, however, the Libyan Arab Foreign Bank has been involved in no new loans for Egypt recently, and even the consortium bank, UBAF, under its Egyptian Chairman Mohamed Abushadi, was forced to withdraw from a $300 million loan which it had been hoping to arrange on behalf of the Egyptian government in 1979.[29] There is little doubt that there is strong pressure on the Arab banks to bow to prevailing political winds, yet it is noticeable that the Cairo based Arab-African International Bank has continued to participate in syndicated loans in co-operation with other Arab banks in spite of the supposed boycott of Egypt. The institution has however been keen to emphasise its international character, and stresses that the Central Bank of Egypt's ownership share is only a 42.4 per cent minority stake.

Despite the political constraints which inhibit the development of international business activity in certain areas by the Middle Eastern commercial banks, overall political factors are undoubtedly an aid rather than a hindrance to growth. The more nationalistic governments in the area have long preferred to channel funds through locally-owned rather than western-owned banks, and the continuing dependence of the Saudi authorities on European and American institutions merely reflects the limited capacity of their own institutions rather than any predisposition towards the West in financial matters. The Kuwaitis have recognised since the 1960s that by dealing with locally-owned banks the profits from international financial operations accrue to their own nationals rather than equity investors in the West.

Undoubtedly the greatest spur of all to the Middle Eastern banks has come since the Iranian revolution. At first Western bankers believed that the sudden nationalisation of the Iranian banking system would cause depositors in the Gulf and elsewhere to think twice about holding their deposits with Arab banks, which might prompt switching to the benefit of European and American institutions. The hasty American freeze on Iranian deposits soon more than dispelled this effect however, and made Middle Eastern depositors nervous about funds held in western institutions generally.[30] Admittedly the freeze only applied to Iranian deposits in the United States financial system and not to Euro-dollar deposits in London or elsewhere, but those holding such funds with American banks, even if offshore, still had their confidence shaken. There was a realisation that the United States banks had to comply with the spirit as well as the letter of the law, and their domestic public image must come first. Although the amount of short-term panic switching to Middle Eastern financial institutions was probably not significant, there is little doubt that governments in the Gulf and elsewhere now see it as being in their long-term interests to encourage the development of their own financial institutions in international financial markets rather than be reliant on the United States banks. There has certainly been a significant change in financial strategy for the 1970s, the results of which may take some time to emerge.

The OPEC countries, of which the states of the Middle East form the major part, have emerged as the second major source of Euro-market funds, after the Western European countries considered collectively. Table 6.3 illustrates their growing significance, which is even greater than that of the United States. As well as the $98.6 billion dollars which was recorded as coming direct from the OPEC countries in 1980, a substantial proportion of the funds recorded as coming from the offshore banking centres also have originated within OPEC. Merely taking account of Bahrain's small share of these funds would be a serious underestimate, as some of the Arab financial institutions are active in other centres such as the Cayman Islands and Nassau. The institutions represented on the former include the Emirates-owned Bank of Credit and Commerce International, the Gefinor Bank which is registered in Geneva but which has Lebanese backing, the Oryx Merchant Bank of Dubai and UBAF Arab American Bank. In the Bahamas the Arab institutions include the Artoc Bank and Trust Limited, a Kuwaiti-financed company, the Islamic Investment Company whose most prominent director is Prince Mohammad bin-Faisal of Saudi Arabia, and the Saudi International Bank.[31]

When the data for the sources of funds and the uses of funds are compared from Table 6.3, it becomes evident, even just taking the OPEC figures, that these countries are the largest net contributors. Although the OPEC countries are emerging as important borrowers in the Euro-markets, and the Middle Eastern banks are heavily involved in this finance, deposits amount to over three times total lending. OPEC countries only used $33 billion of Euro-market funds in 1980, or less than 6 per cent of the total, whereas they directly accounted for almost one-fifth of deposits. Of course most of the deposits in these markets up till now have been channelled through the major western banks rather than the newly emerging Middle Eastern international banks. Nevertheless the data gives some indication of the eventual role

TABLE 6.3   *Euro-market flow of funds, 1977 – 80 ($ billion)*

	1977	1978	1979	1980
Sources				
Western Europe	117.3	144.5	181.0	235.0
OPEC	54.5	54.7	68.6	98.6
Offshore Bank Centres	33.4	45.4	56.9	64.0
United States	25.4	37.0	46.5	56.0
Non-oil LDCs	29.6	39.8	46.0	38.0
Other developed countries	18.8	26.2	31.1	34.0
Canada and Japan	8.4	13.0	14.2	14.0
Eastern Europe	7.0	8.8	8.2	7.0
Unallocated	–	–	7.0	7.3
Total	300.0	377.0	459.5	555.6
Uses				
Western Europe	110.4	139.5	155.6	185.0
Offshore bank centres	43.9	55.0	70.0	90.0
Non-oil LDCs	30.3	40.1	66.0	86.0
Other developed countries	30.8	34.7	39.1	46.5
Eastern Europe	25.7	31.4	34.5	37.5
Canada and Japan	18.7	24.6	28.5	36.5
US	21.3	24.6	32.8	34.1
OPEC	15.7	24.3	28.0	33.0
Unallocated	–	3.0	5.0	7.0
Total	300.0	377.0	459.5	555.6

NOTES   All figures refer to December. Figures for 1980 are projections.

SOURCE   Compiled by Kevin Pakenham of the *Financial Times* from data
issued by the Bank for International Settlements and Amex Bank. (Cited in
the *Financial Times,* 18 February 1980.)

the Middle Eastern banks could play in the international financial
markets, and the scope would appear so great that they may even grow
to rival the major western banks themselves in terms of their scale of
operations.

7 Aid and Development Assistance Agencies

Despite the widespread discussions on the recycling of Middle East surplus funds to help those energy-deficient developing countries who suffer considerably as a result of oil price rises, there is little agreement about the most appropriate institutional forms to channel the funds. There are five main mechanisms to effect such transfers, both intra-regionally within the Middle East and extra-regionally to the other Third World importers. Firstly, there are private investment transfers, either through direct investment by wealthy individuals or companies from the oil exporting countries. Secondly, there is the growing volume of remittances from workers who are citizens of energy-deficient developing countries, but who work in the oil-surplus states. Thirdly, there is the recycling which is carried out by the commercial banks through international capital markets, where Third World countries are heavy borrowers, and OPEC capital is deployed, largely through the major western banks, but also increasingly through Middle Eastern-owned banks as discussed in the previous chapter. A fourth method of recycling is through bilateral state transfers, direct from the government of a petroleum exporting country to the treasury or finance ministry of the energy-deficient recipient. Finally there are the transfers through the established Middle Eastern aid agencies, upon which attention will be focused in this chapter, partly because of their increasing significance, but also owing to the interest they appear to arouse.

Although the Middle Eastern aid and development assistance agencies have attracted most attention, it is important to bear in mind the significance of the other methods of recycling. Thus the major Kuwaiti banks and investment companies together recycle more finance, even intra-regionally, than the Kuwait Fund for Arab Economic Development, and in the case of the banks their paid-up capital is only a small portion of their lending, which is related to deposits, subject of course to a standard reserve ratio. In contrast development agencies have their lending limited by the extent of their capital resources. Whether the lending of the commercial banks and investment companies is as useful from the developmental point of view as that of the agencies is naturally another matter, as for example the National Bank of Abu Dhabi's four branches in Egypt finance trade and real estate purchases, rather than the industrial ventures or agricultural projects on which the Abu Dhabi Fund for Arab Economic Development concentrates its support.

Bilateral government-to-government transfers are also more significant in absolute terms than the assistance directed through development agencies, although again it is debatable how useful such transfers are in terms of development. Most is in the form of general budgetary support, a large portion of which is to finance purchase of military supplies rather than civilian projects. Even the so-called Arab Organisation for Industrialisation, which was financed by Saudi Arabia and the Gulf states, was largely designed to help build up Egypt's production capacity in armaments, and was quickly abandoned in the aftermath of Sadat's Jerusalem visit.[1] Clearly much of the inter-governmental financial transfers both within the Middle East, and outside, have been closely linked with political objectives.

Some Middle Eastern governments have even refused to establish autonomous or semi-autonomous development agencies, as their heads of state or government ministers have preferred to demonstrate their largesse personally to visiting dignitaries from the energy-deficit countries. Libya for instance has no development agency, as President Gadaffi has taken a direct interest in the deployment of funds, while Iraq's government under Sadam Hussein took a similar approach, as, although a Fund for External Development was established with an authorised capital of $338 million, this was a modest amount in relation to the capital of the other Arab funds, and little of even this limited capital has ever been paid in.[2] Since the Iranian revolution of course the Islamic Republic has had no funds to spare for outside assistance, but formerly, when there was a surplus, the Shah, playing the role of imperial ruler, dispensed the funds himself.[3]

QUANTIFICATION OF THE AGENCIES' ROLE

Aggregated amounts of aid and development assistance dispensed by the major Middle Eastern petroleum exporting countries are shown in

Table 7.1, with the states ranked according to the scale of their contributions over the 1975–9 period. From the table no marked trends are discernible, as the annual fluctuations for individual countries are considerable, although overall these seem to some extent to balance out, with the exception of 1978. Although the total value of

TABLE 7.1   *Aid granted by OPEC Middle Eastern countries ($ millions)*

	1975	1976	1977	1978	1979	Total 1975–9
Saudi Arabia	1,997	2,407	2,410	1,470	1,970	10,254
Kuwait	976	615	1,518	1,268	1,099	5,476
United Arab Emirates	1,046	1,060	1,177	690	207	4,180
Iran	593	753	224	278	21	1,869
Iraq	218	232	61	172	861	1,544
Qatar	339	195	197	106	251	1,088
Libya	261	94	115	169	146	785
Total OAPEC[a]	4,879	4,656	5,526	3,919	4,579	23,559
Total OPEC[b]	5,516	5,596	5,866	4,344	4,711	26,033

NOTES   [a] Members of Organisation of Arab Petroleum Exporting Countries. Total aid includes a small multilateral element not recorded in the single country figures.
[b] Non-Middle Eastern members granting small amounts of aid include Venezuela, Algeria and Nigeria.

SOURCE   Organisation for Economic Cooperation and Development, Paris, 1980.

development assistance in money terms has stayed roughly constant, since the 1974 oil price rises it has declined considerably in real terms, reflecting the increasing absorption capacity of the petroleum exporters themselves, and the fall in the real value of petroleum exports until the major price rises of 1979 started to take effect.

By comparing the data cited in Table 7.1 with that presented in Table 7.2 for the individual aid agencies surveyed in this chapter, a perspective can be gained of the relative significance of the agencies in relation to total flows of development assistance from the OPEC producers of the Middle East. Saudi Arabia for example granted developmental assistance worth over $10,000 million over the 1975–9, yet the Saudi Fund for Development, which was founded by the start of this period, had disbursed loans worth only $1408 million by 1978, less than 15 per cent of the total. In Kuwait development assistance was worth $5476 million over the 1975–9 period alone, but the

TABLE 7.2   *Official Middle Eastern aid agencies*

	Founded	Head-quarters	Authorised capital ($ millions)	Paid-up capital ($ millions)	Loans committed ($ millions)	Loans disbursed ($ millions)	Commitments as proportion of authorised capital (%)	Disbursements as proportion of paid-up capital (%)	Disbursements as proportion of commitments (%)
Kuwait Fund for Arab Economic Development	1961	Kuwait	3,600	2,045	2,125	1,080	59.0	52.8	50.8
Arab Fund for Economic and Social Development	1963	Kuwait	1,440	1,332	1,019	425	70.8	31.9	41.7
Abu Dhabi Fund for Arab Economic Development	1971	Abu Dhabi	527	413	777	408	147.4	98.8	52.5
Arab Bank for Economic Development in Africa	1973	Khartoum	738	640	332	195	45.0	30.5	58.7
Saudi Fund for Development	1975	Riyadh	2,985	2,400	1,799	1,408	60.3	58.7	78.3
Islamic Development Bank	1975	Jeddah	2,560	998	987	414	38.5	41.5	42.0
OPEC Special Fund	1975	Vienna	1,660	1,229	927	372	55.8	30.3	40.1

NOTE   Kuwait Fund, Abu Dhabi Fund and Islamic Bank data for 1978 – 9 (1399 AH), Saudi Fund data for 1977 – 8 (1398 AH), Arab Bank data for 1979, Arab Fund and OPEC Special Fund data for 1978. Conversions into dollars at October 1979 values.

SOURCES   Annual reports of institutions listed.

Kuwait Fund for Arab Economic Development had disbursed less than one-fifth of that amount during its entire 18 years of operation up to 1979. Abu Dhabi reveals a similar picture, with its Fund accounting for less than one tenth of its total aid disbursements over the 1975–9 period. This is not of course to deny the qualitative significance of the development assistance agencies, as aid is far from being homogeneous, but in quantitative terms their importance has perhaps been exaggerated in the past. Nevertheless the sheer scale of funding which has been made available for development assistance, representing more than 10 per cent of the gross national products of some of the countries concerned, indicates the scope for expansion which the aid agencies have, providing they can prove their worth.

The data in Table 7.2 also facilitates a comparison between the individual development assistance agencies in terms of their scale of operations and scope for expansion in relation to their existing resources. Authorised and paid-up capital reflects the latter, and as the table shows, the Kuwait Fund for Arab Economic Development has the largest authorised capital, followed by the Saudi Fund for Development and the Islamic Development Bank. This does not reflect the position with respect to paid-up capital, however, as here the Saudi Fund for Development leads, with the Kuwait Fund following, and the Arab Fund for Economic and Social Development in third position. The discrepancy between government pledges and the funds actually paid in may result from governments being too liberal in their pledges in the first place, perhaps to give their agencies added prestige, or it may simply reflect the caution of finance ministries in dispensing funds to autonomous bodies outside their direct control.[4] It is unlikely the funds are not dispensed because of any lack of demand, as the funds the aid agencies themselves have not disbursed are usually invested at commercial rates of interest, which brings in substantial revenues to cover administrative expenses and finance operational expansion.[5]

There is also a considerable discrepancy between the commitments which the development agencies have entered, and the funds actually paid out. Some discrepancies are natural of course when projects can only be completed over fairly lengthy periods, and there are few development schemes which have a start-up period of less than a year while tenders are awarded, and contractors get down to the detail of putting plans into practice. In addition where supplementary finance has to be arranged, as is often the case, even the pre-tender stage can be lengthy. Frequently the development agencies are requested to pledge their financial support in advance, as this increases confidence in the project, and makes it easier to obtain extra funding from commercial sources. The implementation stage will obviously vary with the nature of the project and its location, but around three to five years would seem typical for infrastructure schemes and two to four years for industrial ventures. Spending will often peak in the second and third years. [6]

In these circumstances the large difference between pledges and expenditure indicated in Table 7.2 is scarcely surprising with the proportion of disbursements to commitments varying from 40 per cent in the case of the OPEC Special Fund to over 78 per cent in the case of the Saudi Fund for Development. The latter largely funds projects, while the former has deployed some of its finance to support other agencies, including the United Nations Development Programme. This undoubtedly accounts to some extent for its less rapid disbursement of funds. Another factor may be the length of time an agency has been in existence, as the OPEC Special Fund, as a comparatively young agency, has made many pledges in its early years which there has been insufficient time to carry out. This probably partly accounts for its lower disbursement rate than those of the Kuwait or Abu Dhabi Funds. Conservative administrative practice and finance caution may also play a part, however, and multinational institutions in general are notorious for their reluctance to part with funds until they are precisely certain about how the money has been spent.

The development agencies naturally make an allowance for the time lag between commitments and payments, and can pledge greater amounts than would be the case otherwise. Most in fact believe that if payments become due sooner than expected, so long as they have remained within their authorised capital, their government backers can always step in and increase their subscriptions. Thus it seems relevant to take their proportion of commitments in relation to authorised capital as a measure of financial prudence. As Table 7.2 shows most of the agencies have a relatively modest amount of commitments in relation to their authorised capital, the exception being the Abu Dhabi Fund for Economic and Social Development, whose authorised capital has subsequently been increased, without putting any strain on the vast resources of its government backer. [7] In fact it was the largesse of the Abu Dhabi government rather than the Fund itself which resulted in the seemingly precarious financial position depicted in the table.

Looking at disbursements as a proportion of paid-up capital however shows that even the Abu Dhabi Fund was able to cover its own payments without recourse to external borrowing, while three of the other agencies, the Arab Fund, the Arab Bank and the OPEC Special Fund, have disbursed less than one-third of their paid-up capital. This of course means they can hold their surplus funds profitably, although commercial investment is not the primary purpose of an aid agency, nor was that the intention when these agencies were established. The agencies argue nevertheless that the problem is not any unwillingness on their part to commit funds or delay disbursements, but rather a shortage of sound projects which they can usefully support. It seems there is a lack of aid recipients rather than aid donors, or at least too few potential recipients who can put forward technically feasible and economically viable projects.

A sectoral distribution of Middle Eastern aid agency commitments is presented in Table 7.3, revealing the fields in which viable projects have been approved. Rather surprisingly no agency has committed more than one-quarter of its funds for agricultural projects, perhaps

TABLE 7.3 *Sectoral distribution of Middle Eastern aid agency commitments (per cent)*

	Agriculture and rural development	Industry and mining	Transport and communications	Electricity, water, sewerage and other services
Kuwait Fund for Arab Economic Development	20.9	27.2	35.7	16.2
Arab Fund for Economic and Social Development	9.4	18.9	36.8	34.9
Abu Dhabi Fund for Arab Economic Development	3.6	81.3	6.2	8.9
Arab Bank for Economic Development in Africa	23.7[a]	18.8	44.8	12.7
Saudi Fund for Development	16.1	23.3	33.2	27.4[b]
Islamic Development Bank	10.4	45.1	27.7	16.8[c]
OPEC Special Fund	21.2	26.6	17.3	34.9

NOTES   [a] Includes 4.5 per cent emergency aid.
   [b] Includes 5.6 per cent for social services.
   [c] Includes 3.3 per cent for social services.

SOURCES   Annual reports of institutions listed.

reflecting the limited agricultural potential of the Arab and Muslim countries where assistance has been concentrated.[8] Another factor however may have been the inability of potential recipient countries to formulate agricultural schemes, or the lack of emphasis on rural development, as it is notable that even the Arab Bank for Economic Development in Africa assigned only 23.7 per cent of its funds to agriculture. Overall it appears the main emphasis has been on supporting projects involving basic infrastructure, such as transport and communications networks, or utilities such as electricity, water and sewerage. This emphasis may reflect the early stage of development of most of the recipients where the need is to create the pre-conditions for industrialisation and modernisation, before carrying out more directly productive activities. It may also reflect the belief of some of the agencies that it is not their job to finance industrial projects which can obtain funds through normal commercial channels if they are viable, but which should not be backed if they have no profit potential. Their task is essentially supportive, to complement rather than act as a substitute for commercial finance. From Table 7.3 it seems that only the Abu Dhabi Fund has assigned most of its finance in support of industrial projects.

An examination of the geographical distribution of aid agency funds reveals, not surprisingly, that most of the projects financed

TABLE 7.4   *Geographical distribution of Middle Eastern aid agency commitments (per cent)*

	Arab world	African non-Arab states	Asian non-Arab states	Other
Kuwait Fund for Arab Economic Development	67.7	10.8	20.9	0.6
Arab Fund for Economic and Social Development	100.0	—	—	—
Abu Dhabi Fund for Arab Economic Development	84.0	4.1	11.0	0.9
Arab Bank for Economic Development in Africa	—	100.0	—	—
Saudi Fund for Development	65.2	10.3	13.3	11.2
Islamic Development Bank	50.1	12.4	37.5	—
OPEC Special Fund	27.4	22.0	44.4	6.2

NOTE   Others mainly accounted for by Latin America and Malta.

SOURCES   Annual reports of the institutions listed.

have been within the Arab world. As Table 7.4 shows, around two-thirds of Kuwait and Saudi Fund projects are in other Arab countries, and 84 per cent of those backed by the Abu Dhabi Fund. The activities of the Arab Fund are confined by its charter to Arab states, and only the Arab Bank has concentrated on non-Arab African states, as its articles of association state it should. The Islamic Development Bank of course assists only Muslim states as indicated in Chapter 4, but over a third of these have been in non-Arab Asia, including Bangladesh, Pakistan and Malaysia, while the 12 per cent of total assistance to non-Arab Africa has been shared by Mali, Niger, Uganda and Upper Volta. Only the OPEC Special Fund, to which the Arab states merely subscribe half the capital, has been a truly international aid agency, with beneficiaries throughout the Third World.

THE KUWAIT FUND FOR ARAB ECONOMIC DEVELOPMENT

The Middle Eastern aid agencies can be usefully divided into different categories. National aid agencies such as the Kuwait Fund, the Abu Dhabi Fund and the Saudi Fund can clearly be considered together as they have much in common, and to a considerable extent the two latter agencies have profited from the longer experience of the former, which has been very willing to respond to any assistance requested. The other more specialised agencies are also dealt with at the same time, although this is more from convenience, as the approaches and objectives of the Arab Fund, the Arab Bank for Economic Development in Africa, and the OPEC Special Fund have little in common. Nor do they draw on each other's experiences to the same extent as the other national funds. However, as all the Middle Eastern agencies meet together at least once a year, there is fortunately some general awareness of what each agency is trying to achieve.

Kuwait's Fund for Arab Economic Development is of course the longest established agency as Table 7.2 indicates, as it was founded on 31 December 1961.[9] Its initial capital was $140 million, but during its first year of operations this amount was doubled, in a seemingly generous gesture by the government, as this new sum was equivalent to one-quarter of Kuwait's annual gross national product at that time. There is little doubt that generosity on such a scale was not merely motivated by altruism, but by political factors.[10] Kuwait had just become a fully independent nation and lost its direct political protection by Britain which was reducing its presence east of Suez. As revolutionary Iraq had territorial claims on Kuwait and its oil wealth, the Kuwaiti ruler and government saw the urgent priority of winning friends and influencing government policy in other Arab states. The Kuwait Fund was the vehicle through which this was to be carried out, by buying support with the one asset which the young state had available. At the same time it was realised however that merely granting loans indiscriminately could be counter-productive. If funds were used for unsound projects, then repayment would prove impossible, and debtors seldom feel warmly towards their creditors or give them much support. Nor would grants be appropriate, as this would only tempt a wasteful use of the funds, and perhaps fuel corruption, and there would be nothing concrete to show for the assistance given.

As a consequence of this thinking, from its inception the Kuwait Fund has granted only assistance for specific projects rather than general budgetary support. Strict investment appraisals are carried out, with outside firms of western consultants brought in to advise where appropriate, and the criteria for ultimate approval of a particular project are modelled on those adopted by the World Bank in Washington. Such strict criteria have not precluded the Fund's success, indeed most within the Fund would argue that they were essential for that success, and helped win the agency considerable international respect. Nor did the application of such criteria rebound adversely on the government, in fact Kuwait was admitted as a full member of the Arab League, and it received diplomatic recognition from all other independent Arab states, including Iraq. Although there have been subsequent border incidents with Iraq, these have been settled for the most part amicably, and Kuwait has no problem in finding Arab nations willing to mediate on its behalf.

The high regard in which the Kuwait Fund is held owes much to the personality of its founder and director-general, Abdtalif Al-Hamad, who insisted that it should have a legal personality distinct from government from the start.[11] As the original political objectives were achieved at an early stage, this undoubtedly freed Al-Hamad's hand considerably, but it is his untiring efforts which have resulted in the Fund acquiring a fully professional and extremely competent staff, untarnished by the corruption which is so rife in government departments in many Middle Eastern states. Over 142 separate loans had been processed by 1979,[12] and few are in arrears, which says much for the skill of the staff in handling project appraisal and in disbursing the funds. The repayments record compares favourably with the World Bank, and is better than that of many western aid agencies.

As already indicated, a major problem facing the Kuwait Fund since its inception has been a shortage of suitable projects to support. To some extent this is a result of its strict investment appraisal standards, as many government ministries, in the Arab world as in other developing regions, have difficulty in formulating potentially sound projects. These need to gain approval on grounds of economic viability using standard appraisal techniques. The ministries lack both the trained staff to devise suitable projects, and the imagination to see where development potential lies. For this reason the Kuwait Fund has tried to build up its own team of technical assistance experts from an early stage, and has not hesitated to call in outside consultants, usually from Western Europe and North America, where it has thought that would be appropriate. [13] This is not a complete answer, however, as the Kuwait Fund, like other development agencies, responds to requests for assistance rather than taking the initiative itself, as recipient countries might regard that as usurping their prerogative. A further problem is that civil servants of potential recipient countries often take it as an affront if the aid agency is seen to be doing their work, or perhaps worse, if western experts hired by the agency impinge on what is viewed as domestic responsibilities. The distinction between help and interference is often difficult to draw in practice, especially where sensitivities are as great as they are in many recently independent countries with first-generation public servants.

Nevertheless, despite such pitfalls, the Kuwait Fund provides not only direct project aid, but also technical assistance grants to cover the cost of employing outside consultants for feasibility studies. Proper project design is seen as essential, not only to ensure that financial requirements can be correctly assessed, but also to determine the necessary time scale for implementation, which may affect the overall viability of the project. This information is also needed to ascertain the most appropriate loan terms, including the necessary grace period, the optimum repayments time taking account of the fund generating nature of the scheme, and of course a suitable interest charge. The latter is viewed as necessary not so much from the Kuwait Fund's point of view to ensure some return on its lending, but to demonstrate to the recipient that the finance is not costless, and therefore the emphasis must be on maximising returns. Grants or free money in the Kuwait Fund's view, would often only be wasted money.

Usually, lending for agricultural projects or communications and other basic infrastructure is provided on more generous terms than that for industrial projects or energy developments such as power plants or electricity grids. Interest charges for the former typically average 2 per cent or less, whereas funds for industrialisation schemes often are advanced at a minimum interest rate of 4 per cent. An allowance is of course made for the location and nature of the project as both these affect returns, and therefore influence the decision about an appropriate rate of interest. An agricultural project located in a remote area of the Sudan for example is likely to yield less immediate benefits than one in Syria or Egypt where other ancillary services are already developed, and local farmers are more aware of the advantages which new schemes can bring. Accordingly 1 per cent higher interest may be levied in Egypt or Syria compared with a similar project in Sudan.

A country's capacity to repay in general is also taken into account when fixing loan terms, and the Kuwait Fund officials will usually look at the recipient's overall balance of payments position, and the adequacy of its foreign exchange reserves. Although all lending is for specific projects, and is not in the form of general balance of payments support, the macro-economic environment cannot be ignored; if the country has chronic foreign exchange shortages, then even if the project yields reasonable returns, there may be other claimants on any convertible currency earnings as well as the Kuwait Fund. This factor is particularly relevant in determining the length of the grace period, which typically varies from two and a half years to over five years in exceptional circumstances.[14] Many of the African countries recently supported by the Kuwait Fund have obtained grace periods of around four and a half years on borrowing, whereas Arab countries, including those without oil revenue, have shorter periods of two to three years to repay. Even poor and under-developed Arab countries such as North Yemen have substantial foreign exchange inflows because of remittances, but this is not the case for most African states.

Of course the grace period also must take account of the time necessary to implement a project, and the start-up period before yields are forthcoming. Naturally the Kuwait Fund expects that any foreign exchange yields from the project will be firstly used to service its loan, rather than being diverted to meet other commitments. Obviously projects in more remote areas and agricultural schemes often take longest to come into operation, and accordingly longer grace periods are allowed than is usually the case with industrial projects. An attempt is made to quantify precisely the necessary grace period in terms of months as well as years, and the actual dates when repayments are due are clearly set out in each loan agreement, so that both parties know exactly their commitments. Rarely are the grace periods extended, as this would imply the Kuwait Fund admitting that either its own feasibility study was incorrect, or that the implementation was being incompetently administered.[15] In addition if the borrower saw that the grace period could easily be extended, then there would be less hope of subsequent payments being met on time. The emphasis on financial discipline is because it is the main means the Kuwait Fund has of ensuring efficient project implementation. To date the longest grace period allowed was nine years on a loan to the remote Comoros Islands in the Indian Ocean, a loan in which only 1 per cent interest was levied, which was also exceptional.[16]

Repayments periods also vary considerably according to the nature of the project and the overall economic circumstances of the country concerned. Less weight is given to the latter with respect to repayments scheduling, however, as over a long time span a country's economic fortunes can change considerably, and it is extremely hazardous to predict one, or even two decades into the future. Partly for this reason, Kuwait Fund officials prefer to concentrate on the potential future income generated by the project itself, adopting in other words standard micro-appraisal techniques and ignoring macro considerations. Loan periods are usually shorter for directly productive projects in the industrial field. Fifteen years was allowed, for example, for a phosphate fertiliser project in Jordan,[17] while a fisheries scheme in Malta was allowed 14 years. Infrastructure schemes are usually allowed longer repayments periods as they are less directly productive, 20 to 25 years being the typical period. The longest period ever allowed was for the Comoros Islands road scheme already mentioned, as in this case repayments were spread over 30 years, giving a total loan period for the project of 39 years when the lengthy grace period is added. All repayments are on a bi-annual basis, and the Kuwait Fund has tried to ensure that the repayments for different projects are paid at dates spread throughout each six month period, to facilitate a reasonably even cash flow.

To calculate the grant element in any development assistance through lending, it is necessary to take account of both the length of the grace period and the difference between the concessionary interest rate charged and full commercial rates of interest. The grant element in Kuwait Fund lending usually varies from around one-third to two-thirds, the subsidy again being highest for infrastructure projects and agricultural schemes in the poorest recipients, and lowest for directly productive industrial projects, reflecting of course what has already been indicated with respect to interest terms and grace periods. Not surprisingly, the Comoros loan appears to have had the largest grant element to date, amounting to 77 per cent according to the Kuwait Fund's calculations.[18] In recent years the grant element has risen, reflecting the general increase in commercial rates of interest in the Kuwait financial market. When calculating the grant element the Fund takes the current bank rate on Kuwait dinar loans to prime borrowers which are made by local financial institutions in Kuwait. These are lower than rates on Euro-dinar loans in Bahrain, and most rates in international financial markets generally, as the Kuwait authorities have been keen to restrain domestic interest charges. To this extent the grant element is underestimated. However, as the Kuwait dinar is a fairly strong currency, and has tended to appreciate against most European currencies and the United States dollar, this must be considered an offsetting factor, as all loans are denominated in dinar.[19]

COMPETITIVENESS AND COMPLEMENTARY ASPECTS OF NATIONAL AID AGENCIES

The other national aid agencies were founded later than the Kuwait Fund, as Table 7.2 indicates, and to a large extent have followed its example in their lending practice. When oil revenue was beginning to become more significant in the early 1970s for Abu Dhabi, Sheikh Zayed, its ruler, decided to set up an aid agency, as he was conscious of the vulnerable position of his small sheikhdom. He was well aware of the recognition and allies that the Kuwait Fund had won for its own government, and hoped his aid agency would prove as politically successful. At the same time there was a realisation that the mere fact that Kuwait had a well-publicised agency would mean that Abu Dhabi, with even more surplus wealth in relation to its small indigenous population, would be open to criticism if some formal aid mechanism was not established. As Abu Dhabi and the other Emirates of the lower Gulf had been more closely involved with the British than even Kuwait, and as the union of the Emirates was to a large extent a

British creation, Sheikh Zayed realised that his country was open to the charge of being an instrument of neo-colonialism, a common cry in radical Arab quarters at that time. Interestingly, however, although the major means of Abu Dhabi ensuring its political independence from its neighbour across the Gulf was through the union with the other lower Gulf emirates, the aid agency was a specifically Abu Dhabi-run body, and not a federal institution representing all the emirates. If Abu Dhabi was to act as paymaster, then it was to obtain the political credit, and run the agency itself.

There is little doubt that the Abu Dhabi Fund for Arab Economic Development enjoys less autonomy from local political decision making than the Kuwait Fund,[20] as the tradition of largesse being personally in the hands of the ruler remains to a greater extent in the lower Gulf. Heads of state and ministers visiting Abu Dhabi are often promised assistance by the ruling family, and then the request is passed on to the Abu Dhabi Fund to work out the details. Such a subordination of function would not be acceptable to Abdtalif Al-Hamad of the Kuwait Fund, but there is no similar strong personality at the Abu Dhabi Fund, and Kuwait is governed in a much more decentralised way in any case. It would be mistaken to believe however that the Abu Dhabi Fund does not adopt as high a standard of project appraisal as the Kuwait Fund, it is merely that some projects appear in its books owing to rather arbitrary factors in the first instance, and it is the Fund, in collaboration with the relevant ministries in the recipient countries, that has to try to translate promises into viable projects. There is little question that some schemes have been quietly dropped, often to the satisfaction of all parties, at least at the administrative level, if not at top government level.

The Saudi Development Fund has been even more susceptible to political pressure than the Abu Dhabi Fund, given the politically conscious environment of Riyadh. Whereas the board of directors of the Kuwait Fund tends to pass most executive decisions without much discussion, and Abdtalif Al-Hamad usually steers the meetings himself, government ministers are certainly more influential on the board of the Saudi Fund, and the Minister of Finance and National Economy attends and chairs most meetings. In theory the Kuwaiti Prime Minister is chairman of its Fund's board, but he often delegates his authority to someone else, who is perhaps less well-briefed about procedures and the commitments supposedly being monitored. Nevertheless the confidence of the executive officers in their own decision-making ability has been increasing in recent years, and there are signs that the autonomy of the organisation is increasing. Whether the agency would ever refuse to implement pledges made by the ruling family or senior ministers must nevertheless be questioned. As the sample listing of recent loans cited in Table 7.5 shows however, the conditions of lending are not much at variance with those of the Kuwait Fund. The table cites one at least partly politically motivated loan, that by Abu Dhabi to Oman for oil development, which would otherwise have been less viable, and in which the oil companies showed less interest before Abu Dhabi's support. All Omani requests have to be seriously considered, given its proximity to the Emirates, despite its serious state of under-development. The oil development funded was partly in Oman's previously politically troubled south.[21]

Potential borrowers from the Arab national aid agencies should be aware that if they are rejected by one agency, or find its terms unfavourable, there is little point in going to another agency, as the various agencies freely swap information. Although there is some degree of competition in the sense that each wishes to be the first to participate in any new sound project that is put forward, there is no evidence that particular Arab agencies work to exclude their counterparts in other countries. Indeed they work closely together, and even invite each other to participate in particular projects as a means of spreading the risk. This can also save on administrative overheads, as usually only one agency carries out the project appraisal, and the others trust its judgement when they participate, much as participants in a syndicated loan have faith in the lead manager. In the majority of cases it is the Kuwait Fund which has taken the initiative and carried out most of the appraisal work itself while inviting the other agencies to subscribe, but the newer agencies have been getting more venturesome in recent years, and there are some cases where the Abu Dhabi and Saudi Funds have taken the lead.

The instances where a single agency will cover the entire aid element of a project are now becoming fewer, and often apply only to the smaller schemes. Many involve collaboration with non-Arab development assistance agencies such as the World Bank, United Nations aid bodies, and United States and European government agencies. A complete assistance package is often put together, with individual Arab agencies subscribing 10 to 20 per cent of the total costs of the project. Other external aid agencies may provide up to half the total costs, while the recipient government will meet local currency costs, and finance at least a portion of foreign exchange costs

TABLE 7.5 *Sample national aid agency lending*

Borrower		Purpose	Amount ($ million)	Interest (%)	Repayments period (years)	Grace period (years)	Grant element (%)
Kuwait Fund (1979)	Jordan	Potash	34.1	4.0	20	5.7	40
	Mauritania	Highway	20.4	0.5	24	4.5	67
	Morocco	Dam	23.8	3.0	24	4.3	48
	Sudan	Sugar	20.4	4.0	19	3.4	37
	Senegal	Irrigation	5.4	3.0	24	3.9	48
Abu Dhabi Fund (1979)	Morocco	Agriculture	10.5	4.5	15	5.0	N/E
	Oman	Oil development	174.9	4.0	5	2.0	N/E
	Malagasy	Hydro-energy	4.2	3.4	10	5.0	N/E
	Seychelles	Oil-fired power	0.8	4.5	10	2.0	N/E
Saudi Fund (1978)	Gabon	Railways	21.0	4.0	20	5.0	35
	Somalia	Sugar	75.8	3.0	20	5.0	44
	Morocco	Phosphate port	35.8	4.0	20	5.0	35
	Brazil	Power transmission lines	57.9	5.0	20	5.0	29

NOTE N/E = not estimated.

SOURCE Annual reports of the institutions cited.

by borrowing on international capital markets. The participation of the Arab aid agencies in the less commercially viable aspects of a particular project has often raised potential returns on the remainder of the project, and increased overall confidence in the scheme. This has enabled recipient governments to borrow the commercial share of the funding through the Euro-markets on more favourable terms than might otherwise have been the case. [22]

Where more than one agency is involved in funding, it reduces the likelihood that national political pressures will be brought to bear over the allocation of development assistance. Significantly only the Abu Dhabi Fund participated in the loan for Omani oil development, an operation which alone has accounted for almost a quarter of all the agency's total commitments by 1980. In contrast the Abu Dhabi Fund only committed 16 per cent of the total project costs of a drainage system loan to North Yemen in 1978, while the Saudi Fund and the United States Agency for International Development contributed the remainder. The Abu Dhabi Fund contributed a mere 12 per cent of the total foreign currency requirements for the Gharb agricultural scheme in Morocco, while the Saudi Fund and the Arab Fund for Economic and Social Development contributed the rest. Similarly a highway project in Mauritania in 1979 was aided by the Kuwait Fund which took a 24 per cent stake of the foreign currency loan, while the Saudi and Abu Dhabi Funds committed themselves to similar shares. [23]

Despite the attention which academic economists and development specialists give to shadow pricing, none of the Arab development agencies have relied on these techniques of project appraisal to any significant extent. The wages of domestic workers are taken as those prevailing locally in the project area, while expatriate staff are costed at internationally competitive salaries for those working in harsh environments. No attempt is made to allow for the marginal productivity of labour approaching zero, and the emphasis is seldom on the employment-creating aspects of particular projects. Implementation is to be carried out at minimum cost, whether labour or capital costs, and the emphasis is on the increased output contribution which the projects will bring, and not on input utilisation. Fund managers believe shadow pricing for labour is inoperative in practice, as it is impossible to agree on what the shadow price should be, and it only distracts from determining what is viable, as well as making comparisons between projects more difficult. Capital however is costed at international prices, and not those prevailing under tariff conditions. This tends to lower the cost of capital *vis-à-vis* labour, and introduce a bias towards capital intensity, but the agencies and their consultants justify this on grounds of efficiency and speedy project implementation.[24] Many of the projects are in remote areas where labour is hard to find in any case, and even where recipient countries have under-employed labour in the cities and in agriculture, this cannot be easily redeployed. In any case projects are often only labour intensive at the implementation stage, and the problem of redeploying construction labour on a scheme's completion is often acute.

Project managers in all the Arab national aid agencies are keen to point out how their aid is untied, in comparison to western aid from national agencies, which should help to lower capital costs. In western countries with substantial industrial bases, government aid is often tied to the purchase of capital equipment or other products which the donor country produces. This helps its own industries, while at the same time minimising the foreign exchange cost of the aid, except in so far as there is an opportunity cost involved as the goods could be sold in other export markets. As this has seldom been the case, given the demand deficiencies for capital goods, especially in the 1970s, the case for tied aid has increased. The major Arab aid donors have only limited industrial capacity, however, and none have capital goods industries. Therefore the finance they provide can be spent on goods from anywhere, regardless of national discrimination, and the only criteria for purchase is the price and suitability of the goods. In this sense it is argued the Arab national aid agency assistance can be utilised much more appropriately, and projects can be implemented at a lower price than otherwise. Certainly it seems justifiable to compare Arab aid in this respect with multilateral assistance from the World Bank or United Nations agencies, rather than with bilateral western aid which is usually tied to some extent.[25]

SPECIALISED DEVELOPMENT INSTITUTIONS

The Arab Fund for Economic and Social Development was the earliest aid agency of a specialist type, its specialisation being in the purposes designated for its lending rather than its methods of providing assistance, as is the case with the Islamic Development Bank considered in Chapter 4. Merely looking at the conditions specified with Arab Fund loans in terms of the grace periods offered, interest rate structure and repayments schedules, reveals little difference from the national aid agencies, except that the grant element is slightly higher, reflecting generally lower interest rates, and marginally longer grace and repayments periods. Unlike the Kuwait, Abu Dhabi and Saudi Funds, however, the Arab Fund is a multinational, yet wholly Arab organisation, in which all the member states of the Arab League have a share of the capital, although the organisation is completely independent of the Arab League itself.[26] Subscriptions are left to the individual members to determine for themselves rather than being worked out on the basis of national income level, and Kuwait, which took the initiative to found the Fund, is the largest shareholder, followed by Saudi Arabia and Libya. Kuwait alone accounts for over one-fifth of the capital and together with Saudi Arabia and Libya commands a majority of the shares, and hence a majority of the votes on the board as these are related to share subscriptions. Only 25 per cent of the votes are required to call a meeting of the board of directors, and a resolution can be passed by a two-thirds majority.[27] The voting system is thus similar to that in a commercial company, but it means that Kuwait's vote is almost nineteen times greater than that of the Lebanon or Bahrain, and over thirty-three times greater than that of Palestine which is also represented in the organisation.

In practice Kuwait, where the Fund has been located since its inception in 1968, dominates most of the proceedings, and Abdtalif Al-Hamad, the head of the Kuwait Fund, is also represented on the board of directors of the Arab Fund. When there was dissatisfaction with the way the Fund was being run in 1977, and charges of administrative incompetence, the Kuwaitis instigated the dismissal of the president, and Al-Hamad took over himself until a new president was appointed. At that time new lending was suspended for a two-year period while an investigation was carried out on behalf of the directors, but under a new Syrian president the Fund became fully operational again.[28]

When the Arab Fund was created there was a deliberate intention of making its lending objectives different to those of the Kuwait Fund, so that it would not be a mere duplication despite the contrast in ownership structure. Therefore it was decided that it should concentrate on projects involving two or more Arab countries, in border zones for example, or irrigation works affecting contiguous states in a river valley, or schemes where exports would be promoted from one Arab country to another. As a multinational Arab institution this emphasis on projects involving inter-governmental co-operation was seen as particularly appropriate. In addition it was proposed that the Fund should support social projects such as housing, hospital building, provision of domestic water supplies and other community services. The Kuwait Fund primarily backed productive ventures such as industrial or agricultural development or infrastructural schemes which would contribute to economic advance. There was thought to be a gap in the provision of finance for socially desirable services, which it was hoped the Arab Fund would help fill. It was even envisaged that both Funds could usefully collaborate, with the Arab Fund providing the social support for particular project areas, while the Kuwait Fund financed the more directly productive aspects of any scheme.

In practice these ideas did not work out, as it was extremely difficult to find projects involving more than one Arab state which would help promote co-operation. Thus the Arab Fund concentrated most of its lending on projects within individual countries, in much the same way as the Kuwait Fund. The only inter-Arab schemes supported were for telecommunications facilities between Algeria and Morocco, and the Aden–Taiz highway linking North and South Yemen.[29] Even the fertiliser schemes funded in Egypt were primarily to serve Egyptian farmers, and it was not envisaged that the Talkba project would produce surplus fertiliser for export. The major scheme proposed for inter-Arab collaboration involved agricultural development in the Sudan, which was viewed as a potential breadbasket for the Arab world as a whole, and a crucial source of food for the desert states of Arabia just across the Red Sea from Port Sudan. As the agency entrusted with inter-Arab co-operation, the Arab Fund drew up an ambitious development strategy for the country, including many new rural development, export-orientated projects.[30] Getting these projects beyond the feasibility study stage has proved a problem, however, given the backward conditions prevailing in Sudan. The Arab Fund itself has funded three road schemes and one railway project in the Sudan to facilitate marketing of agricultural products, and the giant Kenana sugar scheme, which is funded by the Kuwait Fund, will benefit from this new infrastructure. Apart from sugar, however, other export crops remain at the planning stage, and it seems likely to be decades rather than years before Sudan will ever supply a wide range of agricultural produce to other Arab countries.

The Arab Fund's project list does not differ markedly from that of the national aid agencies, as most projects involve infrastructure work, and, although there are a few water supply and sewerage projects on its books, there are not many other obviously social schemes. Housing projects are conspicuously absent for instance, as are health and hospital schemes. One reason for this is simply the Arab Fund's limited resources, which means it can only undertake a few feasibility studies itself. It has therefore been easier to support schemes in collaboration with the national aid agencies, which they found sound as a result of their own feasibility studies, or as a result of the findings of consultants they commissioned. The administrative capacity of the Arab Fund is severely limited, and even the supervision of the work of privately-hired consultants has been far from easy.[31] As the Arab Fund was obliged to employ only Arab staff, and as the number of suitably qualified personnel remains in short supply, this has aggregated its difficulties, especially as the national aid agencies are competing for the same people. Often there is a preference for working for national agencies as decisions get taken more speedily, and there is not the same potential for disputes amongst board members as in a multinational institution. Those wanting to work in Kuwait usually prefer to be with the Kuwait Fund, especially given the autonomy of its executive, and the professional way it has been run by Abdtalif Al-Hamad.

There is little doubt that inter-Arab political disputes have interfered with the smooth running of multinational Arab aid agencies such as the Arab Fund. The periodic tensions between Kuwait and Iraq have meant that sometimes the Iraqi governor has not attended board meetings, while those between Morocco and Algeria have not facilitated the implementation of their co-operative project. The greatest tensions of all however have arisen over Egypt, the largest single beneficiary of Arab Fund lending. Egypt's membership of the Fund was suspended following the establishment of diplomatic relations between Sadat's government and Israel, and an Egyptian representative no longer attends board meetings. No new loan commitments are being made to Egypt, although existing agreements are being honoured, and disbursements are continuing for projects under implementation. The same applies to national aid agency lending, although in these cases of course Egyptian nationals never sat on the board of directors.

Inter-Arab political differences have caused even greater problems for the Arab Bank for Economic Development in Africa (BADEA),[32] as, although the headquarters of this organisation was originally agreed to be in Khartoum, which made sense given the regional focus of the institution, during the mid-1970s this did not prove to be an ideal administrative centre because of the city's poor communications and lack of back-up facilities. Much of the routine administration was therefore carried out from the Cairo representative office in Giza, but as Egypt was suspended from BADEA in 1979, much of the work had to be transferred to the Khartoum office. This has proved less convenient, however, given BADEA's desire to collaborate with the Arab League, which has now moved its headquarters from Cairo to Tunis, and with various United Nations regional agencies which were strongly represented in Cairo, but not in Khartoum.

Despite these administrative difficulties BADEA has achieved a considerable degree of success with its lending activities and 37 major agreements were signed by 1980, with loans to aid 14 different countries agreed in 1979 alone.[33] BADEA has won considerable respect in sub-Saharan Africa, and has helped improve the Arab image throughout the continent. In this sense it has lived up to the objectives which originally motivated its establishment, as, although it is an economic organisation, the support for it was largely political. Two basic reasons were behind its creation, the first being to win friends for the Arab cause in Africa in the conflict with Israel. The Jerusalem government had already provided some aid and considerable technical assistance to a large number of African countries,[34] and the Arab nations felt they should be doing the same to counter Israeli influence.[35] A second factor was to deflect the growing criticism of the Arab petroleum exporters, especially in some parts of sub-Saharan Africa, as these states struggled to pay for their petroleum imports. The aid provided by BADEA however only represented a minute fraction of their increased oil import bills after the 1973–74 price rises, but at least the Arab petroleum exporters could point to something concrete which they were doing to alleviate any problems caused.

Like the other Arab aid agencies, BADEA provides only aid for specific projects, and not general budgetary or balance of payments support, although it has advanced some programme aid, notably emergency assistance to the drought-stricken Sahel countries of the Western Sahara. As a result of its own limited administrative capacity, it also collaborates wih other agencies lending to Africa from outside the continent, including the Arab national agencies, which saves it doing all the project appraisal work itself. In addition it has recently made lines of credit available to development banks in Africa which are already heavily involved in project finance, and hopes to extend this type of activity in the future. The Industrial Development Bank of Kenya for example was given help in this way, as was the West African

Development Board, which supports Senegal, the Ivory Coast, Upper Volta, Togo, Benin and Niger. In both these cases BADEA extended loans worth $5 million, repayable over 12 years with a three-year grace period. [36] The interest charged on the Kenyan loan was 7 per cent, while that on the West African loan was 6 per cent, but this is more generous than it appears relative to lending by agencies such as the Kuwait Fund, as credits are denominated in United States dollars which have tended to depreciate against Gulf currencies such as the Kuwaiti dinar. BADEA interest charges averaged 4 per cent during its first six years of operation, and repayments periods averaged twenty years.

Collaboration between BADEA and the OPEC Special Fund has been especially close, as the latter has made almost one-quarter of its commitments to the non-Arab African states which BADEA supports. The two agencies have jointly supported loans to Angola, Chad, The Gambia, Lesotho, Mali and Rwanda, mainly to finance infrastructure development or agricultural schemes. [37] The loan to Angola for example was to support repair work and improvements on the Benguela railway, with BADEA supplying $10 million and the OPEC Special Fund $3 million. The Chad loan was for agricultural development with BADEA committing $7.8 million while the OPEC Special Fund offered $4.85 million. Both agencies share one objective for their lending in Africa, namely to alleviate some of the criticism of the petroleum exporting countries by Third World states that the new financial surplus states are indifferent to the plight of their poorer neighbours. The OPEC Special Fund is however not a specifically Arab agency, as Iran also contributes, nor is it even a specifically Middle Eastern agency, as Nigeria, Ecuador, Indonesia and Venezuela are represented on its board as OPEC member states. [38] Hence it does not share the Arab concern about the need to influence states concerning the conflict with Israel.

Unlike BADEA, the OPEC Special Fund has not confined its assistance to project lending, but has also given wider balance of payments support. Between 1976 and 1978 over $190 million was lent in this way, with funds spread over the 49 developing countries most seriously affected by the petroleum price rises. [39] This amount is rather meagre in relation to the needs of these countries, but the terms of the balance of payments support have been extremely generous, as there is usually a five-year grace period, and 15 years for repayment of the original sum lent, with no interest charged to most beneficiaries. Interest is only required from those with potentially favourable balance of payments positions, due to mineral resources or other primary products such as hardwoods, for which there are good export prospects. In these cases an interest charge of 4 per cent is usually levied. Similar terms are granted on project lending, with no interest required from countries in chronic deficit.

Perhaps because it was late in entering the field of development assistance, OPEC's Special Fund has tried to carve out a distinctive role for itself, and has been more venturesome in its types of funding. Being located in Vienna is an advantage from the point of view of staff recruitment, and it is able to draw qualified personnel from all OPEC member states, and not just the Middle East. In addition, it has instigated much research and technical assistance work, and aided the United Nations Development Programme with respect to the Caribbean regional food plan and the integrated scheme for the development of the Suez Canal region.[40] The OPEC Special Fund is assisting with the establishment of an Industrial Vocational Training Complex in the canal area, which will provide facilities for skilled and semi-skilled workers.

The OPEC Special Fund also administers the disbursement of assistance from its member countries to the United Nations International Fund for Agricultural Development, and takes charge of the distribution of profits from the International Monetary Fund which accrue as a result of the latter selling its OPEC members gold subscriptions. These profits, which totalled $31 million by 1978, have been used to help developing countries through a trust fund.[41] A further task has been the preparation of papers for the United Nations Conferences on Trade and Development concerning the stabilisation of primary product prices, proposals which have been supported by OPEC member states. The Fund also compiles statistics on overall OPEC aid, and in general tries to provide useful back-up facilities which the foreign ministries of OPEC countries can use to help them determine their stance on various policy questions, especially those concerning the North–South dialogue and other related issues. Despite its short time in existence, the OPEC Special Fund is growing in stature and influence, and there is little doubt much more will be heard of the organisation in the future, not only in a Middle Eastern or OPEC context, but also in relation to the growing debate over development priorities worldwide.

Postscript

This study has aimed to provide a long-term view of the evolution of banking and finance in the Arab Middle East. The approach has been to place contemporary developments in a historical perspective. A book is anyway an inappropriate medium to portray the latest events: economic journalists can better report upon the most recent banking news. Excellent coverage of current developments in Arab finance is provided by *Euromoney* and *Middle East Economic Digest,* both published in London. *Euromoney* usually contains a survey of Arab banking at least once a year, and *Middle East Economic Digest* has issued a new quarterly publication, *Arab Banking and Finance.* A bi-monthly publication was launched in 1981, *Arab Banker,* the journal of the Arab Bankers' Association in London. An Annual *Arab Banking and Finance Handbook* is being issued by Falcon Publications of Bahrain from 1983. Features on Arab banking also appear regularly in *The Middle East, Arabia* and *Saudi Business,* as well as in British newspapers such as the *Financial Times* and *The Times,* and in the professional bankers' journal *The Banker.*

An author of a book has the advantage of being able to take a more leisurely and reflective approach. Hence it is sometimes possible to perceive trends that those reporting daily news may fail to detect. Frequently too much weight is given to a particular event, which in retrospect turns out to be less important than appears at the time. As financial markets often over-react, it is scarcely surprising that those who comment on their behaviour have the same tendency to exaggerate. Since the original manuscript of this book was completed over a year ago, several events have occurred which are worthy of mention. They are best seen, however, in the context of the trends which have been discussed in this book. Not surprisingly the major developments in Arab banking during 1981 and 1982 have all occurred in Saudi Arabia and the Gulf. It is this part of the Arab world that has witnessed the most rapid change in banking and finance during the last decade, and it is here that events continue to move swiftly.

The first major development is affecting the moneychangers and moneylenders whose operations are described in Chapter 1. In January 1982 new regulations were introduced by the Saudi Arabian Monetary Agency (SAMA) to control the activities of the moneylenders. The "informal" banking sector which consisted largely of the moneylenders had long prevented effective control of the kingdom's financial system. SAMA was unable even to monitor their domestic lending, or to control capital transfers abroad through these "souk" banks. Some measures to bring the moneylenders into line with the rest of the banking system were thought to be desirable, not because powers to control money supply or capital transfers were seen as an urgent necessity, but rather due to concern that in the future some control might be needed if the kingdom's economic circumstances changed adversely. The move to introduce controls was precautionary, not imperative.

In addition, there were worries in SAMA about the viability of some of the moneylenders themselves, and whether the collapse of one establishment would cause a loss of confidence in the Saudi financial system, which might have repercussions for the major banks. These worries were perhaps exaggerated, but in the summer of 1982 the Damman-based company of Abdullah Saleh Al-Rajhi collapsed as a result of unprofitable bullion dealings. The 40-branch chain had used clients' deposits to take spot and forward positions in the hazardous silver bullion market, and had lost heavily. As a result it was unable to meet demands for withdrawals. The other members of the Al-Rajhi family in Riyadh and Jeddah had long since disassociated themselves from their Damman cousin because of his speculative dealings. Hence they refused to help. The bankruptcy had international repercussions as Abdullah Saleh Al-Rajhi owed Thomas Cook $5.5 million for travellers' cheques, while Kreditbank, Belgium's third largest bank, was left with debts of $4.2 million. Kreditbank had acted on Al-Rajhi's behalf in the dealings with Mocatta and Goldsmid, the bullion-dealing subsidiary of Standard Chartered Bank.

The regulations which SAMA introduced to control the "informal" banking sector were wide ranging. Moneychangers were obliged to apply for licences to continue their operations. These licences were granted for a three-year period, and would only be renewed subject to scrutiny of the moneychanger's accounts by SAMA itself. Moneychangers were to confine their activities to the exchange of currency and travellers' cheques. Transfer services for remittances or the payment of foreign exporters were permitted provided moneychangers maintained a minimum capital reserve of 2 million riyals ($590,000), plus an additional 500,000 riyals for each additional branch they operated. Furthermore, moneychangers were given until 1985 to liquidate all business not directly associated with changing currency. The taking of new deposits was to be prohibited from the spring of 1983, and existing deposits were to be refunded once outstanding loans were liquidated.

If moneychangers wished to continue lending and deposit-taking activity, then they were obliged to apply for registration as fully fledged commercial banks. This would imply a stricter control by SAMA, and the maintenance of the usual banking reserve requirements, amounting to 2 per cent for savings deposits and 7 per cent for demand deposits as indicated in Chapter 4. The conventional banks in Saudi Arabia had long complained to SAMA that the moneylenders had an unfair advantage, in not being required to maintain unprofitable cash reserves, or non-interest bearing deposits with the monetary authority. SAMA's new measures will effectively eliminate this allegedly unfair competition, as most of the moneylenders are expected to revert to being moneychangers. Only the firm of Suleiman Al-Rajhi is thought likely to register as a fully fledged commercial bank, given the size of its deposit-taking and lending business. This registration will have to be completed during 1983 under the regulations, but such a move should formalise the Suleiman Al-Rajhi group's position as the third force in Saudi commercial banking after the National Commercial and Riyadh Banks.

The second major development in finance in the Arabian peninsula in 1982 was in the Kuwait stock market. Kuwait's role as an investment centre was described in Chapter 5, including the significance of its stock market as the largest in the Middle East or the Arab world as a whole. The country has in fact two stock markets, the official market which is regulated by a securities commission, and an unofficial market, the Souk Al-Manakh. There are 42 Kuwaiti public companies quoted on the official market, all of which have to produce detailed annual accounts and submit to a full audit. Shares in companies registered in Bahrain and the United Arab Emirates are, however, traded on the unofficial Souk Al-Manakh, as neither Bahrain nor the United Arab Emirates have stock markets of their own as already indicated. It is perhaps not surprising that it was on the unofficial market where problems arose, although this also affected the official market even if only temporarily, as share price movements in one market tend to reflect changes in the other.

Many companies whose shares are traded on the Souk Al-Manakh of course produce some accounts, but the authorities in Bahrain and the United Arab Emirates did not require the kind of information that would be normally needed for a stock market quotation, as that was not their concern. Some of the companies offering share issues were originally much smaller than would usually be considered adequate for a stock market quotation in London or other Western centres. The Kuwaiti authorities had relaxed their regulations to permit non-Kuwaiti Gulf companies to register on the official market, but only two had taken advantage of this, Gulf Real Estate and Gulf Agriculture. A minimum capital of 5 million dinars ($17.5 million) was required for registration, and in addition the company had to report two profitable years. Some of the companies whose shares were traded on the Souk Al-Manakh had not even been in existence for two years, and had capital bases well below the limit for an official quotation.

During 1981 and the first half of 1982 the rise in share values on the Souk Al-Manakh was so rapid that hitherto small companies became substantial operations, at least on paper. The Bahrain International Bank, for example, which first issued shares on the unofficial market in January 1982, found its shares rising by 270 per cent in the first few weeks following the issue. Share prices were also rising rapidly in the official market during the 1981–2 period, but the rises in the unofficial market were much more impressive. Whereas the Kuwaiti all-share index doubled between April 1981 and April 1982, the unofficial share index more than trebled over the same period. With such enormous potential gains, investors from Kuwait and other Gulf states rushed to buy shares through the 40 brokers who dealt in the unofficial market. Small investors in particular were attracted to the unofficial market, as to deal on their own account an initial investment of only 40,000 dinars was needed, less than half the amount required for dealing on the official market.

Unlike the official market, and untypically for Kuwait, Souk Al-Manakh operated from extremely shoddy premises. Most of the dealing was carried out on the ground floor shopping area of a rather run-down office block. There was a shortage of telephones, and a general atmosphere of chaos prevailed for much of the time. Despite the conditions confidence remained high, and it was felt that if a catastrophe occurred, the government would always intervene to rescue the fortunes of the investors. Once before, in 1977, when the official market was threatened with collapse, the government had launched a 150 million dinar rescue operation, which had turned the market round, and saved many from bankruptcy. Ironically it was the government's efforts to preserve an orderly market, and restrict the number of new shares issued on the official market, that aided the rise of Souk Al-Manakh. There was an unsatisfied demand for Gulf investments, and Souk Al-Manakh was to rise as the means of response. To some extent the market was also fuelled with funds from those who had become disillusioned with investments in Western stock markets in view of the exchange risks involved. The appreciation of the dinar against many Western currencies brought losses for Kuwaiti investors on conversion that more than wiped out any capital gains on their stock holdings.

The ultimate collapse of Souk Al-Manakh in August 1982 was brought about by several factors, not least some profit taking, and worries over the consequences for Kuwait of Iraq's reversals in the Gulf War with Iran. The main cause of collapse however was when the system of purchasing shares with post-dated cheques ran out of control, and some large payments started to fall due. This system had arisen when the size of the market started to outstrip the ability of Kuwait's banking system to provide sufficient liquidity to cover transaction needs. Rather than investors accepting the constraint offered by the funds they had available, or could borrow from the banks, some investors started to acquire shares with post-dated cheques. Such was the confidence in those dealing in the market, and the degree of trust, that sellers were prepared to accept these cheques. Honesty in dealings had always been one of the more attractive features of the Kuwaiti financial community, where everyone knew everyone else, and a coffee house atmosphere prevailed as described in Chapter 5.

The post-dated cheques were nevertheless only accepted at a premium, and by the summer of 1982 some buyers were writing cheques for up to 300 per cent of the value of the shares they were buying. Two speculators in particular, Najib Al-Mutawa and his cousin Jassim Al-Mutawa, had written post-dated cheques valued at 5.7 billion dinars and 3 billion dinars, respectively. Both cousins, however, held substantial amounts of post-dated cheques themselves which other investors had used to purchase their share holdings. Nevertheless rumours started to circulate that Najib Al-Mutawa's net liabilities were a staggering 1.5 billion dinars, and those of Jassim Al-Mutawa were 0.5 billion dinars. Neither cousin was thought likely to be able to meet his commitments when the cheques were drawn upon, even if the underlying values of the shares continued their rapid rise. These rumours were sufficient to cause share prices to start falling, and the authorities were forced to intervene to close the market before too much damage was done. By then the total value of the 28,861 post-dated cheques outstanding had reached an astronomical 26.6 billion dinars.

The collapse resulted in heated questions in the Kuwaiti parliament, and even unprecedented calls for the resignation of the Finance Minister, Abdtalif Al-Hamad, formerly the head of the Kuwait Fund for Arab Economic Development as mentioned in Chapter 7. It required someone with Al-Hamad's financial ability however to sort out the problems, and he remained in power to carry out this task. Unlike the earlier 1977 crash of the official market there was no rescue package, with the government subsidising market speculators. Instead a new body, the Kuwait Clearing Company, was established under Hilal Al-Mutairy of the Kuwait Investment Company. The Clearing Company compiled a register of all the post-dated cheques, and netted out the transactions. After this was done 7 billion dinars were left outstanding. The Clearing Company was then empowered to write down the value of the outstanding debt by eliminating most of the premiums paid for accepting post-dated cheques. A maximum premium of 16 per cent was allowed in excess of the value of the stock purchased. Then those small investors who were owed 100,000 dinars or less were compensated immediately in cash by the Clearing Company. Those owed up to 250,000 dinars were compensated by bonds due to mature in February 1983. Successively longer periods for the bonds to mature were decreed for those owed large amounts. Those owed up to 1 million dinars were compensated in bonds which were not due to mature until June 1987. This eased the payment commitments for the government given the enormous amounts involved. At the same time bond holders were permitted to discount their bonds at the banks, which enabled them to obtain cash to discharge their debts. In this way it was hoped the liquidity of the Kuwaiti economy would be restored, especially if the bonds were substituted for some of the banks' foreign asset holdings.

The maximum sum which the government was prepared to pay out as compensation to any single individual was limited to 2 million dinars. As the eight largest investors in the market together accounted for 18.5 billion dinars, or two thirds of the total amount outstanding, this group clearly stood to lose heavily. Some of these, however, had their debts written off by their creditors as people rallied round their friends in Kuwait's tightly-knit financial circle. One investor, Humud Al-Jabri, a member of Kuwait's parliament, had debts of 16 million dinars cancelled. Only the Al-Mutawa cousins faced the prospect of total bankruptcy, and few regretted their fate, as they were partly responsible for the collapse of the market. Those in the most serious difficulties were the non-Kuwaitis who had entered the market, as the Kuwaiti authorities did not feel obliged to compensate them. Bahraini investors were owed more than 11 million dinars, and those from the United Arab Emirates were owed almost 40 million dinars. The UAE Chamber of Commerce and Industry however registered the claims of all UAE citizens, and is pressing their claims with the Kuwaiti authorities.

The equitable and ingenuous solution found to the crisis seemed to satisfy most Kuwaiti investors and critics of Al-Hamad. In fact, notwithstanding the problems non-citizens faced, the competence shown by the authorities in coping with the aftermath of the Souk Al-Manakh collapse increased confidence in Kuwait as an investment centre. There were no indications of business being transferred to other Gulf centres, and prices on Kuwait's official market started to rise again soon after the whole affair was dealt with. The unofficial Al-Manakh market itself reopened in October 1982, less than 2 months after the collapse. This resilience of the Kuwait market must be encouraging for the future, as it illustrates the durability of the financial structures being created in the Gulf. The only casualty in the long-term has probably been the mutual trust that formerly prevailed in the Kuwait market amongst investors, but such a loss may be unfortunately part of the process of maturing.

Developments since 1980 have tended to reinforce the specialised roles of the different Gulf centres outlined in Chapter 5. Bahrain's role continued as a money market centre, and offshore banking thrived despite the turndown in petroleum revenues in Saudi Arabia and the Gulf as a whole. Profits of Bahrain's 65 offshore banking units totalled $344 million in 1981, a 76 per cent increase over the previous year. In contrast, by 1982 the Bahrain aluminium smelter, the major industrial employer in the economy, was running at a loss. This favourable performance of the banking sector must be regarded as a justification of the policy of the Bahrain authorities in offering encouragement to service activities on the island, especially as it has involved virtually no government financial outlay, unlike industrial investments.

The offshore banking units have become increasingly Arab in their overall composition, particularly since the establishment of the Arab Banking Corporation with its headquarters on the island. By mid-1982 the Arab Banking Corporation's total assets had already reached over $6 billion, most of which were redeposited with other banks. Commercial loans and advances accounted for around a quarter of all assets, but this is expected to increase substantially in 1983. In its first two years of operation the Arab Banking Corporation concentrated on asset growth, most of its deposits also coming from other banks. As its staff expands from the 1982 level of just 170, it is expected to move away from merely wholesale banking into having more direct customer contact with industrial borrowers, especially from the Gulf region. One recent development may threaten this kind of business move however, not only by the Arab Banking Corporation, but by all the other offshore banks. The commercial banks in Saudi Arabia are increasingly resentful that banks in Bahrain are encroaching upon some of their most profitable lending business. In response to their lobbying, SAMA has threatened to introduce a withholding tax which domestic borrowers would have to pay on funds advanced from Bahrain. Although the rate proposed, 15 per cent of the interest payable, is modest, it would be sufficient to eliminate any competitive edge which the Bahraini banks might have.

Of even more fundamental significance were the measures announced by the new Central Bank of the United Arab Emirates. Soon after this centralised body was established at the end of 1980, it sought to consolidate the commercial bank sector in the Emirates, where there were thought to be too many institutions competing, some of which were inadequately funded. Two small banks were forced into liquidation in the Emirates in 1977 as a result of lending for real estate speculation. Once the real estate boom came to an end and land and apartment prices fell, the borrowers were unable to repay the banks, and both institutions had inadequate reserves to cover their bad debts. Under Union Law no. 10 of 1980, the Central Bank instructed all banks operating in the Emirates to increase their paid-up capital to a minimum of 40 million dirhams ($10.9 million) by the end of 1982. Virtually all the banks have now complied with this law, which it was hoped would help avoid future bankruptcies in the financial sector.

In addition, in order to strengthen the position of the indigenous banks the Central Bank decided to limit the foreign banks to maintaining a maximum of 8 offices each in the Emirates. As there were 28 foreign banks operating in the Emirates and 21 indigenous banks, this measure had drastic implications. Over 83 foreign branch banks are being closed over the 1982–3 period, with the British Bank of the Middle East and the Bank of Credit and Commerce being the most adversely affected. Although the latter is partly owned by interests from Abu Dhabi as indicated in Chapter 3, it is nevertheless still regarded as a foreign bank in the United Arab Emirates. The changes in ownership structure, which BCC's president Agha Hasan Abedi brought about, have certainly not proved beneficial as far as the bank's retail banking business in the Emirates is concerned. The future for foreign banks in the Emirates has become more uncertain in the 1980s, although the Central Bank stated in May 1982 that it had no desire to proceed further and indigenise the foreign banks by stipulating a 60-per cent local ownership share, as the authorities in Saudi Arabia have done. Nevertheless a new company law was approved in Abu Dhabi in October 1982 stating that all companies operating in the Emirates should be under majority local ownership. This law is not to be applied to the banking sector, but even the foreign merchant banks operating out of Dubai are beginning to feel uncomfortable.

These moves in the Emirates will probably enhance Bahrain's position as the only centre in the Gulf where the future for foreign banks seems reasonably secure. However, the Central Bank in the Emirates has also acted against an outflow of capital to Bahrain. Banks in the Emirates lending funds offshore have been obliged since May 1982 to deposit with the Central Bank, interest free, the equivalent of 30 per cent of the value of these loans if the funds are offshore for more than a year, and 15 per cent if the capital is exported for longer than 3 months. This has effectively ended the market for dirham loans in Bahrain, but at the same time it has eased the upward pressures on interest rates in the Emirates by increasing capital availability. Despite the moves towards greater economic co-operation which have resulted from the formation of the Gulf Co-operation Council in 1981, in the banking field at least, many of the Gulf states are behaving in a more, rather than a less, nationalistic fashion.

National controls cannot easily be extended or enforced overseas of course, although in some fields this may be a cause for regret. In the Islamic banking field, the major development of the 1980s has been the creation of Dar Al-Maal Al-Islami, the House of Islamic Funds. This new institution, which claims to be the first multinational Islamic bank, was founded by Prince Mohammad bin Faisal. As already mentioned in Chapter 4, Prince Mohammad is the chairman of the

International Association of Islamic Banks, and he has long been one of the main figures in the Islamic banking movement. His new bank is Geneva based, but was registered as a company in the Bahamas in 1981. Its planned capital is $1 billion, but the initial paid-up capital was $200 million, $60 million of which was accounted for by the Islamic Investment Company, in which Prince Mohammad has a major stake. The bank's business is monitored by an 18-man board of Islamic financial specialists to ensure that its operations accord with the Sharia Law. Although the director is a devout Egyptian Muslim, Ibrahim Kamel, many of the other staff are non-Muslims, as the company's policy was to recruit on merit.

Prince Mohammad's plans for Dar Al-Maal Al-Islami are extremely ambitious as the size of the planned capital indicates, and it is hoped to establish branches in Malaysia, Sri Lanka, Turkey, Pakistan, Brunei, Guinea and Morocco, but not in Saudi Arabia, the Prince's own country, or in the Gulf. It is anticipated that most of the capital and deposits will come from the devout of the Gulf. The initial response was poor however, and when a $200 million public share issue was launched in October 1981, few took up subscriptions. There is some scepticism about the bank's ability to find projects in the developing non-Arab states which it hopes to support, and much of its initial business involved redepositing with Western banks. Furthermore, the way the bank is incorporated to take advantage of tax haven status and Swiss bank secrecy laws is not approved of by many potential depositors. If the institution gets into difficulty, no Arab or Islamic government is likely to mount a rescue operation. The fear is that any problems encountered by this unusual multinational will rebound adversely on the rest of the Islamic banking community. There is a feeling that the new institution is trying to move too far and too fast. Many of those considering investment in Dar Al-Maal Al-Islami are waiting to see what its profit record is before committing themselves.

The significance of the advent of new financial institutions such as Dar Al-Maal Al-Islami can of course only be judged after several years of operational experience. Therefore this is perhaps the best point to conclude this postscript. To venture an assessment of such institutions at this stage would be to tread on very unsure ground indeed. This is best left as the terrain of the economic journalist.

November 1982

Statistical Appendix

TABLE A.1   *Total assets and liabilities of the commercial banks ($ millions)*

	1973	1974	1975	1976	1977	1978	1979	1980
Saudi Arabia	1,340	2,160	4,315	7,161	9,940	14,138	17,414	21,138
Kuwait	2,559	3,325	4,099	5,821	8,132	10,560	12,855	16,460
Egypt	4,271	6,387	8,501	10,719	13,524	16,601	11,158	14,579
UAE	878	2,191	3,620	5,983	7,359	8,922	11,088	12,172
Lebanon	3,440	4,900	5,537	4,433	5,268	6,436	7,678	9,196
Libya	1,365	2,170	2,863	3,352	3,924	4,201	4,955	N/A
Iraq	1,149	1,991	3,101	3,396	4,113[b]	N/A	N/A	N/A
Syria	808	1,249	1,820	2,482	2,797	3,074	3,753	N/A
Jordan	310	401	606	882	1,116	1,756	2,322	2,806
Bahrain	307	565	880	1,264	1,440	1,586	1,774	2,090
Sudan	415	509	719	918	1,400	1,707	2,006	1,981
Qatar	212	337	573	781	1,087	1,382	1,580	1,666[a]
Oman	118	422	519	691	711	800	931	1,190
North Yemen	61	84	164	411	460	568	649	775
South Yemen	58	64	104	146	231	241	332	418[a]

NOTES   N/A = not available; [a] = 2nd quarter, [b] = 3rd quarter. Conversions into dollars at average market rates used by IMF for trade conversions for each year. Falling values may therefore reflect depreciating exchange rates.

SOURCE   IMF, *International Financial Statistics*, Washington, February 1981.

TABLE A.2   *Commercial bank demand deposits ($ millions)*

	1973	1974	1975	1976	1977	1978	1979	1980
Saudi Arabia	602	900	2,131	3,875	6,295	8,832	9,226	10,154
Egypt	1,085	1,410	1,800	2,164	3,043	3,491	2,427	2,827
Libya	596	1,051	1,135	1,666	2,004	1,890	2,394	N/A
Kuwait	343	388	649	905	1,186	1,672	1,642	2,061
Syria	250	480	713	799	934	1,246	1,416	N/A
UAE	176	279	499	923	980	1,052	1,126	1,284
Lebanon	533	705	687	622	749	953	972	1,058
Jordan	125	174	264	343	425	489	606	723
Iraq	209	314	507	627	637[b]	N/A	N/A	N/A
Qatar	75	103	194	304	400	447	470	570[a]
Bahrain	111	112	136	237	275	328	357	344
Sudan	26	34	42	54	79	110	167	241
Oman	28	56	95	155	161	143	140	161
South Yemen	22	30	41	51	78	78	119	153[a]
North Yemen	16	20	46	100	120	144	159	145

NOTES   As Table A.1.

TABLE A.3   *Commercial bank time and savings deposits ($ millions)*

	1973	1974	1975	1976	1977	1978	1979	1980
Kuwait	1,234	1,667	2,072	2,826	3,762	4,782	5,768	7,342
Lebanon	1,959	2,823	2,950	2,172	3,032	3,730	4,686	5,633
Egypt	838	1,269	1,452	2,105	2,969	4,247	3,561	4,795
UAE	322	1,062	1,555	3,032	2,639	3,046	3,129	3,795
Saudi Arabia	384	546	892	1,221	1,662	2,244	2,792	3,792
Libya	512	871	834	995	1,345	1,304	2,088	N/A
Jordan	112	148	199	298	410	739	989	1,178
Iraq	405	586	871	1,067	1,160[b]	N/A	N/A	N/A
Bahrain	101	213	268	445	513	595	591	778
Qatar	91	123	189	284	374	467	535	688[a]
Syria	83	122	167	213	283	364	455	N/A
Oman	62	105	132	178	272	332	351	450
Sudan	84	115	138	178	263	312	331	320
North Yemen	22	32	56	151	169	269	275	340
South Yemen	27	29	48	62	103	70[c]	94	113[a]

NOTES AND SOURCE   As Table A.1, except note[c]. This indicates the re-assignment in 1978 for South Yemen which accounts for a large part of its fall that year.

TABLE A.4 Ratio of time and savings deposits to demand deposits (*$ millions*)

	1973	1974	1975	1976	1977	1978	1979	1980
Lebanon	3.67	4.00	4.29	3.49	4.04	3.91	4.82	5.32
Kuwait	3.60	4.30	3.19	3.12	3.17	2.86	3.51	3.56
UAE	1.83	3.81	3.12	3.28	2.69	2.89	2.78	2.95
Oman	2.21	1.87	1.39	1.15	1.69	2.32	2.51	2.79
North Yemen	1.37	1.60	1.22	1.51	1.41	1.87	1.73	2.34
Bahrain	0.91	1.90	1.97	1.88	1.86	1.81	1.65	2.26
Iraq	1.94	1.86	1.72	1.70	1.82[b]	N/A	N/A	N/A
Egypt	0.77	0.90	0.81	0.97	0.98	1.22	1.47	1.70
Jordan	0.90	0.85	0.75	0.87	0.96	1.51	1.63	1.63
Sudan	3.23	3.38	3.28	3.30	3.33	2.84	1.98	1.32
Qatar	1.21	1.19	0.97	0.93	0.93	1.04	1.14	1.21[a]
Libya	0.86	0.83	0.73	0.60	0.67	0.69	0.87	N/A
South Yemen	1.22	0.97	1.17	1.22	1.32	0.89[c]	0.79	0.73[a]
Saudi Arabia	0.63	0.61	0.42	0.31	0.26	0.25	0.30	0.37
Syria	0.33	0.25	0.23	0.27	0.30	0.29	0.32	N/A

NOTES   As Tables A.1 and A.3.

SOURCES   Computed from Tables A.2 and A.3.

TABLE A.5 *Commercial bank lending to private sector ($ millions)*

	1973	1974	1975	1976	1977	1978	1979	1980
Saudi Arabia	637	1,248	1,909	2,799	3,085	4,235	7,955	10,117
Kuwait	846	1,212	1,748	3,195	4,316	5,693	7,687	9,600
UAE	407	849	1,437	2,651	4,056	5,002	5,553	6,582
Lebanon	1,789	2,460	2,967	2,499	2,616	3,351	4,022	4,458
Egypt	1,038	1,502	2,255	2,935	3,934	4,582	3,427	4,046
Libya	915	1,525	2,178	2,507	2,893	3,139	3,541	N/A
Jordan	181	253	378	591	696	1,023	1,479	1,778
Bahrain	184	305	406	678	786	840	985	1,121
Sudan	283	354	534	655	759	913	1,083	1,015
Qatar	126	190	286	393	623	745	884	924[a]
Oman	54	188	245	343	477	566	636	779
Syria	171	187	233	297	342	421	599	N/A
Iraq	268	347	401	450	529[b]	N/A	N/A	N/A
North Yemen	30	47	73	193	282	351	382	477
South Yemen	N/A	N/A	N/A	N/A	N/A	41	40	45[a]

NOTES   As Table A.1.

TABLE A.6 *Exchange rates*

	1974	1975	1976	1977	1978	1979	1980	Jan. 1981
Bahrain ($ per dinar)	2.53	2.53	2.53	2.53	2.58	2.62	2.65	2.66
Egypt ($ per dinar)	2.56	2.56	2.56	2.56	2.56	1.43	1.43	1.43
Iraq ($ per dinar)	3.39	3.39	3.39	3.39	3.39	3.39	3.39	3.39
Jordan ($ per dinar)	3.12	3.13	3.01	3.04	3.26	3.33	3.35	3.23
Kuwait ($ per dinar)	3.41	3.45	3.42	3.49	3.64	3.62	3.70	3.69
Lebanon (pounds per $)	2.33	2.31	2.90	3.07	2.96	3.24	N/A	N/A
Libya ($ per dinar)	3.38	3.38	3.38	3.38	3.38	3.38	3.38	3.38
Oman (rials per $)	0.34	0.34	0.34	0.34	0.34	0.34	0.34	0.34
Qatar ($ per riyal)	0.25	0.25	0.25	0.25	0.26	0.26	0.27	0.27
Saudi Arabia (riyals per $)	3.55	3.52	3.53	3.52	3.40	3.36	3.33	3.32
Sudan ($ per pound)	2.87	2.87	2.87	2.87	2.66	2.35	2.00	2.00
Syria (pounds per $)	3.73	3.70	3.85	3.92	3.92	3.92	3.92	3.92
UAE (dirhams per $)	3.96	3.96	3.95	3.90	3.87	3.81	3.71	3.67
North Yemen (riyals per $)	4.57	4.57	4.56	4.56	4.56	4.56	4.56	4.56
South Yemen ($ per dinar)	2.89	2.89	2.89	2.89	2.89	2.89	2.89	2.89

NOTE All dollars US; annual rates from monthly averages of daily data.

SOURCE IMF, *International Financial Statistics*, March 1981.

TABLE A.7   *Top twenty Arab Middle Eastern banks ($ millions)*

	Assets (less contra accounts)	Total deposits	Capital and reserves	Total revenue	Pre-tax earnings
1. Rafidain Bank, Iraq	8,764	7,818	375	559	402
2. National Commercial Bank, Saudi Arabia	7,768	7,177	349	350	164
3. National Bank of Abu Dhabi, UAE	4,879	4,492	58	386	14
4. Arab Bank, Jordan	4,233	4,007	186	361	47
5. Riyadh Bank, Saudi Arabia	4,226	3,307	398	282	13
6. National Bank of Egypt	4,216	2,014	91	226	134
7. Union de Banques Arabes et Francaises (UBAF), France	4,035	3,826	78	419	16
8. Bank of Credit and Commerce International (BCC), Luxembourg	3,919	3,566	226	390	35
9. National Bank of Kuwait	3,584	3,314	255	N/A	35
10. Gulf Bank, Kuwait	3,320	3,132	183	N/A	16
11. Commercial Bank of Syria	3,055	1,353	91	N/A	N/A
12. Al-Ahli Bank of Kuwait	2,985	2,818	168	N/A	13
13. Bank Misr, Egypt	2,821	2,007	72	208	97
14. Commerical Bank of Kuwait	2,715	2,234	197	204	20
15. UMMA Bank, Libya	2,598	543	283	N/A	N/A
16. Banque Arabe et Internationale d'Investissement (BAII), France	2,259	2,107	61	212	7
17. Banque du Caire, Egypt	2,200	1,624	257	72	N/A
18. National Commercial Bank, Libya	2,107	1,422	199	N/A	N/A
19. Saudi International Bank, United Kingdom	1,747	1,605	93	22	12
20. Bank of Alexandria, Egypt	1,671	1,443	163	147	N/A

SOURCE   *The Banker*, December 1980, pp. 155 – 61.

Notes

CHAPTER 1   TRADITIONAL BANKING PRACTICE

1.   The terms are sometimes used interchangeably, but of course lending money and exchange of currencies are two distinct activities. The terms are specifically used in relation to each activity in this chapter.
2.   Originally called Yathrib but changed to Madinat al Rasul or City of the Prophet as it is where Mohammed died.
3.   Zanzibar being an important source.
4.   The term "bazaar" is generally used in Turkey and Iran, and "souk" in the Arab world.
5.   Their importance of course fluctuated with the fortunes of the communities based in each centre, and this was reflected in the prosperity of the moneychangers.
6.   Both terms are used to describe these silver coins.
7.   An island off the Kenya coast largely colonised by Arabs.
8.   Many of whom were of Iranian origin, and shared a common form of Islam with Iran.
9.   The author surveyed charge structures in Riyadh and Jeddah in detail, and more casual investigation in other souks in Dubai and Cairo reveals a similar lack of variation in charges.
10.   Nor are there any moves to establish separate moneychanging establishments for women as in the case of the banks in Saudi Arabia as described in Chapter 4.
11.   Which the author carried out in March and April 1980.
12.   The number of branches cited by the Al-Rajhi company themselves.
13.   Which are not counted in the 120 offices cited above.
14.   Rodney Wilson, "Currencies Changed with Swiss Efficiency", *The Times Report on Saudi Arabia,* 9 December 1980, p. 6.
15.   See the Al-Rajhi announcement in *The Times Report,* ibid., p. 20.
16.   Although it would be a mistake to describe them as Islamic banks like those described in Chapter 4. The latter normally have a religious advisory committee to help ensure operations accord with the Sharia, and are registered banks. The moneychangers and moneylenders operate much more informally.
17.   Yet many Arab and other Middle Eastern banks would claim they have a distinct, non-western character. See Rodney Wilson, "Wider Range of Services than in West", *The Times Report on Finance in the Arab World,* 6 March 1981, p. 5.
18.   Rodney Wilson, "The Evolution of the Saudi Banking System and its Relationship with Bahrain". Paper presented to the University of

Exeter Centre for Arab Gulf Studies Conference on Saudi Arabia, July 1980, p. 15.

19. Nigel Harvey, "Moneychangers: Serving the Public, without Rules", *Saudi Business,* 13 October 1980, pp. 20–5.

20. Rodney Wilson in *The Times Report on Saudi Arabia,* op. cit.

21. The evenings would appear to be their busiest period.

22. Many of the Swiss dealings are through the Union Bank of Switzerland, but Saudi involvement in that country includes an ownership share in the Bank for Saudi-Swiss Trade and Finance, with the Union Bank as the main Swiss shareholder, and the Al-Rajhis amongst the Saudi shareholders.

23. Formerly the British Bank of the Middle East which owns 40 per cent of the equity of the Saudi British Bank.

24. Formerly Citibank which similarly owns 40 per cent of the equity in the Saudi American Bank.

CHAPTER 2   EMERGENCE OF MODERN BANKING

1. For a useful description of Egypt's economic background during this period see C. Issawi, "Egypt since 1800: a Study in Lop-sided Development", *Journal of Economic History,* Vol. 21, No.1 (1961).

2. Mohammed Ali Rifaat, *The Monetary System of Egypt* (London: Allen and Unwin, 1935) pp. 77–8; David S. Landes, *Bankers and Pachas* (London: Heinemann, 1958) pp. 67–8 and 136; M. Kamel A. Malache, *Etude Economique et Critique des Instruments de Circulation et des Institutions de Credit en Egypte* (Paris: Presses Universitaires de France, 1930) pp. 251ff.; Pierre Arminjon, *La Situation Economique Financière de L'Egypt* (Paris: Librairie Générale de Droit et de Jurisprudence, 1911) p. 422.

3. E. R. J. Owen, *Cotton and the Egyptian Economy 1820–1914* (London: Oxford University Press, 1969) p. 83.

4. Albert Baster, "The Origins of British Banking in the Middle East", *Economic History Review,* Vol. V, No. 1 (October 1934) pp. 80–1.

5. Riffaat, op. cit., p. 78.

6. Ibid.

7. Ibid., p. 90.

8. Information from unpublished records of the Ottoman Bank.

9. For further details of British policy see E. R. J. Owen, "The Attitudes of British Officials to the Development of the Egyptian Economy, 1882–1922", in M. Cook (ed.), *Studies in the Economic History of the Middle East* (London: Allen and Unwin, 1970). See also Anon., *Histoire Financière de l'Egypt depuis Said Pacha, 1854–1876* (Paris: Guillaumin et Cie, 1878) pp. 209ff.

10. Rifaat, op. cit., pp. 105–9. All of Chapter IV of this work is concerned with the National Bank. Theodore Rothstein, *Egypt's Ruin: A Financial and Administrative Record* (London: A. C. Fifield, 1910) pp. 241–72, discusses the role of Lord Cromer.

11. Ibid., p. 110.

12. J. Ducruet, *Les Capitaux Européens au Proche-Orient* (Paris: Presse Universitaires de France, 1964) p. 346; Fouad Sultan, *La Monnaire Egyptienne* (Paris: Librairie Nouvelle de Droit et de Jurisprudence, 1914) pp. 106–13, describes the role of the National Bank of Egypt in managing the note issue.

13. Rifaat, op. cit., p. 112.

14. Ibid., p. 113.

15. Ibid., p. 111.

16. Ibid.

17. Details given by Marius Deeb, "Bank Misr and the Emergence of the Local Bourgeoisie in Egypt", in Elie Kedourie (ed.), *The Middle Eastern Economy: Studies in Economics and Economic History* (London: Frank Cass, 1976) p. 70.

18. Ibid., p. 71.

19. Fawzy Mansour, *Development of the Egyptian Financial System up to 1967: A Study in the Relation between Finance and Socio-Economic Development* (Cairo: Ain Shams University Press, 1970) p. 26.

20. Albert N. Forte, *Les Banques en Egypte* (Paris: Librairie Technique et Economique, 1938) p. 149.

21. Hossam M. Issa, *Capitalisme et Sociétés Anonymes en Egypte* (Paris: Librairie Générale de Droit et de Jurisprudence, 1970) pp. 241ff. gives details of Bank Misr's cartelisation policy.

22. Rifaat, op. cit., p. 145.

23. Ibid.

24. Ibid.

25. Ibid., p. 148.

26. Ibid., p. 152

27. Fawzy Mansour, op. cit., pp. 27ff.

28. Ibid.

29. Ibid., p. 73.

30. A detailed account of the structure and operations of the Banque de Syrie et du Grand Liban is given by Said B. Himadeh, *Monetary and Banking System of Syria* (Beirut: American Press, 1935) Chapter XI, pp. 137ff.

31. Ibid., pp. 165–6.

32. Ibid., pp. 166–7 and pp. 225–33.

33. Ibid., pp. 167–8.

34. Ibid., p. 174.

35. One commentator notes how in the inter-war period there was little lending for agriculture or industrial projects: see Edmund Y. Asfour, *Syria: Development and Monetary Policy* (Cambridge, Mass.: Harvard University Press, 1959) pp. 60–2.

36. Himadeh, op.cit., p. 174.

37. Ibid.

CHAPTER 3 GROWTH OF ARAB FINANCIAL EXPERTISE

1. The American schools conducting United States examinations, the French schools standard French examinations etc.

2.   Many of whom wanted to undertake courses such as those prescribed by the British Institute of Bankers.

3.   A profile of Abdul Hameed Shoman was given by Robert Graham in the *Financial Times,* 15 June 1976.

4.   These predominated in the local Arab economy in any case, as there were no large industries at the time.

5.   There were considerable economic tensions between Jewish immigrants and the local Arab population even in the 1920s, and the immigrants' practice of dealing with their own establishments and institutions whenever possible caused resentment.

6.   Information supplied by the Arab Bank.

7.   Robert Graham, op. cit.

8.   Amman's development was aided generally by the demise of Jerusalem, of which the transfer of the Arab Bank headquarters was only one manifestation.

9.   Following the example of the Jordanian government which also continued to pay its West Bank employees after the occupation.

10. Data from the annual reports of the respective banks.

11. These were forced to leave Jordan.

12. Arab Bank (Overseas) Ltd of Zurich and Geneva, and Arab Bank (Nigeria) Ltd, in which it has a 40 per cent stake. The latter was established in 1969, and by 1980 had eight branches.

13. Through this some Saudi and Kuwait deposits are recycled.

14. Citizens of Qatar only.

15. There are seldom developed markets in government securities.

16. Its formation in 1971 marked the final elimination of foreign banking in Kuwait.

17. The foreign banks mainly finance international trade and the foreign businesses involved in Egypt.

18. Donald C. Mead, *Growth and Structural Change in the Egyptian Economy* (Homewood, Ill.: Irwin, 1967) pp. 194–5.

19. Charles Issawi, *Egypt in Revolution* (London: Oxford University Press, 1963) pp. 249–50.

20. Patrick O'Brien, *The Revolution in Egypt's Economic System,* (London: Oxford University Press, 1966) pp. 125–6.

21. Jean Ducruet, op. cit., pp. 411–13.

22. Charles Issawi, op. cit., p. 249

23. Alan Mackie, "Egypt Must Channel Funds into Investment", *Middle East Economic Digest, Special Report on Arab Banking,* London, May 1980, p. 81.

24. Usually in the state-sector industries, including services, or directly in the bureaucracy.

25. J.N. Bridge, "Financial Growth and Economic Development: a Case Study of Lebanon", Ph.D. thesis, University of Durham (1975) pp. 151 ff. and Appendix 1 for a summary of the law.

26. Which would not have been great in any case until the generalised floating of currencies in the 1970s, particularly in the Arab world where there were few devaluations or revaluations.

27. Especially after floating in the early 1970s.
28. Only 10 per cent of bank deposits were withdrawn in the course of the war. See Raymond Mallat, *Seventy Years of Money Muddling* (Beirut: Aleph Publishing, 1977) p. 214.
29. There were also direct flights to Prague, East Berlin, Moscow and Yerevan, the capital of Soviet Armenia.
30. Mallat, op. cit., p. 215. The reserve requirement is 5 per cent.
31. Johnny Rizq, "Lebanese Banks Flourish, Despite Unrest", *Middle East Economic Digest, Special Report on Arab Banking,* London, May 1980, p. 79.
32. Ibid.
33. It is largely in the hands of the Ghosn family.
34. *Know Your Bank,* publication prepared by the Energy Division of BCC, April 1979, pp. 3–5.
35. Nicholas Colchester, "The Man Who Adds a Touch of Mysticism to Banking", *Financial Times,* 17 May 1978.
36. As quoted in the London market.
37. Where it had a representative office only in New York, as Bank of America represented its interests.
38. It owns 45 per cent of Ghana's Premier Bank.
39. See *The International,* No.2 (1980) p. 13 (staff magazine of BCC).
40. The Luxembourg branch advertises extensively in the press in Saudi Arabia and the Gulf.
41. Nicholas Colchester, op. cit.

CHAPTER 4 ISLAMIC BANKING IN PRINCIPLE AND PRACTICE

1. *The Koran,* translation by N. J. Dawood (London: Penguin Books, 1956) p. 314.
2. Ibid., p. 352.
3. Ibid.
4. Ibid., p. 353.
5. Ibid.
6. Ibid., p. 351.
7. Abd-al Rahman Azzar, *The Eternal Message of Mohammed* (London: Quartet Books, 1979) p. 92.
8. *The Koran,* op. cit., p. 352.
9. For a survey describing the economic implications of this see Rodney Wilson, *The Economies of the Middle East* (London: Macmillan, 1979) Chapter 6, pp. 90ff. especially.
10. Maxime Rodinson, *Islam and Capitalism* (London: Penguin Books, 1977) p. 154.
11. Nigel Harvey, "World Islamic Finance Based on Community Banks", *Saudi Business,* 20 March 1981, p. 28.
12. Ibid.
13. This amounted to a guarantee of employment for life.
14. Islamic Development Bank, *Fourth Annual Report,* Jeddah, 1979, p. 36.

15.   Ibid.

16.   Such as the Badr housing complex.

17.   This is independent of the Islamic Investment Company of the Gulf, a Sharjah-based company which also acts in accordance with the Sharia law. It was founded in 1981 in association with the Banca della Svizzera Italiana, a Lugano-based institution, which provides some of the management services. See the *Guardian,* 23 March 1981, p. 16.

18.   Hence the ban on local registration of insurance companies in Saudi Arabia. See Rodney Wilson, "The Economic Consequences of the Islamic Revival", *Contemporary Review,* May 1980, p. 243.

19.   Johnny Rizq, "Kuwait Finance House Proves the System Works", *Middle East Economic Digest, Special Report on Arab Banking,* London, May 1980, pp. 33–5.

20.   Ibid.

21.   See Rami G. Khouri, "The Dictates of Islam", *Financial Times Report on Arab Banking and Finance,* 16 July 1979, p. 3.

22.   For some details on Prince Mohammad's role see Simon Proctor, "Principles Stem from Koran", *Middle East Economic Digest, Special Report on Arab Banking,* London, May 1980, pp. 31–2. Also Michel Szwed-Cousins, "Islamic Ethics in Banking", *Eight Days,* 22 December 1979, pp. 34–5.

23.   Nigel Harvey, op. cit.

24.   Its two founder shareholders, Ali Hajtarkhani and Seyyed Mohammed Beheshti, have 60 per cent of the equity.

25.   Rodney Wilson, "The Evolution of the Saudi Banking System and its Relationship with Bahrain". Paper presented to the University of Exeter Centre for Arab Gulf Studies Conference on Saudi Arabia, July 1980, p. 4.

26.   Largely through making loans to less reputable customers who had been refused credit by the National Commercial Bank. The Riyadh Bank had difficulty in getting into a monopolised market, and nearly failed in the attempt.

27.   Rodney Wilson, "Gifts Entice the Depositors", *The Times Report on Saudi Arabia,* 9 December 1980, p. 6.

28.   Edmund O'Sullivan, "Branching Draws a Scattered Market", ibid., p. 13. The article profiles the Saudi American Bank.

29.   Rodney Wilson, "Fears that Inflation may Soar Once Again", ibid., p. 7.

30.   Rodney Wilson, "Gifts Entice the Depositors", ibid.

31.   For details of the inheritance laws see *The Koran,* op. cit., pp. 355–6.

32.   It subscribed over a quarter of the total capital, compared to 16 per cent for Libya and 14 per cent for the United Arab Emirates. See the Islamic Development Bank's *Fourth Annual Report,* Jeddah, 1979, p. 101. As voting rights largely reflect subscriptions, these three countries, together with Kuwait, command an overall majority of votes.

33.   Calculated by the author from Islamic Development Bank trade data.

34.   Islamic Development Bank, *Fourth Annual Report,* Jeddah, 1979, pp. 30–3.

35. Ibid., p. 34.
36. The bank provided the finance for the purchase of the vessel *Solidarity* by the Islamic Solidarity Shipping Co. of Sharjah, which is being leased to the Bangladesh Shipping Co. The latter will become the eventual owner. See Nigel Harvey,"Islamic Banking", *Saudi Business,* 20 March 1981, p. 22.
37. Islamic Development Bank, *Articles of Agreement,* Jeddah, 1977, Article 17, Clause 2, p. 13.
38. Ibid., Clause 7.
39. Ibid., Clause 6.
40. Islamic Development Bank, *Fourth Annual Report,* Jeddah, 1979, pp. 62–3.

CHAPTER 5   FINANCIAL SPECIALISATION IN THE GULF

1. R. J. A. Wilson, "Banking: Competition for Beirut's Role", *Middle Eastern Yearbook* (London: International Communications, 1978) pp. 90–2.
2. M. W. Khouja and P. G. Sadler, *The Economy of Kuwait: Development and Role in International Finance* (London: Macmillan, 1979) pp. 165ff.
3. Details of the board of directors are given each year in the company's annual report.
4. *Middle East Financial Directory 1980* (London: Middle East Economic Digest, 1980) p. 132.
5. Including bond issues, portfolio management, syndicated loans and guarantees, project financing, real estate development, construction management and equity participation.
6. Such as *Business Week, The Economist* or *Investors' Chronicle.*
7. For details see *Middle East Financial Directory, 1980*, op. cit., pp. 123ff.
8. Antoine Asseily, "Banking and Financial Centres in the Arab East: Kuwait". Proceedings of a regional financial conference on "The Role of Arab Capital in the Economic Development of the Arab East", Beirut, 8–10 May 1980, unpublished.
9. Nigel Dudley, "Bond Market: the Next Two Years will be Crucial", *Middle East Economic Digest, Special Report on Kuwait,* London, February 1980, pp. 15–16.
10. "Kuwait Bond Market Gains Prestige", special issue of *Arab-British Commerce on Arab Banking and Finance* (London: Arab-British Chamber of Commerce, November 1979) p. 24.
11. Peter Field,"Bond Market Blues Hit Kuwait", *f uromoney,* London, April 1980, p. 104.
12. Nigel Dudley, "Confidence Remains Despite Problems, for KD Bonds", *Middle East Economic Digest, Special Report on Arab Banking,* London, May 1980, pp. 41–2.
13. Nigel Dudley, "Secondary Market: Bankers are Confident of Market's Success", *Middle East Economic Digest, Special Report on Kuwait,* London, February 1980, p. 18.

14. Antoine Asseily, op. cit.

15. As in December 1977 for example. See M. W. Khouja and P. G. Sadler, op. cit., p. 186.

16. Rodney Wilson, *The Economies of the Middle East* (London: Macmillan, 1979) pp. 73–6.

17. For a brief history of the island's development as a financial centre see Alan Moore, "The Development of Banking in Bahrain", in May Ziwar Daftari (ed.), *Issues in Development: The Arab Gulf States* (London: MD Research and Services Ltd, 1980) pp. 138–53.

18. Rodney Wilson, "The Evolution of the Saudi Banking System and its Relationship with Bahrain". Paper presented to University of Exeter Centre for Arab Gulf Studies Conference on Saudi Arabia, July 1980, p. 31.

19. Information from unpublished lists from Bahrain Monetary Authority, 1980.

20. Meguerditch Bouldoukian, "Banking and Financial Centres in the Arab East: Bahrain". Proceedings of a regional financial conference on "The Role of Arab Capital in the Economic Development of the Arab East", Beirut, 8–10 May 1980, unpublished.

21. Although often in times of uncertainty early morning dealings in Bahrain are rather thin before European markets open.

22. Nigel Dudley, "Credit Card Habit Slow to Grow", *Middle East Economic Digest, Special Report on Arab Banking,* London, May 1980, p. 50.

23. Alan Moore, "The Arabs Seek a Bigger Role in Recycling their Funds", *Euromoney,* London, April 1980, p. 106.

24. David Ashby, "New Euro-currency Centres", Grindlays Bank, unpublished paper, p. 2.

25. Estimate by the Bahrain Monetary Authority.

26. Which may prevent banks leaving in difficult periods. See Nigel Dudley, "Tough Times for Bahrain Offshore Banks", *Middle East Economic Digest, Special Report on Arab Banking,* London, May 1980, pp. 47ff.

27. Data from Bahrain Monetary Authority, *Annual Report,* 1978, pp. 9–10.

28. Nigel Dudley, "Political Pressures Harm Banking Centre", *The Times Special Report on Bahrain,* 6 December 1980, p. 3.

29. The offshore banking units have been roughly categorised by Atef Sultan: see "Bahrain OBUs: a Bustling Outpost in the Gulf", special issue of *Arab-British Commerce on Arab Banking and Finance,* op. cit., pp. 25–6.

30. John Townsend, "Offshore Banking: a Highly Successful Operation", *Financial Times, Survey of Bahrain,* 5 June 1979, p. 4.

31. Peter Field, "Offshore Banking – Supremacy of Bahrain", *Middle East Annual Review,* London, 1979.

32. "The ABC of Arab Banking", *Euromoney,* London, April 1980, p. 98.

33. Although official funding does not go through Bahrain, most of the funds being from the private commercial banks.

34. "The Merchants of Dubai", *Euromoney,* London, April 1980, p. 96.

35. As is the case with most other Dubai banks: see Doina Thomas,

"Banking: Keeping a Low Profile", *Financial Times Survey of the UAE,* 26 June 1978, p. 26.

36. In its own annual reports.
37. John Whelan, "UAE Banking Faces Same Problems as Federation", *Middle East Economic Digest, Special Report on Arab Banking,* London, May 1980, p. 58; Nigel Dudley, "Oil Wealth Masks Banking Weakness", *Middle East Economic Digest, Special Report on the UAE,* London, December 1979, p. 18.
38. As well as perhaps certificates of deposits: see R. C. B. Smith, "A Fledgling CD Market is Hatched", *Euromoney,* London, April 1980, pp. 141–2.

CHAPTER 6   THE ROLE OF COMMERCIAL BANKS IN RECYCLING

1. Yet this is still being urged. See Nigel Dudley, "Recycling Petrodollars – Western Bankers Need Help", *Middle East Economic Digest, Special Report on Arab Banking,* London, May 1980, p. 3. Also David Blake, "Changes in Recycling Oil Funds Needed", *The Times Special Report on Arab Banking,* 11 March 1980, p. 1.
2. Data from IMF, *International Financial Statistics,* Washington.
3. Usually Dubai, although Chase Manhattan's office is in Abu Dhabi.
4. Because of worries about potential monopolies, United States anti-trust legislation has always been enforced rigorously as far as the banks were concerned.
5. Whose main Middle Eastern presence had become restricted to the lower Gulf.
6. The salaries offered were often 50 per cent higher than their European counterparts, and since the late 1970s the strengthening of the dollar has considerably increased differentials.
7. A market in dollars had long been present in Paris.
8. There has been nevertheless a considerable growth in holdings of smaller currencies in recent years, especially the Swiss Franc and, to a lesser extent, the Australian, Canadian and even Hong Kong dollar.
9. Britain was after all in effect the colonial power in Iraq and the Gulf.
10. Beirut, until the civil war, and Bahrain, today, being the only places in the region which could be regarded as communications centres.
11. The Scandinavian Bank is largely British owned, in fact, despite its name, which reflects its traditional trading interest.
12. Especially in Kuwait.
13. Many young Beirut bankers were trained in Paris under agreements between the French and Lebanese banks. They were therefore fully conversant with French banking practice.
14. See FRAB Bank, *Annual Reports,* Paris.
15. Like other consortium banks, FRAB has participated in many Euromarket loans to clients in Western and Eastern Europe, North America and even Latin America.
16. A useful account of UBAF's operations was given by Cary Reich,

"UBAF's Fragile Future" in *Institutional Investor,* August 1979, pp. 93–104.

17. UBAF's annual reports explain this ownership structure.

18. "Tombstones" being the announcements in the press of syndicated loans and bond issues.

19. During the Nasser period the banks were more preoccupied with domestic issues, including their own nationalisation.

20. The author's own estimate using their annual reports and the aggregative data presented in Table 6.1.

21. This sequence of events is generally agreed; see Peter Field, "Euromarkets – Their Role in Middle Eastern Finance", *Middle East Annual Review* (London: International Communications, 1980) pp. 149ff.

22. See David Cudaback, "Where Do the Arab Overseas Banks Go From Here", *Institutional Investor,* August 1979, pp. 51ff.

23. "London : Home from Home for Arab Banks", *Arab-British Chamber of Commerce Report on Arab Banking,* p. 27.

24. Details in the annual reports of the Saudi International Bank. See also Nigel Dudley, "London : a Base for International Markets", *Middle East Economic Digest, Special Report on Arab Banking,* London, May 1980, p. 12.

25. Some even provide non-banking services for their clients such as arranging hotel accommodation and medical treatment.

26. As the annual reports of the Arab banks involved in this business for those years show.

27. See Hikmat Sharif Nashashibi, "The Developing Pace of Arab Financial Intermediation", *The Banker,* March 1980, pp. 29ff.

28. *Libyan Arab Foreign Bank 1972–1977,* Tripoli, 1978.

29. Cary Reich. op. cit., p. 93.

30. Interest payments on Iranian deposits were also suspended. See David Blake, op. cit., p. 1.

31. An offspring of the London company.

CHAPTER 7   AID AND DEVELOPMENT ASSISTANCE AGENCIES

1. The plants it was set up to support have since received some assistance from the United States and other western countries, although some projects were abandoned, notably that for assembly of Lynx helicopters.

2. Nor does the Iraq Fund enjoy administrative autonomy, or even its own headquarters. It is merely part of the finance ministry.

3. Some funds were dispensed through the Pahlavi Foundation, but this was under the control of his wife, the Empress Farah.

4. Especially in a fund's early years of operation.

5. Around one seventh of the assets of the Kuwait Fund are in fact held in bank deposits, mainly yielding interest, while over 40 per cent are invested in securities. See, for details, the Fund's *Seventeenth Annual Report for 1978–9,* p. 89.

6. Earlier for infrastructural schemes than for industrial ventures where expensive machinery and equipment are often installed only at the final stages.

7. In per capita terms the United Arab Emirates have the highest income level in the world, and if the oil-deficient Emirates were excluded, Abu Dhabi's per capita income figure would be several times that of any other country.

8. The definition of what constitutes an agricultural project and the differentiation between these and transport projects, for example, is not always easy, but the agencies listed in the table have standardised their categorisations.

9. Several books have been written on the Kuwait Fund, including Robert Stephens, *The Arabs' New Frontier* (London: Temple Smith, 1973) and Soliman Demir, *The Kuwait Fund and the Political Economy of Arab Regional Development* (New York: Praeger, 1976). The earliest account of its activities was in Ragaei El Mallakh, *Economic Development and Regional Co-operation: Kuwait* (University of Chicago Press, 1968) Chapter 6, pp. 181ff. especially. A brief account also appears in Rodney Wilson, *Trade and Investment in the Middle East* (London: Macmillan, 1977) Chapter 5, pp. 101–4.

10. Rodney Wilson, "Arab Aid Funds: Moving out of the Middle East", *Wall Street Journal,* 7 December 1979, p. 15.

11. Which he points out leads to "a business-like style, free from routine restrictions, and geared to sound financial standards" ("Bilateral Development Aid: the View from the Kuwait Fund", paper presented by Abdtalif Al-Hamad to the "Symposium on Diplomacy, Development and International Cooperation", Khartoum, January 1974, p. 10).

12. See the Kuwait Fund, *Seventeenth Annual Report, 1978–79,* p. 13.

13. The Kuwait Fund encouraged the formation of the Arab Fund for Technical Assistance to African and Arab Countries, which started operating in Cairo in 1978 under the aegis of the Arab League. This body has made a limited number of experts available to help in project formulation in recent years.

14. Especially as foreign exchange shortages can delay implementation in any case, particularly where the government itself is making some contribution to the project out of its scarce reserves.

15. The preference is for putting back the starting date when the loan should come into effect if the project is only in the early stages of implementation before the first disbursement.

16. See the Kuwait Funds, *Seventeenth Annual Report,* op. cit., p. 46.

17. Ibid., p. 19.

18. Ibid., p. 83.

19. Ibrahim Shihata, *The Kuwait Fund for Arab Economic Development: A Legal Analysis* (Kuwait, 1973) p. 17.

20. Especially as under its charter Sheikh Zayed himself is chairman of its board of directors. See Abu Dhabi Fund for Arab Economic Development, *Law and Regulations* (Abu Dhabi, 1972) p. 10.

21. See Abu Dhabi Fund for Arab Economic Development, *5 nnual Report 1978–9,* country page on Oman (unnumbered).

22. The increasing participation of Arab financial institutions in these markets also helps, as they are keen to support projects the Arab agencies support.

23. See Abu Dhabi Fund, *Annual Report, 1978–9,* op. cit., details under countries cited in text.

24. Where countries have a more favourable exchange rate for capital imports, this exchange rate is used, which adds to the bias. For a general discussion of appraisal techniques used by the Arab funds see Traute Scharf (ed.), *Trilateral Co-operation* (Paris: OECD, 1978) Vol. 1, *Arab Development Funds and Banks,* pp. 57–64.

25. Rodney Wilson, "Arab Aid Funds: Moving Out of the Middle East", op. cit.

26. For an account of its history and purpose see Soliman Demir, *Arab Development Funds in the Middle East* (New York: Pergamon Press, 1979) Chapter 3, pp. 40ff.

27. Ibid., p. 42.

28. Dr Mohammed Imadi, a former Minister of Economy. See Kathleen Evans, "Policies – a Model for Other States", *Financial Times Report on Kuwait,* 25 February 1981, p. 11.

29. See listing of projects in the Fund's *Annual Report for 1978.*

30. Rodney Wilson, "Oil Exporters Emerge as Important Source of Aid", *Times Report on Banking in the Middle East,* 18 February, 1977, p. 2.

31. Although the Arab Fund has been criticised for the size of its wage bill, which was over 1.5 million dinar in 1978, compared to under 1 million for the Kuwait Fund, which is a larger organisation. Even its travel expenses bill was 50 per cent higher than that of the Kuwait Fund.

32. Banque Arabe pour le Développement Economique de l'Afrique.

33. See its 1979 *Annual Report,* pp. 7ff.

34. See Shimeon Amir, *Israel's Development Co-operation with Africa, Asia and Latin America* (New York: Praeger, 1974).

35. For an African perspective of what was wanted from the Arab world, see E.C. Chibwe, *Arab Dollars for Africa* (London: Croom Helm, 1976).

36. 1979 *Annual Report,* op. cit., pp. 41–2.

37. Ibid., p. 56.

38. OPEC Bulletin Supplement, *Agreement Establishing the OPEC Special Fund,* Vienna, 30 June 1979, p. vii.

39. OPEC Bulletin Supplement, *Third Annual Report of OPEC Special Fund,* 18 June 1979, p. v.

40. Ibid., pp. xii–xiii.

41. Ibid., p. xv.

Index

201